Cotton Capitalists

American Jewish Entrepreneurship in the
Reconstruction Era

Michael R. Cohen

NEW YORK UNIVERSITY PRESS

New York

NEW YORK UNIVERSITY PRESS
New York
www.nyupress.org

© 2017 by New York University
All rights reserved

References to Internet websites (URLs) were accurate at the time of writing. Neither the author nor New York University Press is responsible for URLs that may have expired or changed since the manuscript was prepared.

ISBN: 978-1-4798-7970-0

For Library of Congress Cataloging-in-Publication data, please contact the Library of Congress.

New York University Press books are printed on acid-free paper, and their binding materials are chosen for strength and durability. We strive to use environmentally responsible suppliers and materials to the greatest extent possible in publishing our books.

Manufactured in the United States of America

10 9 8 7 6 5 4 3 2 1

Also available as an ebook

COTTON CAPITALISTS

THE GOLDSTEIN-GOREN SERIES IN AMERICAN JEWISH HISTORY

General Editor: Hasia R. Diner

We Remember with Reverence and Love: American Jews and the Myth of Silence after the Holocaust, 1945–1962
Hasia R. Diner

Is Diss a System? A Milt Gross Comic Reader
Edited by Ari Y. Kelman

All Together Different: Yiddish Socialists, Garment Workers, and the Labor Roots of Multiculturalism
Daniel Katz

Jews and Booze: Becoming American in the Age of Prohibition
Marni Davis

Jewish Radicals: A Documentary History
Tony Michels

1929: Mapping the Jewish World
Edited by Hasia R. Diner and Gennady Estraikh

An Unusual Relationship: Evangelical Christians and Jews
Yaakov Ariel

Unclean Lips: Obscenity, Jews, and American Culture
Josh Lambert

Hanukkah in America: A History
Dianne Ashton

The Rag Race: How Jews Sewed Their Way to Success in America and the British Empire
Adam Mendelsohn

Hollywood's Spies: The Undercover Surveillance of Nazis in Los Angeles
Laura B. Rosenzweig

Cotton Capitalists: American Jewish Entrepreneurship in the Reconstruction Era
Michael R. Cohen

For Shira

CONTENTS

List of Figures	ix
List of Maps	xi
Acknowledgments	xiii
Introduction	1
1. The Antebellum Cotton Economy	24
2. The War Years	58
3. Timing Is Everything	82
4. Networks from Above	124
5. Networks from Below	153
6. The End of the Niche Economy	181
Conclusion	199
Notes	203
Index	247
About the Author	259

LIST OF FIGURES

Figure 1.1. "Cotton Levee in New Orleans." Image courtesy of the
Library of Congress (LC-USZ62–4928).   25
Figure 1.2. "King Cotton and His Slaves, Greenwood, Mississippi."
Image courtesy of the Library of Congress
(LC-USZ62–36638).   26
Figure 1.3. "A Cotton Plantation on the Mississippi." Image
courtesy of the Library of Congress (LC-USZ62–345).   27
Figure 1.4. "Caricature of Jewish Merchant and Steamboat."
Image courtesy of the Jacob Rader Marcus Center of the
American Jewish Archives, Cincinnati, Ohio (MSS 601,
box 5, folder 1).   35
Figure 1.5. "Julius Weis." Image courtesy of the Jacob Rader
Marcus Center of the American Jewish Archives, Cincinnati,
Ohio (PC-4687).   44
Figure 2.1. "Sutler's Tent." Image courtesy of the Library of
Congress (LC-B8171–2448).   65
Figure 2.2. "Caricature of Jewish Sutler." Image courtesy of the
Jacob Rader Marcus Center of the American Jewish
Archives, Cincinnati, Ohio (PC-4585).   66
Figure 2.3. "The Levee at Vicksburg Miss., February, 1864." Image
courtesy of the Library of Congress (LC-USZ61–1597).   71
Figure 2.4. "Main Street, Little Rock, Arkansas, 1860–65." Image
courtesy of the Jacob Rader Marcus Center of the American
Jewish Archives, Cincinnati, Ohio (PC-2688).   72
Figure 3.1. "View from Catholic Hill, St. Francisville, LA, toward
Bayou Sara." Image courtesy of the Louisiana State University
Special Collections, Elizabeth Dart Collection (121:9, box 3).   85
Figure 3.2. "Preparing Cotton in Bayou Sara." Image courtesy of
the Louisiana State University Special Collections, Elizabeth
Dart Collection (121:9, box 14, folder 1).   85

Figure 3.3. "Cotton Scene in Houston and Texas Central Railway Yards." Image courtesy of the Library of Congress (LC-USZ62–29471). 87

Figure 3.4. "Architect's Sketch of Baum Block, Meridian, Mississippi." Image courtesy of the Jacob Rader Marcus Center of the American Jewish Archives, Cincinnati, Ohio (MSS 601, box 5, folder 2). 90

Figure 3.5. "Commercial Street with Wagons Laden with Cotton Bales, Gainesville." Image courtesy of the Library of Congress (LC-USZ62–16565). 91

Figure 3.6. "Cotton Market in Montgomery." Produced courtesy of the American Museum in Britain, Bath (NA 045). 92

Figure 4.1. "Mayer Lehman." Image courtesy of the Jacob Rader Marcus Center of the American Jewish Archives, Cincinnati, Ohio (PC-2946). 127

Figure 4.2. "Receipt for Bonnet from Mrs. B. Gans." Image courtesy of Temple B'nai Israel, Little Rock, Arkansas. 148

Figure 4.3. "Architect's Sketch, Marks & Lichtenstein, Meridian, Mississippi." Image courtesy of the Jacob Rader Marcus Center of the American Jewish Archives, Cincinnati, Ohio (MSS 601, box 5, folder 2). 150

Figure 5.1. "Cotton Receipt from Julius Freyhan & Co." Image courtesy of the West Feliciana Historical Society. 154

Figure 5.2. "Isaac Lowenburg." Image courtesy of the Jacob Rader Marcus Center of the American Jewish Archives, Cincinnati, Ohio (MSS 601, box 2). 169

Figure 6.1. "A Flooded Bayou Sara." Image courtesy of the Louisiana State University Special Collections, Elizabeth Dart Collection (121:9, box 3). 189

Figure 6.2. "Man Surveying a Flooded Bayou Sara." Image courtesy of the Louisiana State University Special Collections, Elizabeth Dart Collection (121:9, box 3). 190

LIST OF MAPS

Map 1.1. Cotton production in the Gulf South, 1880   5

Map 1.2. Percentage of Jewish-owned general and dry goods stores
     in Gulf South towns, 1880   14

Map 1.3. Jewish percentages of the population, store ownership,
     and general and dry goods store ownership, 1880   15

Map 4.1. Lehman Brothers' flow of credit and capital   125

Map 4.2. Vicksburg and the Bends   136

Map 6.1. Incidents of anti-Jewish violence   193

ACKNOWLEDGMENTS

I owe a large debt of gratitude to friends and colleagues who have shaped this project from the start. Jonathan Sarna helped from beginning to end—first inspiring me to undertake this research, and then providing valuable comments throughout. Adam Mendelsohn and Rebecca Kobrin both read the penultimate draft and assisted me through countless conversations as I formulated my argument and narrowed my scope. My discussions with Hasia Diner helped me to situate this project within the field of Jewish history, and my conversations with Sven Beckert helped me to place my work in a broader context within the history of capitalism.

I also benefited greatly from the discussions at the Center for Jewish History's scholars' working group on Jewish economic history, and for that I thank Adam Teller, Derek Penslar, Francesca Trivellato, Jonathan Karp, Susie Pak, Jerry Muller, Judith Siegel, and many others. As I moved into the field of Southern Jewish history, many colleagues helped me to understand the lay of the land, including Stuart Rockoff and Mark Bauman. Special thanks also go to Teri Tillman and Anton Hieke, to whom I am indebted for their valuable feedback on my manuscript.

I am grateful for my Tulane University colleagues in the Department of Jewish Studies, including Brian Horowitz, David Goldstein, Ronna Burger, Sarah Cramsey, Yehuda Halper, Inna Shakster, Allison Mull, and Patrice Nadeau. At Tulane, I have also been incredibly lucky to receive the support of a leadership team that was committed to my success, and I must thank Carole Haber and Scott Cowen for providing me with the space and resources to develop as a scholar.

Because of the significant amount of travel that my archival research required, this project would also not have been possible without the generous financial support that I have received along the way. I received Lurcy and Glick Fellowships from the Tulane University School of Liberal Arts, a Committee on Research grant from the Tulane University

Provost's Office, and a Monroe Fellowship from the New Orleans Center for the Gulf South. I also received support through the New England Regional Fellowship Consortium, and a Louisiana Board of Regents' Award to Louisiana Artists and Scholars. Generous support also came through Mellon and Sizeler Professorships at Tulane University, and I was a recipient of a subvention grant and a Carol Lavin Bernick Faculty Grant at Tulane.

I am also indebted to the many archives and archivists who made this work possible. The staff at Harvard Business School's Baker Library welcomed me with open arms to what became my home away from home and provided more support than I ever could have imagined. Particular thanks are due to Katherine Fox, Ben Johnson, Tim Mahoney, Melissa Murphy, Christine Riggle, Liam Sullivan, and Abby Thompson. I also must thank the staff at Tulane University Special Collections, Louisiana State University Special Collections, the New-York Historical Society, the Columbia University Rare Book and Manuscript Library, the California Historical Society, the Library of Congress, and the National Archives. Special thanks are also in order for Mimi Miller at the Historic Natchez Foundation, to Helen Williams and the staff of the West Feliciana Historical Society, and to Gary Zola, Dana Herman and the staff of the American Jewish Archives. It was through an article in the *American Jewish Archives Journal* that I became convinced that this would become my next book project. Thanks also to the many students who assisted me in my research with this project, including Aaron Silberman, Margaret Abrams, and Sam Furman. Special thanks also to Richard Campanella, who not only designed the maps throughout this volume that allowed me to explain a niche economy to my readers through geographic information systems (GIS), but whose maps also revealed to me the patterns that undergird this study.

My editor, Jennifer Hammer, believed in this project from the start, and she has been essential in seeing it through to completion.

Finally, I must thank my family for all their support. Leonard Nemon, whose knowledge of Civil War history is rivaled only by his wife Nancy's, read a full draft of my manuscript and offered superb advice. To my parents Marlene and Bernard Cohen, your support (and editorial hands) have been essential throughout this project and my life, and I couldn't be prouder to have you as parents. My brother, David B. Cohen, served as digital lead on this project and introduced me to the world of the digital humanities. His unique blend of historical scholarship, business analytics, and patience assisted me in creating databases that uncovered the patterns that shaped my manuscript. And finally, a huge debt of gratitude goes to my amazing wife Shira, without whose support this manuscript would not be possible.

Introduction

Upon his arrival at the Port of New Orleans in late 1845, nineteen-year-old Jewish immigrant Julius Weis boarded a Mississippi River steamship bound for the region at the heart of the United States' cotton production. There, he peddled throughout the countryside, later operating a storefront in the bustling Mississippi River port city of Natchez and then opening what would become one of the most successful cotton commission houses in postbellum New Orleans. For Weis, and most others in the cotton economy, economic success was predicated upon credit. While he had the option of fronting cash to furnish his own stock, he could offer far more variety to his customers if he could acquire credit himself, take delivery of goods before the start of the growing season, and sell staples and luxury goods to his customers.

But extending credit was risky business in an era before scientific credit reporting. To mitigate risk, entrepreneurs relied on trust; indeed, John Pierpont "J. P." Morgan considered trust "the fundamental basis of business." Credit reporters, however, did not trust Jews. They were suspicious of Jewish immigrants like Julius Weis and often advised against extending credit to them. In need of the trust necessary to acquire credit and conduct business, Weis and his fellow Jewish merchants turned to each other. For them, trust generally boiled down to shared ethnicity—a term that I use to emphasize the cultural solidarity and sense of shared past (and future) that bound Jews together. Jews, much like other ethnic minorities, trusted one another more than they trusted strangers with whom they had no connections. Such was the case for Weis, and it was also the case for the prominent Jewish banking house of Lehman Brothers, which relied on ethnic trust networks to conduct business, bringing European investment to the scores of Jewish merchants who fanned out across the cotton-producing regions of the Gulf South. Leveraging these ethnic networks, Jewish merchants created a niche economy in the nation's most important industry—cotton. In so doing, they positioned themselves at the forefront of global capitalist expansion for much of the second half of the nineteenth century.[1]

In many ways, the Jewish economic niche in the cotton industry reflects the quintessential Jewish immigrant experience. As Jews did elsewhere,[2] these cotton capitalists peddled on geographic and economic frontiers and graduated from peddlers to shopkeepers. A visible cohort reached the pinnacle of success. Exploring the Jewish niche in this industry reveals the myriad ways in which economic forces defined the contours of the American Jewish experience as a whole. The golden age for American Jewry that grew out of the cotton industry dictated the ways in which Jews shaped, and were shaped by, the communities in which they lived. Their role in the cotton industry redrew the American Jewish map, changing the internal dynamics of American Jewish communities, redefining Jews' levels of integration in the cities and towns in which they lived, and reshaping the growth and development of the towns themselves.

But this is more than a book about Jews. The story of these American Jewish entrepreneurs also acts as a case study to explore the role of ethnicity in the development of global capitalism more broadly. Ethnic minorities frequently stood at the forefront of entrepreneurship, clustering in narrow sectors of the economy.[3] Yet despite the universality of these minority economic niches,[4] very little scholarship has asked how they emerge and function. This book, at its core, asks how such niche economies come to be.[5]

In the case of the Jewish niche economy in the cotton industry, some would quickly offer a recipe for success highlighted by ingenuity, an enterprising spirit, and an abiding business acumen. But the ingredients are in fact far more complex. This book argues that Jewish entrepreneurs created a thriving niche economy in the cotton industry because of two interrelated forces: first, structural factors unique to this place and time. Certainly timing mattered, alongside a host of often overlooked forces, that created the conditions that allowed Jewish merchants to succeed in the cotton industry.[6] Second, this book also argues that, within this milieu, ethnic networks of trust served as the key force that fueled this niche economy and provided Jews with a competitive advantage.[7] In the face of suspicions that limited access to traditional sources of credit, shared ethnicity and the trust that it instilled provided the glue essential for Jewish success within the cotton industry.

How did these two interrelated forces operate? When Julius Weis stepped off his steamship, he entered a cotton region where structural factors nurtured a Jewish niche economy. Cotton stood at the heart of the global economy. It fostered industrialization, furthered the emergence of global capitalism, and it stood behind many of the world's labor battles. It linked farmers and merchants across the globe to wealthy financiers, bringing rural cotton-growing areas to the forefront of the modern world. Because of these connections, cotton, argues Sven Beckert, "provides the key to understanding the modern world, the great inequalities that characterize it, the long history of globalization, and the ever-changing political economy of capitalism."[8]

Nowhere was cotton production more important in the nineteenth century than in the United States, where the fiber dominated exports between 1803 and 1937. And within the United States, no region was more important in the mid-nineteenth century than the Gulf South, which I define here as Louisiana, Mississippi, Alabama, and parts of Arkansas. The former three states saw their share of the cotton crop grow from 22.7 percent in 1821 to 63.5 percent in 1859, and cotton receipts in New Orleans increased from under 40,000 bales in 1816 to nearly 1 million bales by 1840. Cotton from this region provided the raw materials for New York's garment industry and for textile factories across the world.

While cotton fueled factories, its growth and production was inextricably linked to slavery. The internal slave trade in the mid-nineteenth century forcibly shifted as many as a million slaves to the region, most of whom were compelled to labor upon cotton lands that had been largely expropriated from Native Americans. One nineteenth-century observer noted that "the expanding geographical distribution of slaves and of cotton cultivation affords the most striking evidence of the close connection of the two institutions that can be had." Cotton production was so dependent upon slave labor that slave market prices fluctuated in harmony with cotton prices.[9]

Cotton and slavery came together to make the Gulf South an incredibly important region within the United States' economy, and of particular importance were the towns within it along the Mississippi River in an area contemporaries termed "Vicksburg and the Bends," named for the bends in the river between Greenville, Mississippi in the north and the twin towns of Bayou Sara and St. Francisville, Louisiana in the south. This region, where Julius Weis settled, was inclusive of the Mississippi towns of Natchez, Vicksburg, and the twin towns of Grand Gulf and Port Gibson, as well as small towns and landings alongside the river's banks. These towns were situated in what U.S. internal commerce reports declared to be "the richest and most productive cotton country in the world" and the Gulf South's most fertile cotton land, based on yield per acre. Although there was some other agricultural production in this area, the staple was cotton, and Mississippi River traffic in this region consisted almost entirely of bringing cotton and cottonseed to market or in bringing plantation supplies into the region.[10]

While Vicksburg and the Bends, and the Gulf South more broadly, offered fertile soil for cotton production, the need to bring that cotton to market provided an opening for Jewish merchants. Cotton was a credit-based crop, and farmers and landowners needed supplies and foodstuffs to survive from the beginning to the end of the growing cycle. Farmers were not paid until after harvest, and thus only once the crop was harvested could they repay their debts. In the antebellum years, cotton factors, or brokers, most of whom operated on a larger scale and who were located in port cities, provided credit to planters.[11] In the wake of the Civil War and its concomitant bank failures, however, the importance of cotton factors declined as port cities became less central to the industry. New technologies such as the telegraph and railroad moved the center of cotton marketing to interior towns.[12] Yet the need for credit remained strong.[13] Meanwhile, new labor arrangements replaced slavery,[14] and while the various forms of tenancy and sharecropping did not provide anywhere near the liberties for which freedmen had longed and deserved, they did provide a modicum of economic sovereignty for freedmen, who became an important customer base for interior merchants. Jewish merchants had a history selling across the color line around the globe,[15] and it made good business sense for them to sell to freedmen in postbellum America.[16]

All of this meant that interior merchants, who as a group were on the margins of the antebellum cotton industry, moved to the mainstream in the postbellum years. Many, including Julius Weis, had already scattered

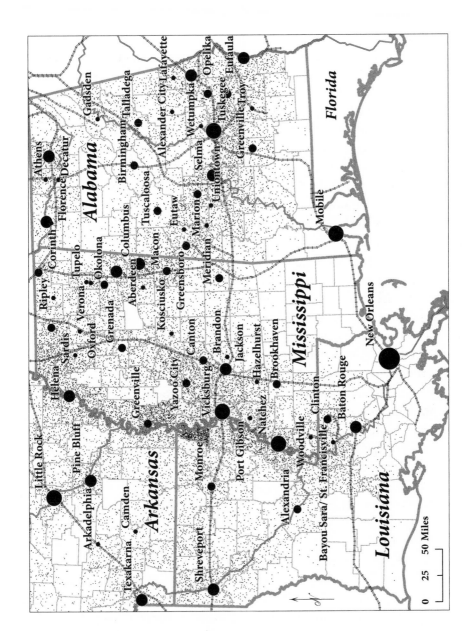

Map 1.1. Cotton production in the Gulf South, 1880. *Note:* Black circles representing cities and towns are sized by their total 1880 population. Shaded gray dots represent 100 bales of cotton produced in 1880, distributed randomly throughout county and parish borders. Railroads depict extent of tracks in 1880.

5

throughout the market towns of the region and were in the right place at the right time. Some had peddled before the war and had already established relationships with farmers and plantation owners. Some had previously opened storefronts where they could sell goods. Some owned warehouses where they could store cotton until prices rose. Other new merchants in search of opportunity came to these towns as New Orleans and Vicksburg fell to federal troops. Together, these interior merchants and shopkeepers filled the void left by Southern banks and cotton factors, and in the postbellum years, they provided the credit necessary to operate the economy.[17]

While these structural forces may have paved the way for Jewish cotton capitalists, ethnic credit networks made their niche economy possible. Merchants and shopkeepers could only thrive in this milieu if they themselves had access to what fueled the economy—credit or capital. Some merchants had stockpiled capital during the war, some by speculating in cotton or currency, many by selling whatever goods they could wherever they could, and still others by blockade-running or smuggling. But for those who did not amass wealth during the conflict, the other primary way to succeed as a postbellum merchant was to find access to credit. And for this, merchants relied on networks that placed them as the intermediaries between the cotton growers of the region and the international markets and financiers of global capitalism. Some merchants rebuilt those networks in the final years of the war, once trade resumed along the Mississippi River, and others waited until after the war officially came to a close. Then, as now, lenient treatment from creditors during an economic downturn often separated success from failure.

But these networks did not operate as nameless and faceless business transactions dictated solely by the free market and rational business decisions. While collateral was certainly important to credit reporters, trust mitigated some of the risks associated with those transactions. J. P. Morgan, for example, often lent money to those whom he trusted, even if they had no collateral to back the loan. He spoke of "lots of men . . . who can borrow any amount, whose credit is unquestioned," without the money or property to back them, and he noted that he had given "a good many" people checks "for a million dollars when I knew [they] had not a cent in the world." When asked why, Morgan pointed to trust:

"A man I do not trust could not get money from me on all the bonds of Christendom."[18]

Conventional thinking may suggest that trust in the economic sphere builds over time as businesses interact with one another profitably. Yet here the opposite is true—economic interactions were *predicated upon* trust. But because of the separate social spheres in which some minorities operated, the opportunities to build trust between members of minority groups and the larger culture were limited. Jews and Gentiles, for example, operated in separate social spheres in nineteenth-century America. Elite Protestant organizations and establishments often discriminated against Jews; in one of the more notorious incidents, the Grand Union Hotel in Saratoga Springs, New York, turned away the wealthy Jewish banker Joseph Seligman because he was Jewish. Joseph's nephew Theodore was later denied membership in the Union League Club of New York City, of which J. P. Morgan was a member, and the *Christian Advocate* claimed that "no motive existed for it except the fact that he is a Jew." All of this is not to say that there were no interethnic business relationships. Although J. P. Morgan operated in a social milieu that confined Jews and Gentiles to largely different social spheres, he nevertheless worked closely with Kuhn, Loeb & Co., which was led by Jacob Schiff. Yet the partners of the firms were not close socially, reflective of the different social spheres that they occupied. The "five o'clock shadow," where Jews and Christians occupied separate social spheres, was a way of life, and these separate spheres made it difficult to nurture trust through social relationships.[19]

Because of this social separation, Jewish firms often turned to ties of family and ethnicity to create the requisite trust networks upon which capitalism relied. Leadership positions within Jewish firms were frequently limited to family members. Goldman Sachs, for example, employed only family members in leadership until 1915, and the same was true for Lehman Brothers until 1924. All of Kuhn, Loeb & Co.'s partners in 1895 were related to another partner, and the firm did not add a partner from outside the family until 1912. As long as partners in the firms eschewed interreligious marriage, the family dynamic within firms left Jewish and non-Jewish firms largely separate from one another. But while Jewish firms had Jewish partners, the same was true in reverse.

J. P. Morgan & Co., for example, did not share familial ties with any of the German-Jewish banks until 1930.[20]

Trust certainly mattered in the composition of firms. It also mattered for the day-to-day, face-to-face interactions between firms that moved capital and credit through the economic system. For example, Marcus Goldman, founder of Goldman Sachs, purchased promissory notes in New York that he would then sell to bankers. Goldman would purportedly take these notes uptown to various commercial banks, where he would meet with bank cashiers or presidents and negotiate, face-to-face, over the value of those notes.[21]

In the case of cotton and the Gulf South, these family and ethnic connections mattered. European banks financed much of America's cotton industry, and businesses such as Lehman Brothers cultivated overseas ethnic trust networks to access their capital. To facilitate these global transactions, Lehman Brothers moved its flagship branch to New York, which was fast becoming the center of both finance and the cotton industry, and which served as a gateway for European investment. Scores of other Southern Jewish merchants also sent family members or Jewish partners to New York, where they cultivated personal relationships with creditors, and some opened branches there that provided them with direct access to credit and goods. These firms then utilized their Southern branches to extend credit to smaller Jewish firms throughout the interior—again, often through economic networks fostered by trust. In this way, Jewish businesses in the Gulf South developed family and ethnic networks that provided desperately needed credit to the war-torn South in a time of economic collapse, bank failure, and currency devaluation. While some non-Jewish businesses followed a similar model, those that had been reliant upon Southern banks or traditional sources of credit found themselves without the credit needed to rebuild in the wake of the Civil War.[22]

Thus access to Northern credit in the years after the war, when that credit was scarce, allowed Jewish merchants to survive years in which crops were devastated by floods or when other circumstances occurred that prevented farmers from paying their debts to their merchants. Surviving and thriving during the postbellum credit crisis is at the center of the story told in this book, and because Jews were able to access credit through these networks, their early toehold in the cotton industry quickly grew into a larger ethnic economy.[23]

But Jews were not the only group in the cotton industry for whom ethnic networks provided a competitive advantage. Some non-Jews cultivated networks between New York and the Gulf South, and other minority groups in cotton-producing regions elsewhere in the world also used trust networks to connect farmers to the global economy. In western Anatolia, for example, Greek and Christian Arab merchants utilized Mediterranean networks to connect rural farmers to Armenian traders. In the late 1840s and early 1850s, merchants, many of whom were Greek, began to purchase cotton directly from Egyptian peasants. Greek networks brought international capital to cotton growers and provided cotton to manufacturers and textiles to consumers around the world.[24]

Those Greek networks operated in much the same way as did Jewish networks. One of the key Greek cotton trading firms of the nineteenth century was operated by the Ralli family. Relationships of trust were important within this firm, as most members were family, and those who were not mostly hailed from the same island. The firm was started by two brothers who went to London to trade, and it soon welcomed a third brother who opened an office in Manchester, a fourth who opened a Persian office, and a fifth who opened a branch in Marseille. By the 1860s the firm had stretched its footprint beyond its initial reach and into Liverpool, Odessa, Constantinople, Calcutta, Karachi, Bombay, and the United States. These networks allowed the Rallis to purchase cotton in the United States and send it to Liverpool and then on to Manchester for production, where the goods that were produced would be shipped and sold around the world. Merchants such as the Rallis played an important intermediary role throughout the global cotton trade, linking the European center to the rural cotton growers of Egypt, India, Anatolia, Brazil, and beyond. The example of the Rallis demonstrates that ethnic networks were not a particular Jewish trait but, rather, a means by which minorities across the globe could conduct business in the broader societies in which they lived.[25]

Greek firms such as the Rallis and Jewish firms such as Lehman Brothers offer prominent examples of ethnic networks in action. But are they anomalies—high-profile firms that played an outsized role in cotton capitalism? Or do they reflect a broader trend in which networks provided opportunities for members of an ethnic group, encouraging a clustering into an economic niche? In the Greek case, twelve Greek mercantile firms had cornered one-third of Alexandria's cotton export market by 1839, and the largest Greek firm exported 11 percent of Egypt's cotton on its own. The Jewish case, however, has not previously been quantified. Contemporaries and historians certainly believed that Jewish merchants played a significant role in the Gulf South's cotton industry, but these assumptions are rooted primarily in anecdotes and micro studies. "In the cotton states, after the war," Mark Twain wrote in 1897 in his *Concerning the Jews*, "the Jew came down in force, set up shop on the plantation, supplied all the negro's wants on credit." Moreover, Frederick Law Olmsted also claimed that "a swarm of Jews, within the last ten years, has settled in nearly every southern town, many of them men of no character."[26]

Others echoed this sentiment. For example, Edward King, a journalist who toured the South and wrote most of his articles in a series in *Scribner's Monthly*, maintained that it was "the shrewd Hebrew, who has entered into the commerce of the South in such a manner as almost to preclude Gentile competition," and suggested that "the Hebrew merchants have large establishments in all the planting districts." Such sentiments and language—the use of the words "mostly," "much," "preclude," "every," and "all"—suggest a perception that Jews were becoming so prominent in the cotton industry that they were cornering that sector of the economy at the expense of "natives."[27]

The Scottish journalist Robert Somers traveled to America in 1870 and in Meridian, Mississippi, observed that "much of the storekeeping business is conducted by sharp, active young men of Jewish aspect, who talk German-English." In New Orleans, he observed that a "new class of houses are springing up, mostly Jews, who, by establishing stores in the little towns near the plantations, are becoming middlemen through whose hands the cotton passes from the growers into the market of New Orleans, and whose conditions of advance are almost necessarily marked by a degree of rigour that was unknown in former times."[28]

These comments certainly suggest a contemporary perception of a niche economy for Jews in the Gulf South's cotton industry, but existing scholarship has told us little about whether this concentration was real or perceived. Roger Ransom and Richard Sutch claim that, "throughout the South, Jews apparently constituted only a small minority of the merchants." They argue that although the "Mississippi River basin [was] an area that particularly attracted Jewish immigrants after the war," they were in no way ubiquitous, as "even in the Mississippi Delta they did not dominate" the business of furnishing supplies. Yet not only do Ransom and Sutch fail to define "small minority" or "did not dominate," but their statistics are also based only on "a *sample* of general store operators throughout the cotton region" (italics mine).[29]

Elliott Ashkenazi closely analyzes several towns and Jewish individuals and convincingly argues that "the story of Jews in Louisiana during the middle of the nineteenth century is best told through their commercial activity." But the strength of his work is in his close analysis and not in establishing how widespread his observations might be. He limits his study to an important group of people and towns, but he has "not attempted to discuss all the Jews who did business in Louisiana during the period." He does expect that the patterns he uncovers "will hold true for the many Jews who go unmentioned," but he has not attempted a quantitative study, although he admits that extant sources "would seemingly make such a presentation attractive from a statistical point of view."[30]

Ransom, Sutch, and Ashkenazi are not alone in their inability to quantify just how widespread Jewish merchants actually were. What percentage, for example, of merchants were Jews? Thomas Clark, in his classic 1966 article "The Post–Civil War Economy in the South," notes of postbellum wholesale mercantile establishments that "many of these houses were operated by Jewish merchants." Moreover, he suggests that "possibly a major portion" of the dry goods and clothing stores in small Southern towns were run by Jewish merchants. While he is correct in noting that "it would be impossible to consider Southern economic and social history with any degree of thoroughness without also considering the history of the Southern Jewish people," he does little to quantify the phenomenon that he identifies beyond his use of the terms "possibly" and "many."[31]

Looking, therefore, at contemporary comments and historiography yields little in the way of specific, quantitative details that might suggest how widespread Jewish merchants were. How can we sort through the contradictory hunches and vague notions and create an accurate quantification of Jewish mercantile life in the postbellum Gulf South? An excellent source comes from the R.G. Dun & Co. records, housed at the Baker Library at Harvard Business School, which include materials that meticulously detail U.S. businesses, including but not limited to those in the Gulf South during the second half of the nineteenth century. Dun agents throughout the country lived in or traveled to cities and towns, large and small—and offered written assessment of each business. Businesses were classified by type and location and in *Mercantile Agency Reference Books* were given ratings for their credit and pecuniary strength. The Dun reports also include narrative descriptions, which generally list the partners and employees of a particular firm, creditors, the net worth of the business, other affiliated firms or branch locations, and various notes about credit worthiness.[32]

While the Dun reports can help us to quantify and understand mercantile life in the region, they cannot always tell us if a particular merchant was Jewish. Jewishness is not always easy to define, and it becomes especially difficult when numbers and percentages matter. It is particularly challenging to account for those who have no synagogue affiliation or those who try to hide their Jewishness. We therefore must recognize at the outset that precision is not possible. Yet we do have several methods through which we can come fairly close to approximating Jewish numbers. First, while the Dun reports do not officially utilize the category of Jewishness, it is clearly indicated in Dun's narrative description of many businesses, as it was a consideration in determining credit worthiness. Jewish business practices were often considered secretive by Gentiles, and thus Jews were not always trusted by non-Jews. Aware of the stereotypical Shylock image, Dun agents were often hesitant to recommend credit to Jews, and thus their reports frequently mention Jewishness. In addition to the Dun reports, extant synagogue and burial records are helpful, as well as both Jewish and non-Jewish census data. Coupled with various other archival sources, and as a final resort suspicions based on last names, we can come close to determining which merchants may likely have been Jewish. We can then link Jewish merchants back to the businesses they operated to quantify Jewish mercantile life in the region.[33]

Utilizing sources such as these, we can paint a clearer, though not perfect, demographic profile of Jews in this era using methodologies of the digital humanities—particularly through geographic information system (GIS) maps. These maps clearly demonstrate that the vast majority of Gulf South Jews lived in market towns that were located first in regions of high cotton production and/or marketing. The most important region that stands out is Vicksburg and the Bends, which, as we saw above, was considered to be the most fertile cotton land in the world. A second cotton-rich region that stands out is the Black Belt of central Alabama and northeast Mississippi, named for its rich soil, which provided some of the most productive cotton land in the region.

But in addition to Jewish concentrations in these two dense cotton-growing and cotton-production areas, Jews were concentrated in towns situated along river and/or rail lines that offered easy transportation access for cotton shipments. Vicksburg and the Bends towns had easy transportation along the Mississippi River, and Black Belt towns had access primarily along the Alabama and Tombigbee Rivers. But following transportation routes also broadens the map to include towns along the Mississippi River's tributaries that were also located in areas of dense cotton production, particularly the Red, Ouachita, Arkansas, and Yazoo Rivers. Moreover, with the expansion of the railroad, the map also indicates Jewish population density in towns in cotton-producing regions alongside railroads such as the Texas Pacific, the Illinois Central, the Tennessee & Virginia, the Louisville, Nashville & Southern, and the Alabama Great Southern.

A closer demographic analysis shows a staggering concentration of Jewish dry goods and general store merchants in these towns, revealing a Jewish niche economy within the Gulf South's cotton industry. As we have seen, these stores were critically important because they provided the goods and credit that fueled the postbellum cotton-based economy. With cotton at the center of the global economy, and as owners of the stores that fueled that vital industry, Jewish merchants in these towns were at the heart of the local and global economies.

When we piece all this information together, and incorporate these data into maps, we uncover a clear economic niche for postbellum Jewry in the Gulf South. Map I.2 demonstrates how, in cotton towns along river and rail lines, Jews operated an inordinate number of general and dry goods stores. The size of each pie chart represents the total number of these stores, and the dark section of the circle represents the best estimate of Jewish-owned stores. These high concentrations are in the towns of the cotton regions, which were located along rivers and rail lines. Percentages in the especially fertile Vicksburg and the Bends are particularly compelling, showing that Jews owned upward of half of these stores.

Map I.3 reveals another pattern to display this niche economy, in which Jews in these cotton towns constituted a larger percentage of the population than their statewide average, owned a larger percentage of the stores in a particular town than their percentage of the population in those towns, and owned an even larger share of general and dry goods stores than their overall share of store ownership. The size of the black circle on the map represents the percentage of Jewish-owned dry goods and general stores in a particular town—not the actual number of these stores. The larger the black circle, the greater the percentage. The gray circle indicates the percentage of all businesses in that town that were owned by Jews, and the white circle indicates the Jewish percentage of the town's population. In nearly every town in the region, although Jews

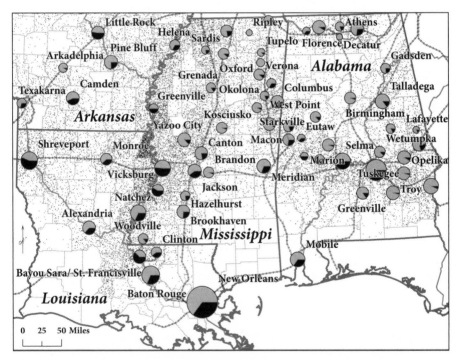

Map I.2. Percentage of Jewish-owned general and dry goods stores in Gulf South towns, 1880. *Note*: Size of pie chart represents total number of general and dry goods stores in each town. Black section of pie chart represents Jewish-owned general and dry goods stores. Shaded gray dots represent 100 bales of cotton produced in 1880, distributed randomly throughout county and parish borders. Railroads depict extent of tracks in 1880.

constituted only about 0.32 percent of the Gulf South states included in our study, their representation in businesses, and particularly in this sector of the economy, vastly outpaced their numbers in the broader population.[34]

The impact of niche economies, however, is not limited to the economic sphere, as economic success begat communal, civic, and social integration for the merchants and communities at the heart of the industry. There is already a very robust literature on Jewish success, communal life, and integration in the Gulf South, and the impact of their success, while important, is not the subject of this book. Yet it is worth

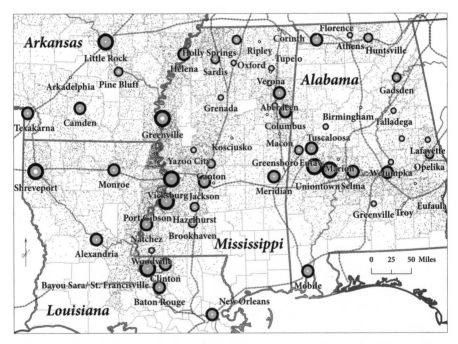

Map 1.3. Jewish percentages of the population, store ownership, and general and dry goods store ownership, 1880.

Note: Size of circles represent percentages, not total numbers. Size of white dot represents percentage of Jews in the town's total population. Size of gray circle represents percentage of Jewish-owned businesses among all businesses in the town. Size of black circle represents percentage of Jewish-owned general and dry goods stores among all general and dry goods stores in the town. Shaded gray dots represent 100 bales of cotton produced in 1880, distributed randomly throughout county and parish borders. Railroads depict extent of tracks in 1880.

stepping back briefly to recognize the ways in which this ethnic niche economy led to a "golden era" for Southern Jews during the roughly two decades after the Civil War.

This Jewish renaissance is often overlooked. For some students of American Jewish history, the story only truly begins in the year 1880, which conjures up images of East European immigrants arriving en masse to Ellis Island, eager to begin life anew in the densely packed Lower East Side of Manhattan. Over 2 million Jews poured into America over the ensuing four decades, marking one of the largest demographic shifts in modern Jewish history. Speaking Yiddish, practicing Eastern European traditions, often living in squalid conditions in a densely packed ethnic enclave, working in sweatshops, and clustering in the garment industry, these American Jews lived what many assume is the "quintessential" American Jewish experience.[35]

But concurrently, a similarly important but oft-overlooked demographic shift was taking place in the Lower Mississippi Valley, as many Southern Jews, who had arrived earlier in the nineteenth century, were beginning to achieve economic success as they fortified their niche in the cotton industry. These Jewish merchants rose to prominence, much as the Sephardic Jews had previously done in America in the seventeenth and eighteenth centuries. The niche economy they created transformed both the Jewish community and the broader Gulf South in several ways. First, it redrew the American Jewish map, so that, as we saw above, it came to resemble the map of the Gulf South's cotton production. Jews moved to market towns in significant numbers, settling down from their peddling-based lifestyles to open storefronts in cotton towns throughout the Gulf South.[36]

Second, Jewish mercantile success allowed Jews to achieve economic stability in a remarkably short period of time. The Jews of Bayou Sara, Louisiana, for example, according to the *American Israelite* in 1876, were "well-to-do, and appear to be liberal in principle and purse." Jewish sojourner Charles Wessolowsky visited Greenville, Mississippi, in 1878 and "admired the beautiful cottages owned by our co-religionists."[37]

Third, the internal dynamics of Jewish communities also changed dramatically. As Jews transitioned from a wandering, peddling-based lifestyle, they built more stable Jewish communities. Successful Jewish merchants throughout the Gulf South invested some of their earnings in purchasing burial grounds, erecting synagogues, hiring rabbis, operating social organizations, and investing in other forms of Jewish life. In Greenville, Mississippi, Jewish merchants Morris Weiss and Nathan Goldstein sold to the Jewish community land that was intended to be used for building a new synagogue. In Bayou Sara, many of the town's most prosperous merchants were members and leaders of its B'nai B'rith lodge, and when the time came for a burial ground, the *American Israelite* reported that Bayou Sara's Jews "went to work in the old Jewish manner, viz: putting their hands in their pockets and pulling out enough to defray all the expenses and retain a handsome balance in hand," and a local merchant hosted the dedication.[38]

When it was time to build a synagogue in St. Francisville, Louisiana, one of the town's leading merchants was elected chairman pro tem of the committee to find a site for the new congregation, and when the congregation opened, its membership rolls included a significant number of the town's leading merchants. When Charles Wessolowsky visited Natchez, Mississippi, he called its grand house of worship a "gorgeous and handsome temple" that "seems to prosper very much." In Meridian, Mississippi, Wessolowsky noted how twenty-two families and about one hundred fifty people in all "have by determination, adequate will and energetic works, erected a structure which today stands with its majestic towers, in grandeur and splendor, as an honor to our people and a pride to the citizens of Meridian." In Vicksburg, he observed that the synagogue building was "handsome and neatly fitted up inside, but it is very much in want of improvement on external appearance," noting however that its members planned to fundraise to "give it a brushing sometime this winter."[39] Jewish merchants thus embraced and nurtured communal life in these cotton towns, creating the institutions of Jewish community where there had been none.

Fourth, this niche affected Jews' general level of integration in their broader societies. Jewish mercantile success facilitated Jewish integration into the towns in which they lived, and that integration is illustrated by their philanthropy toward the community's broader causes. One newspaper noted in Bayou Sara "the generosity and great charity for which our Jewish fellow-citizens are proverbial." The *True Democrat* of West Feliciana Parish declared that, "for over a third of a century," Jewish merchant Julius Freyhan "was closely identified with the rehabilitation of West

Feliciana parish [sic], in which he played no unimportant part." One article claimed that, during a time in which flood relief was necessary, "J. Freyhan and Company shipped 10,000 lbs. of meat, filling an order for that amount." Later, Freyhan donated the chandelier for the West Feliciana Parish courthouse, and he also donated to the construction of levees, roads, and public facilities. A bequest after his death helped to build a public school that was named in his memory—the Julius Freyhan High School.[40]

The same was true elsewhere. In Pine Bluff, Arkansas, as a testament to his stature in the community, townspeople named the local elementary school after Jewish merchant Gabe Meyer—the school was largely demolished in 2014, but a successful crowd sourcing campaign saved the facade. In Greenville, Mississippi, when Jewish merchant Leopold Wilczinski and his kin arrived in town, claimed one 1891 publication, "it was a hamlet of perhaps five hundred people, and no one has done more in various ways to advance and develop her resources than the members of this family."[41]

The Jews' level of integration is also illustrated by their election to important political offices. Merchant Adolph Meyer represented Louisiana in the U.S. House of Representatives from 1891 to 1908, and in the major towns in Vicksburg and the Bends, Jews served as mayors in all but one. By 1891 Port Gibson had a Jewish mayor—Simon Unger. In Greenville, merchants Leopold Wilczinski, Julius Lengsfield, Jacob Alexander, and Nathan Goldstein all served terms as mayor in the 1870s alone. In Natchez, Isaac Lowenburg was elected mayor in 1882 and 1884, and at least thirteen Jews, including cotton merchants Aaron and Albert Jacobs, served as aldermen. E. W. Whiteman worked at the Bayou Sara store of his father, who may have been Jewish, and he later served two stints as the town's mayor. Jews were also elected as mayors elsewhere in the Gulf South. In Montgomery, Jewish Mayor Mordecai Moses, "with his zeal and energy works for the welfare of the city, and his ability as a financier has succeeded in establishing the credit of the city equally as good as that of any other in the Union," Wesselowsky claimed. In 1887, Selma elected a Jewish mayor, Simon Maas, and Ed Weil served as mayor of Alexandria, Louisiana.[42]

The Jews' level of integration is also evidenced by the significant amount of social integration, at least on the surface, between Jews and Gentiles. Natchez's Jews "stand high in the social scale," noted the *American Israelite*, and social columns in Natchez's newspapers reveal that social events were hosted by the now thriving merchant class—most of the members of the merchant class who hosted these social events were Jewish. At Bayou Sara's Jewish weddings, "among the guests were numbered many Christian friends," and at St. Francisville's synagogue dedication, "the sacred building was filled prior to the hour for the services," noted the *True Democrat*, "by a large congregation composed of Jews and Gentiles. It was an hour of rejoicing," the account continued, "and Christian friends, fully sympathetic, rejoiced too." In Greenville, a reverend gave a benediction at a Hebrew Union Congregation event to honor the hundredth birthday of Moses Montefiore. Also in Greenville, non-Jewish children attended Purim parties while Jewish children gave tableaus as benefits for churches, and in 1882, the local Episcopal, Methodist, and Presbyterian clergy joined a local rabbi in condemning anti-Jewish pogroms as "contrary to the spirit of Christianity."[43]

However, despite that significant degree of integration in the communities in which they lived, Jews still in many ways remained "integrated outsiders" and were not treated as full equals by the society around them. Even in the small Southern towns of the region, where Jewish merchants had reached the pinnacle of success, social stigmas, such as those in New York that affected the Seligmans, never quite disappeared.[44]

But this is not a book about Jewish success. Rather, it analyzes the niche economy in the cotton industry that laid the foundations for this communal, civic, and social success and that ushered Jews into the world of global capitalism. The first chapter begins in the decade prior to the Civil War and argues that while Jews did not play a major role in the antebellum cotton industry, three particular developments in these years set the stage for postbellum mercantile success. First, Jewish merchants, who often started by peddling throughout the countryside, began to open general and dry goods stores in the interior towns of the Gulf South. When the old factorage system broke down and general stores became the primary creditors of the region, Jewish merchants were in the right place at the right time and found themselves at the center of global capitalism. Second, many of the antebellum general stores accumulated capital, and their proprietors invested wisely to grow their businesses. Thus, on the eve of the Civil War, a number of Jewish-owned stores were poised to become major players in the postbellum economy. But a third and important antebellum factor that set the stage for postbellum success was the development of family and ethnic networks that linked partners within firms, brought global capital and credit to Southern Jewish firms, and then allowed those firms to offer credit to other Jewish firms throughout the Gulf South. While these networks did not lead to widespread success for Jewish cotton merchants in the antebellum years, they facilitated the later transformation of their toehold in the cotton industry into a much larger niche economy. Antebellum networks were closely tied to postbellum success.

Chapter 2 focuses on the Civil War years, which threatened to undermine the Jews' early presence in the cotton industry. In the early years of the war, a Union blockade brought legal trade to a standstill, and for merchants who relied on trade networks between the North and the South, the blockade appeared catastrophic. But with soaring demand for cotton around the globe, as well as strong demand for goods in the South, opportunities abounded for merchants to engage in clandestine smuggling and blockade-running, and many acquired capital in this fashion. Merchants also conducted legal trade throughout the South in whichever ways they could. Some stockpiled cotton, and some wisely avoided Confederate currency, which would turn out to be worthless after the war. But once Ulysses S. Grant's troops declared victory after the bloody battle of Vicksburg, which opened the Mississippi River for commerce, the landscape changed, and new opportunities emerged. With New Orleans and the Mississippi River in Union hands, legal cotton trade resumed between North and South, and merchants flocked to the interior towns that facilitated this commerce. They also established or reestablished trade networks that closely resembled those that emerged in the antebellum years. But the resumption of trade was slowed by a plethora of factors, including the death and destruction left in the wake of the war and the Confederates' quest to burn cotton rather than see it fall into Union hands. Nonetheless, by the end of the Civil War, firms that had saved capital, reestablished North-South networks, or both, stood on sound footing, prepared to face the vicissitudes of the postbellum economy.[45]

Chapter 3 examines the aftermath of the war and the new environment in which merchants operated. It argues that a myriad of structural forces aligned to position interior general store merchants at the forefront of the cotton economy. Of particular importance was the collapse of traditional financing structures, which could no longer provide the credit necessary to fuel the cotton economy. Instead, interior general store owners, with capital saved from the war years or with credit networks linking them to centers such as New York and Liverpool, became the lifeblood of the Southern economy. But despite the cotton economy moving toward them, success was not guaranteed, nor was it linear. Rather, three distinct periods shaped mercantile life after the war, and the ebbs and flows of these eras very much dictated both *when* and *how* businesses could succeed. Businesses that had saved capital from the war had the reserves to draw upon when crop failures hit in 1866 and 1867, but new businesses often did not. In some of the towns most important to the industry, these new businesses were predominantly operated by non-Jews. These non-Jewish merchants found themselves in the wrong place at the wrong time, as they chased opportunity in the industry during a period where success was doomed by forces beyond their control. The fortunes of the region ticked upward between 1868 and 1873, as crop yields improved, the economy strengthened, and laws passed in response to the downturn greatly benefited merchants. Jewish merchants in particular, who either survived the war or who settled in the region in greater numbers than they had during the downturn, now found themselves in the right place at the right time. These merchants grew their customer bases by working with freedmen, which made logical business sense. But the Panic of 1873 ushered in a period of uncertainty that lasted until 1879 and was accompanied by violence, political instability, disease outbreaks, and other challenges.

While skill, luck, and steady access to capital helped businesses to survive the downturns that were endemic to the postbellum years, survival also required credit. The fourth and fifth chapters closely analyze how two primary tiers of ethnic networks brought that credit from global financiers to the merchants and farmers of the Gulf South. Through the lens of Lehman Brothers, chapter 4 examines the top tier, exploring how networks carried global investment to the Gulf South. This occurred in an era where, as we have seen, business transactions relied upon trust, which was often fostered by shared ethnicity—largely confining Jewish and non-Jewish networks to separate spheres. Lehman Brothers, for example, worked closely with Jewish-owned banking houses such as Lazard Frères, J. W. Seligman & Co., and Kuhn, Loeb & Co., in much the same way that Anglo-American banks such as J. P. Morgan & Co. cultivated networks with other non-Jewish businesses. Utilizing these ethnic networks, Lehman Brothers brought international investment to America, and continuing to rely on ethnicity to build trust, the firm loaned money to scores of cotton businesses in the Gulf South, many of which were also operated by Jews. With access to this credit via ethnic networks, these businesses could survive downturns in the economy and thrive in the postbellum milieu.

Chapter 5 examines the bottom tier of this network, exploring how the Southern firms with which Lehman Brothers worked dispersed this global investment throughout local economies. In some instances, Lehman Brothers' customers sold directly to rural farmers and plantation owners, providing them with the credit necessary to purchase their farming supplies, to put food on their tables, and to purchase luxury goods if they were in a position to do so. But in other instances, firms with which Lehman Brothers worked, including Julius Weis's firm, Meyer, Weis & Co., extended credit to smaller shopkeepers, who could then stock their own shelves at the start of the season, sell goods to their customers on credit, and, if all went well, be repaid by their customers after the harvest. For these smaller businesses, this line of credit was the difference between success and failure, particularly when the vicissitudes of the economy necessitated leniency from creditors. But this leniency was risky for lenders, and to mitigate risk, firms such as Meyer, Weis & Co. utilized trust-based economic networks that were often fostered by shared ethnicity. In this way, Jewish merchants created an ethnic niche in the cotton industry, securing global investment, funneling it to the South, and dispersing it throughout local economies.

Finally, chapter 6 explores the end of the niche economy. By the late nineteenth century, changes to the cotton industry meant that merchants in the Gulf South were no longer as important as they once were. Structural changes to global capitalism, including the rise of investment banking, changed the nature of credit and lending, as networks of trust, which once provided a competitive advantage for Jews, Greeks, and other minorities, began to lose their importance. Additional global forces also mitigated the Gulf South's centrality in the cotton industry, as the world's thirst for cotton pushed European powers to find cheaper places in the world to produce cotton. Localized factors were also marginalizing the Gulf South and its Jewish merchants, as floods and invasive species ravaged cotton crops and a spate of anti-Jewish violence took direct aim at the Jewish niche economy. All of this meant that, in much the same manner that Jewish merchants had once marginalized cotton factors, Jewish merchants themselves were now marginalized, and their niche economy collapsed.

Yet during the heyday of this Jewish niche economy, Jewish merchants were at the forefront of capitalist expansion. Their story, as we shall see, unfolds as more than just a tale of success and integration. It is, instead, the story of how ethnicity mattered in the development of global capitalism.

1

The Antebellum Cotton Economy

One spring day in 1844, Friedrich Gerstäcker was floating downriver approaching Shreveport, Louisiana, when he looked toward the left bank of the river "and was not a little astonished when I saw that the left bank of the bayou, right at the point where it merged with the Red River, was covered with *snow*. Or so it appeared." After a closer examination, however, Gerstäcker "realized that it was *cotton* that covered almost an acre of land as densely as snow." As he continued down the Red and into the Mississippi River, he found himself surrounded by vessels carrying even more cotton downriver to New Orleans. "Wherever my eye gazed, I could see the heavily laden flatboats," Gerstäcker noted, and he also saw steamboats—once per hour, he estimated, and often three or four at a time—that were "capable of loading three or four thousand bales" of cotton. This cotton was destined for New Orleans, where it was then sold and shipped to points across the globe.[1]

In the antebellum years, Jewish merchants were on the margins of this booming cotton industry, but three particular developments in this era laid the groundwork for their postbellum success. First, Jewish merchants began to open general and dry goods stores in interior cotton towns. When the traditional cotton factorage system would later break down, these interior general stores would become the most important institutions in the cotton industry. Jewish merchants would thus be in the right place at the right time, facilitating their entry into the cotton industry and their integration into global capitalism. Second, a number of those Jewish merchants accumulated a significant amount of capital during the antebellum years, providing them with the resources to survive the disruption of the Civil War and to enter the postbellum years on sound footing. And third, Jewish merchants began to establish family and ethnic networks that connected partners within firms, brought global investment through New York to the Gulf South, and provided credit to fellow Jewish merchants in the region. These three developments were prerequisites that allowed Jewish merchants' early toehold in the industry to later blossom into a flourishing ethnic economy.

* * *

By the mid-nineteenth century the region's cotton-propelled economy was rapidly taking market share from the Atlantic Seaboard. Yet it doing so on the backs of slaves—between 1820 and 1860, possibly a million slaves were "sold down the river" via an internal slave trade. Predicated upon slavery, the region's market share increased dramatically to over half of the nation's crop by 1840. Aggregate value of real and personal property more than doubled in Louisiana over the

Figure 1.1. "Cotton Levee in New Orleans." Image courtesy of the Library of Congress (LC-USZ62–4928).

1850s as rural landholders poured more and more of their resources into cotton, favoring immediate profit over long-term diversification. And as more land was cultivated for cotton, the steamboat traffic that Gerstäcker had observed on the Mississippi River increased. Between 1840 and 1860, the number increased from 1,500 to 3,500 steamboats, and the amount of freight shipped increased fourfold, from half a million tons to 2 million tons. The value of that cotton increased as well, from $50 million to almost $2 billion.[2]

But bringing cotton from the fields to market was no easy proposition. For starters, cotton bales were unwieldy. They often weighed 400–500 pounds each, were four to five feet long, and one to three feet wide, and each bale had to be individually wrapped and then tied. In large part because of their size and weight, damage was frequent. Bales were often "skidded," dragged across the ground as they were being loaded or unloaded into boats, resulting in dirt on the bottom and thus a reduction in quality. Rain could leave the surfaces of a bale "wet-packed," caked

Figure 1.2. "King Cotton and His Slaves, Greenwood, Mississippi." Image courtesy of the Library of Congress (LC-USZ62–36638).

Figure 1.3. "A Cotton Plantation on the Mississippi." Image courtesy of the Library of Congress (LC-USZ62-345).

and foul smelling, similarly reducing quality. While selling crops locally could reduce the time in transit and thus minimize the chance of such damage, shipping to cotton markets such as New Orleans increased risk, but more buyers generally meant higher demand and higher prices. Because the slightest bit of damage could be the difference between profit and loss, the simple act of bringing a bale of cotton to market was critically important and by no means an easy task.[3]

While bringing a bale of cotton to market in good condition was a challenge, so, too, was selling that cotton at the highest price possible. Unaware of the daily fluctuations of cotton prices in an age before the widespread use of the telegraph, interior planters had no way of knowing when the time was right to sell. Cotton prices could change by the minute, often fluctuating 10–15 percent over the course of a month and as much as 30–40 percent over a selling season. But news of those changes could not reach interior planters before the information was out of date. One planter estimated that it took a week for letters to make their way upriver, and another called mail service to Bayou Sara, Louisiana, "extremely irregular." Thus planters had little idea as to whether they were selling when supply was limited and prices were high or whether they were shipping cotton to a saturated New Orleans market with depressed prices.[4]

Lacking the requisite knowledge, expertise, and resources, planters frequently turned to cotton factors to market their cotton and maximize their profits. Unlike planters, factors were generally based in port cities, so they weren't limited to selling cotton locally. Prices differed by market, and factors often had agents overseas—in the large cotton markets of Liverpool, for example. Southern factors often had outlets for their cotton in Northern markets as well, as large Northern firms often had agents located in port cities in the South. Thus factors gave growers access to markets across the globe that they would not have otherwise had.[5]

In addition to finding the right place to sell, factors also had to find the right time to sell. A stockpile of cotton from the previous growing year could depress prices early in the season, while little prior stock could lead to high early-season prices. If the bulk of the cotton harvest came to market mid-season, prices might be low. However, that could mean a smaller late harvest, which could lead to a spike in prices if demand were high. Or, if demand were low, it could lead to a glut of cotton on the market at the end of the season, lowering prices. It was one thing to rely on gossip when estimating the size and timing of the harvest, but it was another to have the resources and information to make a more educated decision about the best time to sell.[6]

Sometimes a cotton factor was successful in maximizing profits by choosing the right place and time to sell, but other times he was not. Misreading the market was often the culprit when a factor failed in his task, but so were more nefarious elements. If a factor had cash-flow problems, he might be tempted to sell too soon and before prices had crested, or even more dubious or deceptive business practices might yield a factor more money than was due. In part because planters had so little control over their profits, legal action sometimes followed sales that did not deliver the highest prices of the season.[7]

In addition to marketing and selling cotton, a factor's other primary responsibility was to provision planters with the supplies they needed throughout the year. This might include seeds and planting supplies to produce crops, emergency funds to meet an unexpected expense, staple foodstuffs to feed the planter's family throughout the year, or luxury goods such as books or wine. By provisioning them with goods and supplies while at the same time selling their crop, a factor had an inordinate impact over the lives of the planters and farmers with whom he worked.[8]

The success of the cotton factorage system was possible only because cotton was the security at the center of the South's extensive credit system. Factors borrowed money from banks in New Orleans, New York, or Europe and used this money to purchase the goods that they would then advance to planters. Factors also advanced to planters the costs of marketing the cotton, including transportation and insurance against water and fire damage, and charges for weighing and warehousing the cotton once it arrived in the port city. If the cotton was to be sold in another city, factors would advance additional charges for shipping, and potentially charges for recompression, which were often necessary for European shipments. Factors advanced these services, and when the cotton was sold, the cost of the items, as well as the factors' commissions, would be deducted from the proceeds. Factors would then pay their debts to their creditors and then pay the planters whatever profits—if any—remained. Planters would generally be paid in the wintertime, and the cycle would begin again in the spring.[9]

This form of credit—security in a crop that was not yet grown and a perpetual cycle of credit and debt—was, in the words of one Northerner visiting Mississippi in 1834, "peculiar." An 1841 article declared that it was "well known" that, in the cotton trade, "the harvest of one year is, as it were, mortgaged for the expenses of the next." Such a system, in which money was borrowed against the future crop, was commonplace. "The agriculturalists who create the real wealth of the country are not in daily receipt of money," noted one observer. "Their produce is ready but once in the year, whereas they buy supplies [on credit] year round. . . . The whole banking system of the country is based primarily on this bill movement against produce."[10]

Cotton crops, however, were not always profitable enough to repay the debts incurred by the planter over the course of the year. Too much sun mid-season could lead to a withered crop, and too much rain could also doom the crop, as could a late-arriving spring, an early frost, or a crop infestation. "Day by day you can see the vegetation of vast fields becoming thinner and thinner," one contemporary observed, as the result of a worm infestation. "All efforts to arrest their progress or annihilate them prove unavailing. They seem to spring out of the ground, and fall from the clouds."[11]

When a bad crop year occurred, a planter's debts would be carried over from one year to the next. But a bad crop year also placed a factor at risk, as reduced income often meant that he could not repay his own bank loans. To protect against risk, some bankers tried to limit their exposure to three-quarters of the expected revenue from the cotton. Factors also generally lent money to planters at interest and charged a commission on goods purchased or sold on behalf of the planter in order to limit their own risk. In this way, both the bankers and factors could make money while limiting their risk, although they were not always successful in doing so.[12]

While the factorage system long dominated antebellum mercantile life, the landscape was beginning to shift in the years prior to the Civil War, foreshadowing a major transformation that would reach fruition in the postbellum years and would facilitate Jewish concentration in the industry. In the years prior to the Civil War, factors began to find competition in scores of small general stores that were popping up across the interior—some of which were operated by Jews. As transportation improved and new lands opened for production on the cotton frontier, the number of these towns and stores grew rapidly. In 1840, Louisiana's number of stores per thousand population ranked second in the nation, and while much of this mercantile activity was centered in New Orleans, one estimate counted almost 600 stores in Louisiana outside of New Orleans. Those numbers only grew over time.[13]

Interior river towns became particularly important to the cotton industry in the antebellum years—particularly towns located on rivers that provided access to New Orleans. "The place has gone business mad," one newspaper correspondent wrote of antebellum Shreveport. "There seem to be more stores than residences." Antebellum Natchez was also an important interior cotton center, in close proximity to cotton plantations and along the Mississippi River for easy access to New Orleans. Natchez's river port shipped 50,000 bales of cotton in 1860, and mercantile sales approached $2 million.[14]

Bayou Sara, Louisiana, was another interior river town that played an important role in the cotton industry. Located in West Feliciana Parish on the banks of the Mississippi River, Bayou Sara was the largest port in terms of arrivals and departures between Vicksburg and New Orleans, and it was located in some of the most fertile cotton land in the world. It was the transfer point for freight for the Red and Ouachita Rivers, the landing place of the Ohio River coal fleet, and the terminus of the West Feliciana Railroad, which delivered cotton from the interior and acted much like a tributary of the Mississippi. All of this, according to one census report, meant that it was "a commercial center of greater importance than its size or population would seem to indicate." Few people, the *New Orleans Daily Picayune* later noted, "have an idea of the immense business done at this [Bayou Sara] point, in the receiving, forwarding and dry goods business."[15]

Bayou Sara's importance was clear by the beginning of the nineteenth century. "You would be astonished I am sure, if you could spend one week at the Mouth [*sic*] of Bayou Sarah [*sic*] at this season of the year . . . to see the quantity of produce that passes daily to New Orleans," one resident wrote in 1807 to his cousin who was in the "commercial city" of New York. "As the Rivers break up more northwardly," he wrote, "the Boats come on loaded with every kind of produce that the upper empire affords or that ingenuity can invent, Flour, corn meal, whiskey and Cider, Pork and Beef, live state fed Beaver, Venison and Mutton Hams, great quantities of bacon, Horses in great numbers . . . and every thing else that the country affords, or that is wanted here." One resident described how riverboats brought goods to Bayou Sara from St. Louis and New Orleans, and it was warehoused by a local business. "Merchants came by horse and buggy and with large wagons drawn by yokes of oxen, four or five to a wagon, to pick up goods for resale in their communities."[16]

When J. W. Dorr, a journalist from New Orleans, visited Bayou Sara before the war, he found a "thriving and bustling place" that "contains some of the most extensive and heavily stocked stores in Louisiana, outside of New Orleans." The town had its share of large businesses, as well as "a variety of smaller but apparently prosperous establishments, restaurants, bar-rooms, etc., and all the other aspects of a small city," including a dentist and an apothecary. At the top of the hill was Bayou Sara's twin town of St. Francisville, which, Dorr maintained, was "stronger on the ornamental," but Bayou Sara was "out of sight ahead of her on the practical, for she does all the business and a great deal of business is done, too."[17]

As Bayou Sara grew, it gained a reputation as "a wild, rowdy, riverboat town," while the surrounding plantations reflected wealthy, Southern genteel society. There were several large homes in the surrounding area, including Afton Villa, "with its thirty-four rooms, large ballroom and banqueting hall, towers, balconies enclosed by stained glass doors opening on a terrace above a sloping lawn beyond which winds a live oak avenue." Then there was Wakefield, with "rooms thirty or forty feet long," The Myrtles, "with its ornate iron-railed gallery," and Rosedown, "gleaming white at the end of its long, deeply umbraged, azelia[sic]-bordered avenue of grand old oaks." In 1821, John James Audubon visited the region and noted that "the rich magnolias covered with fragrant blossoms, the holly, the beech, the tall yellow poplars, the hilly ground and even the red clay all excited my admiration."[18]

While towns such as Shreveport, Natchez, and Bayou Sara were on the rise in the antebellum years, the merchants of these towns were beginning to play an increasingly important role in the cotton industry. As proximate farmlands opened to cotton production, the region became friendlier to interior merchants. Peddlers, many of whom were Jews, were often the first merchants to arrive, selling farming supplies and other wares and chasing what little opportunity was available. But as new frontier lands opened for farming, and their scale of business increased, many peddlers made enough money to open storefronts in towns such as Shreveport, Natchez, and Bayou Sara. In Natchez, middle-class merchants gained financial prominence in the 1850s. There were over 100 retail firms in 1858, and the most successful businesses in that era were those that stocked a variety of goods to supply plantations. Some owners of these small general stores, many of whom were Jews, may have been familiar with their clientele and their needs from their days as peddlers, and they would have a decided advantage when general stores ultimately made the cotton factor superfluous. Although these merchants played only a small role in the antebellum cotton industry, they were in the right place at the right time to capitalize on the changes that would soon come.[19]

Initially the functions that those shopkeepers fulfilled mirrored those of the factors, though on a smaller scale. Store owners worked primarily with farmers whose crops were generally too small to interest large-scale factors, and their most important function was supplying goods to those living in rural areas. While some stores sold goods on the cash system, others would sell goods on credit in much the same fashion as the factor. Moreover, just as the factor did for larger clients, general stores also handled the sale of the cotton crop of smaller farmers. Store owners would purchase the small crops from a multitude of farmers, providing them the scale necessary to work with larger factors to market the crop. Additionally, because there were no rural state-chartered banks in Louisiana, many of these firms filled this void by also operating rudimentary banking operations.[20]

As the Gulf South's cotton economy grew in the antebellum period, so, too, did the number and strength of general stores, which began to tread on the economic territory of the factors. Not only were these stores, which were usually small, locally owned, and locally managed, numerous, but a fairly significant number of them also achieved success in the antebellum years. Their success provided store owners with a base of capital that would help them survive the war years and thrive in the postbellum years.[21]

Successful merchants in Bayou Sara included Swedish native Charles Toorain, a dry goods and grocery proprietor, who arrived around 1849 and, like many others, began his career as a clerk. He was soon engaged to the daughter of his employer and shortly thereafter opened his own business. Although initially the "public don't seem to have any great confidence in him," as a credit reporter wrote, this soon changed. His business grew slowly, and although not large, he was "apparently sf. [safe]" for creditors. Toorain purchased his goods and supplies in New York and New Orleans, and by the late 1850s, he "seems to have the confidence of the public."[22]

Toorain was not the only Bayou Sara merchant who capitalized on the growing opportunities in the interior. One of the most prominent businesses in town was Lebret & Hearsey, initially under the direction of Peter and John Lebret, Frenchmen who came "with nothing." They accumulated wealth, purchasing slaves and a plantation in 1844, and by 1847 were doing a "large . . . chiefly cash" business on the mercantile side of their operation. By 1851, son-in-law William Hearsey, formerly a clerk, had become a partner, and Lebret & Hearsey made between 75 and 100 bales of cotton per year and purchased in New Orleans, St. Louis, and Cincinnati. It was deemed the "best firm here, no doubt [about] it" in 1852, but trouble appeared by 1855, as they were sued and were "hard pressed, carrying on a plantation, + doing but little as merchants." By the middle of 1859, they had "retired from commercial [business]," and Hearsey was running for sheriff.[23]

Bayou Sara had many other mercantile establishments. Felix Leake bought out the firm of Clauss & Fisher in 1852 and was considered a "good bus. [business] man" who operated a commission and forwarding business. He owned slaves by 1857, and was elected parish sheriff. J. W. Dorr called this firm one of the "principal merchants of the place" during his visit around 1860. Charles Wolflin operated a store in Bayou Sara that sold dry goods, groceries, boots, and shoes and also doubled as a saloon, which helped to bring potential customers into his store. Wolflin was operational by 1851 and kept a "small shop" of dry goods and groceries. He was a "prud. [prudent] + econom'l [economical] man," who was "[doing] a [small] but apparently a [safe business]" and who also "keeps a large beer saloon." Not all businessmen, however, were successful. Leonard Schneider ran a grocery store with a tavern and coffeehouse, up the hill in St. Francisville, and although he was "[making] money" and was "a hard worker," he was also "a hard drinker." A credit reporter predicted in 1855 that he "will soon die of whiskey," and within two years, Schneider was dead.[24]

Throughout the interior, some stores attracted customers by doubling as precinct polling places or post offices. Such a status was coveted for the amount of foot traffic it drove. Many served as community meeting spaces, where individuals who were dispersed throughout the countryside could come together and share news or gossip. Other stores served liquor, undoubtedly facilitating social interaction but also creating rowdy and often unpleasant gatherings. Nonetheless, a fairly significant number of interior stores achieved success in the antebellum years at the expense of cotton factors, paving the way for a dramatic increase in these stores in the postbellum period.[25]

Jews, who largely operated as peddlers and interior store owners, were in the right place at the right time—perfectly positioned to capitalize on the trend. On the eve of the Civil War, approximately 33,000 Jews were scattered throughout the South, and the Gulf South saw a

Figure 1.4. "Caricature of Jewish Merchant and Steamboat." Image courtesy of the Jacob Rader Marcus Center of the American Jewish Archives, Cincinnati, Ohio (MSS 601, box 5, folder 1).

particular concentration of Alsatian and Bavarian Jews—due in large part to chain migration as friends and family members followed some of the early migrants. Many of these Jews became peddlers, a role that was familiar to them from their days in Europe and that also integrated them into the American economy. Jews would place packs on their backs, travel to rural interior areas where there was little competition, and bring goods to far-flung places. This was a nationwide pattern, and as new interior cities such as Chicago, St. Louis, Cincinnati, and scores of smaller towns opened, Jewish peddlers were also quickly on the scene to provision early settlers. As they became more successful, Jewish peddlers often opened storefronts, and some store owners would then provision other peddlers.

This economic niche shaped Jewish settlement patterns across the country, but particularly in the Gulf South, and the timing could not have been better. By the mid-nineteenth century, Jews were acquiring the means necessary to open stores just as the general store model was beginning to challenge the factorage system. By opening interior general stores that purchased cotton from farmers and sold them goods on credit, Jews found early success in the cotton industry that served as a harbinger of their postbellum niche economy.[26]

Lehman Brothers provides an excellent example of this phenomenon. Henry Lehman emigrated from rural Bavaria in 1844 at age twenty-one, and after brief stops in New York and Mobile, Alabama, he settled in Montgomery, Alabama, where he was joined in 1847 by his brother Emanuel, and in 1850 by his brother Mayer. In Montgomery, the Lehman brothers opened a store selling merchandise such as crockery, glassware, tools, dry goods, and seeds, and as early as 1850, the partners would "buy cotton," claimed a Dun recorder. "Cotton was used instead of currency in the South in those days," recalled Mayer Lehman's son. "The farmers would come in to town with their cotton and trade it for shirts, shoes, fertilizer . . . and all the necessities." This, he maintained, was "how they got started in the cotton business." The brothers would often extend credit to planters and regularly received payment in cotton rather than currency.[27]

In addition to Lehman Brothers, other Montgomery Jewish businesses fit this model. Weil & Kohn, operated by two "shrewd" German Jews, opened a clothing and dry goods store and did a small "retail business principally with that class of farmers who sell them 2 or 3 bales of cotton, + buy from them a sm. [small] quantity" of dry goods and groceries. Additionally, they employed peddlers in the countryside. Jacob Abrahams also conducted a "country trade" and speculated in cotton. "Good today—cotton may take them tomorrow," warned a credit reporter in 1858.[28]

Bayou Sara, which as we have seen had a strong mercantile presence, also had its fair share of Jewish-owned businesses within the cotton economy. While it is difficult to define the term "cotton economy" with precision, I generally use the term to include those firms that loaned money and/or sold plantation supplies. Stores defined as general or dry goods stores, among others, fit this criterion. Nonetheless, in 1860, based on the best data available, somewhere between 35 percent and 45 percent of firms in the cotton economy were operated by Jews, and of the businesses that credit reporters deemed strong, about half of them were Jewish owned. One of the strongest firms in town was Charles Hoffman & Co., owned by Jews, which by 1849 was said to do "a more extensive [business] than any other [merchant] in the [parish]." A partner in Hoffman's firm, Isaias Meyer, backed I. Meyer & Co., a store operated by a relative, P. Adolphus. Another firm, L. Bach & Co., was considered to be "the largest retailers here" in the mid-1840s. Abram Wolf's small general store was operational by 1853, doing a very safe business. By 1857 his business was described as a commission and forwarding business, yet on the eve of the Civil War, he had "no means except [a small] country store." Another Jewish firm was the grocery and provision store of J & C Whiteman, which had opened by around 1850. John Whiteman was a widower who was considered a good businessman, and in addition to his children, he was assisted for a time by W. D. Hatch. Hatch was likely not Jewish, demonstrating that, while most Jewish shopkeepers formed partnerships with fellow Jews, there were exceptions. Soon the firm was doing a profitable dry goods business, purchasing goods principally in St. Louis and Cincinnati, and its proprietors owned slaves. The firm had warehouses to hold either cotton or goods, and J. W. Dorr also included it among the "principal merchants of the place" during his visit.[29]

In addition to these firms, two other Jewish firms emerged on the eve of the war that would come to play critically important roles in the town's postbellum growth. The first firm was that of Julius Freyhan, who was likely born in 1830 and who arrived in America in 1851. Little is known about his early life in America, but he operated a business in Jackson, Louisiana, in 1853, and a Dun recorder noted in that year that he was told Freyhan had moved to Bayou Sara. By 1856 he was in neighboring East Feliciana Parish, having applied to take the oath of citizenship, and he was a resident of West Feliciana Parish by 1860, when he was called a "young man who has been clerking for [several years]." At that point he ran a "[small business] on the cash system," and one credit reporter believed that he "will not do much." That credit reporter couldn't have been more wrong, as Freyhan would soon operate the most successful postbellum business in Bayou Sara, and he would later work with Lehman Brothers at Lane Cotton Mills in New Orleans.[30]

Another Jewish merchant who came to town shortly before the war, and who would also play an important role after the war, was Moses Mann. When he first arrived, Mann and his partner Abraham Hirsch were "comparatively strangers" who "live somewhat secluded," and they operated a "[small] store." Within a couple of years, however, business was increasing, and Mann owned two slaves. He soon purchased some stores and town property and appeared to be making money. In the postbellum years, Mann would also become one of the town's most important merchants.[31]

Bayou Sara was not the only town in the antebellum Gulf South to see an influx of Jewish businesses. Isaac Brown and Alexander Kuhn were operating a small grocery store in Vicksburg by 1859, and S. Bernheimer & Bro were running a dry goods store in Port Gibson by 1852. Nearly two dozen Jewish-owned businesses were operating in Natchez in the antebellum years, including Aaron Beekman's dry goods and clothing business. In Baton Rouge, Jacob Farnbacher established a dry goods store in 1860, after having "commenced peddling some years since," and M. Levy and Gabriel Meyer's dry goods, etc., shop in Pine Bluff, Arkansas, was in business by 1858. Solomon Block and Edward Feibelman's dry goods store had set down roots in Camden, Arkansas, by 1852, and it also had a presence in Columbia County.[32]

But Bayou Sara played a particularly important role in the cotton economy, and because of its significant mercantile presence and its genteel wealth, the town was closely intertwined socially and economically with New Orleans. New Orleanians, wrote the *Daily Picayune*, "are so intimately allied with those of Bayou Sara, by ties of personal friendship and business connections" and "in the frequency of communication, and the identity of feeling with us," that it was "almost a fifth district of New Orleans."[33]

While interior towns were gaining in stature, there is no question that New Orleans continued to play a dominant role in America's cotton trade in the antebellum period. Although its importance was slipping as the Civil War approached, New Orleans was nevertheless strategically situated at the mouth of the Mississippi River, and large quantities of cotton from the fertile cotton lands nearby were shipped downriver for pressing and baling and then were ultimately sold throughout the world. "For commercial purposes," observed one contemporary, "New Orleans occupies a very superior and commanding situation. It is the natural entrepôt for supplies destined to all parts of the Mississippi Valley, as well as the depot for those products of that salubrious region which seek a market seaward." The Crescent City's cotton receipts increased from less than 40,000 bales in 1816 to almost 1 million by 1840, leading one person to declare that "no city of the world has ever advanced as a market of commerce with such gigantic strides as New Orleans." Over the 1850s, New Orleans's prosperity increased so much that one newspaper declared that "New Orleans is destined to be the greatest city in the Western Hemisphere."[34]

By most outward appearances, New Orleans was booming in the antebellum years, yet the city's prosperity masked fundamental flaws that would hinder its long-term development. Convinced of its geographically driven invincibility, the city placed all its eggs in the cotton industry's basket—largely at the expense of more sustainable industries that could have established a basis for long-term success. Moreover, its infrastructure stagnated without a viable railroad system, and it also did not maintain its waterways—failing, for instance, to remove navigational hazards in the Mississippi River. On top of its notorious history of corruption, as well as its frequent disease outbreaks, New Orleans's levee system lacked needed upgrades, its docks were falling apart, and the city charged extremely high port fees. Much of this was a testament to its misplaced sense of invincibility. Moreover, the city's prosperity in the antebellum years also masked underlying financial issues. Louisiana was not encouraging of foreign investment, and New Orleans had gained an international reputation as a risky place to invest long-term capital. As a result, the Crescent City was losing market share.[35]

Not surprisingly, although New Orleans remained central to the Gulf South's cotton industry, there was an increasing push among interior shopkeepers to decrease their dependence on it. Merchants increasingly purchased supplies in cities such as Louisville, Cincinnati, St. Louis, and New York, but this was particularly galling to many Southerners, who resented the increasing Northern role in Southern trade. For example, the *Vicksburg Daily Whig* declared that New York "sends out her long arms to the extreme South; and with avidity rarely equaled, grasps our gains and transfers them to herself—taxing us at every step and depleting us as extensively as possible without actually destroying us." Although interior merchants may have been torn as to whether to purchase from the North, by avoiding New Orleans they could offer their customers lower prices and thereby generate more business and increased revenues. Pitting loyalty against profits, most storekeepers opted to bypass New Orleans whenever possible.[36]

As New Orleans's centrality to the cotton industry was shrinking, New York's role was on the rise. After recovering from the Panic of 1837, New York increased its exports by 139 percent and its imports by 97 percent between 1850 and 1857—making it America's most important port. By the eve of the Civil War, two-thirds of U.S. imports and one-third of exports went through New York. This trade spurred the city's booming industrial sector, as the amount of capital invested in manufacturing rose by 60 percent over the course of the 1850s. This made New York not only the most important port in the United States but also the most important manufacturing center.[37]

In addition to its advantageous geographic location, New York grew in large part because it was "like a spider in the web of the American economy," argues Sven Beckert, "drawing resources into the metropolis, transforming them, and sending them to places near and far." This placed New York in the center of Pennsylvania's iron works, Cuba's sugar plantations, America's railroads, and, for our purposes, the South's cotton plantations. New York's centrality to the nation's economy only continued to further enhance the city's importance.[38]

As it was growing as a mercantile center, New York was also becoming a major hub of American Jewish life. As the city's population grew to over 1 million by 1860, the Jewish presence increased as well. According to one estimate, by 1840 there were about 10,000 Jews in New York, and on the eve of the Civil War, 40,000 Jews lived in the city. Other population estimates vary, but numbers undoubtedly rose significantly during this period. The Jewish mercantile presence was also maturing. In 1853, at least 105 of the city's "principal" wholesalers were of Jewish firms. That same year, the *Merchants' and Bankers' New York City Reference Guide* listed fourteen "established wholesalers and bankers" in the dry goods business, and that number jumped to forty-one in 1859.[39]

By the mid-nineteenth century, the primary source of profits for New York's mercantile sector was the Southern cotton economy. One observer in the 1850s noted that New York was "virtually an annex of the South, the New York merchants having extensive and very profitable business relations with the merchants south of the Mason and Dixon line. The South was the best customer of New York." The system was fairly straightforward. New York merchants would purchase cotton from the South, often to send via ships to Liverpool. Those ships would return from Liverpool with British goods that the merchants could then sell to Southern plantation owners, as well as to Northerners and Westerners. In this way, many New York merchants connected Southern plantations to the British economy, realizing economic benefits along the way.[40]

In addition to its important role in the country's mercantile industry, New York in the 1850s was also rapidly becoming the nation's financial center. The shift from mercantile activity toward banking was natural, as one of the primary roles of merchants was to advance credit—New York merchants were already providing credit for future crops and goods that were not yet sold. Between 1845 and 1860, Northern banks increased in number from 301 to 567, and their capital increased from $88 million to $193 million—all of this while the South's banks stagnated.[41]

While some of this capital was domestic, much of New York banks' capital came from Britain and Europe. One of the city's most important bankers, August Belmont, came to New York in 1837 to represent the European banking House of Rothschild, which was Jewish owned. So, too, did George Cabot Ward come to represent London's Baring Brothers, which was not owned by Jews. These bankers provided their European firms with access to the American market and affected the contours of French, German, and British investments in American markets.[42]

While Belmont and Ward represented two of the more prominent firms, they were not alone in connecting New York to international investment. Lazard Frères began in the dry goods business in New Orleans and then San Francisco but soon transitioned into banking, focusing largely on exchange services for the foreign currency market. This activity led them to open a Parisian branch in 1852, and they developed close ties with the French government and the Banque de Paris, en route to becoming one of the most important banking firms in Paris. They also began arbitrage services, later opening a London office to access that financial market, and organized a New York branch of the firm.[43]

Despite these connections, there was trouble lurking beneath the surface. First and foremost was the cotton industry's reliance on slavery. Slave market prices varied based on the cotton market, and as the Gulf South's cotton economy boomed between 1820 and 1860, the number of slaves increased sevenfold while the amount of cotton increased fortyfold. New York's dependence on the cotton industry thus made it financially challenging for New York merchants to oppose slavery. One contemporary rhetorically asked what New York would be without slavery and answered by suggesting that "the ships would rot at her docks; grass would grow in Wall Street and Broadway, and the glory of New York, like that of Babylon and Rome, would be numbered with the things of the past." One merchant noted that slavery was "a great evil, a great wrong," but its abolition would wreak economic disaster on New York. "There are millions upon millions of dollars due from Southerners to the merchants and mechanics alone, the payment of which would be jeopardized by any rupture between the North and the South." Slavery, he maintained, was "a matter of business necessity." Moreover, New York bankers took slaves as collateral, so if slavery were abolished, financiers would have little recourse if plantation owners defaulted. The vast majority of loans in East Feliciana Parish, Louisiana, for example, utilized human slaves as collateral, so the end of slavery could spell financial disaster for New York's mercantile firms and banking houses.[44]

In addition to the industry's reliance on slavery, the close relationship between New York and the Southern cotton trade was being challenged by new investment opportunities. Some financiers were turning their attention toward the West, as the gold rush presented a plethora of opportunities, particularly for Jewish firms. The cotton trade also found competition in both manufacturing and New York real estate, which similarly attracted the investment capital of New York bankers and financial elites, offering them a means of diversification with the looming political crisis and threat of war. All of this portended challenges for the South.[45]

As New York's economic importance was on the rise, Southern cotton businesses utilized networks to foster economic connections to the city.

A direct line of credit could mean profitability, but how could a small Jewish general store owner in rural Louisiana or Mississippi convince a large New York business to sell them goods on credit, particularly when societal stigmas of Jews bled into the economic sphere? Credit reporters frequently arrived at Jewish businesses only to find owners who were reluctant to open their books to strangers. This lack of information, coupled with the stereotypical Jewish Shylock image, often fostered a lack of trust, which meant that reporters were often hesitant to recommend Jews for credit. One reporter, for example, declared Lazarus and Leon Bloom of Clinton, Louisiana, to be "as reliable as Jews are generally," and one cautioned that a partner in a firm was "responsible now, but [he] is a Jew; there is no telling how long he will remain so." A credit reporter also warned that "prudence in large transactions with all Jews should be used." Thus, if a New York firm were to rely solely on credit reports to decide whether to trust a particular Southern merchant, Jewish merchants would be at a decided disadvantage.[46]

But by relying on familial and ethnic ties, Jews could sidestep the impact of these reports and build economic relationships based upon trust, which, as we have seen, J. P. Morgan called "the fundamental basis of business." Stores were frequently run as family businesses, as partners were often relatives, and clerks the sons of partners. Moreover, partners would also choose spouses for their children with an eye to the economic impact of a particular match. Family connections could stretch across the country and the globe, as partners in the firm would settle in different cities—including New York—to facilitate trade and credit flows between those with whom they shared trust. When family networks weren't possible, or when a business outgrew them, shared ethnicity between partners still offered a far higher level of trust than a random business interaction.[47]

In addition to connecting partners within firms, family and ethnicity also cultivated networks that moved capital and credit on two primary levels. First, ethnic networks brought foreign and domestic capital into the Gulf South. Often a partner would open a branch in New York, where he or she could develop face-to-face relationships with financiers who had global connections, many of whom were Jewish. Family and ethnic connections such as these were not limited to Jews. The firm of Robert Habersham & Son, for example, would sell in the South, while

I. Rae Habersham led the New York branch of the firm. In addition to family connections, ties of ethnicity also undergirded networks between Southern and Northern firms. "As far back as 1846," Julius Weis recalled, his firm "imported some drygoods from Switzerland, for which Lazard Freres [*sic*]," operated by fellow Jews to whom he was not related, "had given their acceptance."[48]

Additionally, family and ethnic networks operated at a second level. Once capital reached wholesale and retail firms in the Gulf South, those businesses then utilized ethnic networks to distribute capital and provide credit to other Jewish firms within the local economies. For example, when wholesaler A. Beer & Co. went bankrupt in 1855, approximately two-thirds of the customers who owed it money were fellow Jews. Ethnic credit networks often allowed lenders to be more lenient in allowing a trusted customer extra time to pay. For example, when

Figure 1.5. "Julius Weis." Image courtesy of the Jacob Rader Marcus Center of the American Jewish Archives, Cincinnati, Ohio (PC-4687).

a yellow fever outbreak decimated Julius Weis's business and "the payments came due for our goods," Weis noted that his Jewish creditors "had confidence in me and helped us out," and he was soon "paid up in full."[49]

These family and ethnic networks stood at the center of many of the largest and strongest Jewish businesses in the antebellum Gulf South's cotton industry. For Goldsmith, Haber & Co., family and ethnic networks within and without the firm ran deep, allowing its partners to accumulate capital during the antebellum years and positioning them for success after the war. Lewis Goldsmith emigrated from Bavaria to Mobile, Alabama, in 1836 around the age of twenty-five, where he married Esther Haber, and he also met members of the Forcheimer family, with whom he would later partner. Goldsmith began peddling in the Mobile area, and by 1844 he had opened a wholesale clothing firm that conducted business primarily with Jewish peddlers and rural shopkeepers. By 1846, Goldsmith had opened Goldsmith, Haber & Co. in New Orleans with his brother-in-law Abraham Haber and Haber's brother Isaac, which began inauspiciously enough. Dun agents reported that it was composed of unknown Jews, though they "seem to understand" the business. Goldsmith, Haber & Co. quickly became successful, and in 1855 the firm moved to a "fine new store in a better location" and was "selling a good many goods." By 1857, they were doing a "good wholesale business," supplying other firms with the goods they could acquire in New York. In 1858, a credit reporter considered them to be as good as any firm in the city.[50]

As New York was growing in importance over the 1850s, Goldsmith, Haber & Co. sought a direct connection with the New York market. To that end, they sent Isaac Haber to New York to purchase goods for the firm, and he opened Morrison, Haber & Co., together with Lewis Morrison, who was the father-in-law of one of the Habers. The roots of the New York branch dated back to the 1840s, and it had begun under Morrison's tutelage. The firm frequently bought at auctions and conducted a large clothing business in the South, in California, and elsewhere in the West. By 1855, the firm was a "first-class" clothing house that "stands as well as it ever did." In 1859 it was doing well, and the New York branch continued to do a general wholesale business, manufacturing and selling where they could, although they had no house abroad.[51]

The New York branch's business was deeply interconnected with the Southern trade. In 1854, the firm had reorganized into two branches—Morrison, Haber & Co. of New York and Goldsmith, Haber & Co. of New Orleans. The New Orleans branch would "issue no paper," and its purchases were made by Morrison, Haber & Co. of New York, "who give their own paper in payment." The New York branch's "trade is mostly South + West," but in 1855, it reduced its California trade in favor of its Southern trade. By late 1859, the firm added another clerk who was "well acquainted with the southern trade," and at this point its business was "mostly Southern."[52]

With Northern connections in place that provided access to goods and credit, Goldsmith, Haber & Co. in turn provided those goods on credit to other Jewish-owned firms throughout the region. Drawing on the resources it accessed through Morrison, Haber & Co. of New York, Goldsmith, Haber & Co. then worked with other firms throughout the region, often selling goods to Jewish mercantile firms at wholesale, which would then sell retail to customers throughout the Gulf South. In New Orleans, down the street from Goldsmith, Haber & Co. was a bonnet-and-hat store operated by Lewis Goldsmith's brother Manuel, together with the brothers Simon and Emanuel Forcheimer; the Goldsmiths and Habers had met the Forcheimer family in Mobile. The "new Jew concern" ran a "small, safe" business in 1851, but after having "lost money in their California operations," claimed to have failed in 1853 with liabilities of over $90,000. It appears that they settled with their creditors for between ten and twenty cents on the dollar.[53]

Upon the failure of Goldsmith, Forcheimer & Bro., Manuel Goldsmith and the Forcheimer brothers went their separate ways, although they still remained tapped into this network. By 1857, and after carrying on business in the name of his brother Lewis, Manuel had opened his own business in New Orleans. On his own, however, Manuel's "standing [was] not very good," as he had "little stock" and hardly conducted enough business to justify continuing. His business skills appeared to be lacking as well. "He is said to live *fast* in the upper part of the town," wrote one credit reporter, who also noted that Manuel "usually gets down to the store late in the day + leaves early, leaving the [business] principally in the care of his two clerks." While his business was "fair," opinions of his firm seem to have been buoyed because of the backing of his brother and his network.[54]

While Manuel Goldsmith turned to his brother Lewis to get back on his feet after the bankruptcy, Simon Forcheimer turned to his brother-in-law Louis Meyer. With Meyer as the capitalist, the two opened Forcheimer & Meyer in New Orleans, and by 1857, they were doing a "fair business" and were in "good credit." The firm also had two interior stores. Meyer had been operating a store in Harrisonburg, Louisiana, since the early 1840s, and by the 1850s, that firm's principal debts were in New York, although he also purchased in New Orleans, where he resided. With Meyer living in the Crescent City, his brother Moritz operated the Harrisonburg branch for a time. The firm's other interior store was in Farmersville, Louisiana, and it was under the direction of Alexander Shlenker.[55]

Meanwhile, the Goldsmiths and Forcheimers also had business interests in Florida. M. Goldsmith was a silent partner of the Forcheimer & Bro. general store in Milton, Florida, which was operational by the early 1840s. The Forcheimers were considered "safe Jews, who by [industriousness] and attention, have during the last 5 years, made all they have." With debts in New Orleans, in 1853, they sold out their business to Abraham and Gerson Forcheimer, and within five years the reorganized business was deemed "as good as any house in the South."[56]

The Goldsmith, Haber, Forcheimer network did not stop there. Forcheimer & Bro. of Milton was also connected to M. Goldsmith's own business in Pensacola, Florida. Goldsmith, Forcheimer & Bro. also had a branch in Mobile, and the firm also appears related to Meyer, Forcheimer & Gutman of Cincinnati, which itself was affiliated with a hat-and-cap shop in New York.[57]

While Goldsmith, Haber & Co. equated ethnic networks with trust, not all of its financial relationships with Jewish firms turned out well. The firm sold goods to rural Jewish merchants throughout the region such as H. Levy & Bro. in Bayou Sara. Henry and Gabriel Levy were in business in neighboring East Feliciana Parish and arrived in Bayou Sara by 1852 with "a pretty [large stock] of goods." The firm purchased in both New Orleans and New York, but they weren't always prompt with their payments when they owed money to Goldsmith, Haber & Co. In 1853, Goldsmith, Haber & Co.'s New York branch tried to recoup debts, advertising via the *New York Herald* a $500 reward for Henry Levy if he was captured alive—or $200 if he was recovered dead. In New York, they had "not promptly met their debts," which "permitted some of their best friends to suffer by their refusing to pay a draft upon them."[58]

Their financial record in New Orleans was not much better. In 1858, a judgment against H. Levy & Bro. in favor of Goldsmith & Haber was sent from New Orleans in the amount of nearly $28,000. Shortly thereafter the Levys "transferred all of their property" to Goldsmith, Haber & Co., which seized the store itself, as well as its inventory, two parcels of river-front lots, and two slaves. The very next day, however, Gabriel Levy leased the store, the slaves, and one of the parcels of land, apparently now con-ducting business on behalf of Goldsmith, Haber & Co. The Levy brothers also used the Goldsmith name to buy goods in New York, but despite the assistance from their co-religionists, the firm soon failed, and the brothers left the parish, apparently without paying their debts.[59]

Thus the Goldsmith, Haber, and Forcheimer network was extensive. It connected the credit and goods of New York to the Gulf South, and it provided goods and credit to firms throughout the region. With the bonds of family and ethnicity, the members of the firm developed an economic network with those whom they trusted, but despite their suc-cess, not everybody trusted them in return. They were in good stand-ing, had "excellent" credit, and "some of our best [business] men [had] great [confidence] in this firm" because they had "ample means" and "pay promptly." Yet some credit reporters still had reservations, having "not confidence in any of these men," wrote one reporter, and "I can not feel so confident of them."[60]

One explanation for this lack of trust may have been a lack of honesty in their business dealings. They were said to be "uneducated," and there were rumors that they were not honest and would "cheat any man if they had a chance," noted one reporter, and "they have done some dirty tricks that I know of." But another possible explanation is that trust was lacking because of their Jewishness. Reporters noted that the New York branch was a "wealthy Hebrew House," whose members were "of the better class of Israelites." Moreover, they called the New Orleans branch "perfectly [good] (for the tribe)," as it was operated by "good Israelites." Such language belies a lack of faith in Jews and that the Goldsmiths, Habers, and Forcheimers were exceptions who needed to be closely watched. It was in this environment that the partners of the firm utilized a family and ethnic network to grow their businesses while overcoming any such prejudices.[61]

While Lewis Goldsmith stood at the center of an economic network that directly connected the goods and credit of New York to the Gulf South's interior, so, too, did Henry, Mayer, and Emanuel Lehman. By the 1850s, Lehman Brothers was a growing Montgomery firm that sold supplies on credit to cotton farmers and often took cotton in return. The firm did a "large country trade with regular customers," was "punctual in all their transactions . . . good for their contracts," and the brothers owned a large house, slaves, and real estate and steadily, quickly made money. With a "prosperous business and a very successful warehouse," Mayer Lehman was also socially well connected—he was friends with the governor of Alabama and an acquaintance of Jefferson Davis, the future president of the Confederacy.[62]

Desirous of growing the business, Lehman Brothers relied on family and ethnic networks to expand. Emanuel Lehman grew the business in the Alabama interior, capitalizing the Richmond, Alabama, dry goods, etc., store of Joseph Tannenbaum & Co. This large and "popular" store sold "the finest kinds only" and was financially successful. It was a "prosperous" business that sold over $50,000 worth of carriages, clothes, and dry goods in 1859, and it was deemed "responsible for their engagements, especially so while [Lehman] continues interested." Two months before the battle of Fort Sumter, Joseph Tannenbaum & Co. sold out its interests in Richmond and Montgomery, although Meyer Lehman would remain in Montgomery. Lehman Brothers also entered the New Orleans market by sending Henry Lehman to the Crescent City. After he died of yellow fever on a business trip, Mayer took his place and shortly thereafter married into a New Orleans Jewish mercantile family.[63]

While the importance of New Orleans was declining and New York's star was rising, Lehman Brothers wisely sought access to the growing Gotham market. Initially, Emanuel traveled to New York to purchase supplies, negotiate with cotton manufacturers and exporters, and secure capital so they could run an informal banking operation in Montgomery. Emanuel later partnered with Moses Ferst, a twenty-eight-year-old who had been in the cigar business, and they operated their own importing business. With the partners deemed "frugal," "close," and "reliable for reasonable credit," the New York operation grew. By the eve of the Civil War, Lehman & Ferst had "enlarged" the business and had the credit to "cover all their wants."[64]

Because Lehman & Ferst had been created in large part to supply Lehman's Southern operations and "friends South," the business was, not surprisingly, reliant upon the Southern trade. It conducted a "brisk + safe Southern bus.," observed one credit reporter, noting that the firm "sent pretty much all their goods to Montgomery." Lehman had made money in the South, and continued to visit the South personally "to form new acquaintances + to extend" their business.[65]

Lehman Brothers expanded into the New York market via a family network—Emanuel moved to New York while Mayer remained in the South. Establishing face-to-face contact with New York wholesalers and financiers was far more effective than relying solely on credit reports to ingratiate themselves with distant New York firms. Those credit reports were less than stellar, as, despite Lehman Brothers' success, credit reporters were skeptical because the Lehmans were Jewish. One Alabama credit reporter was sure to note in 1849 that the Lehmans were German Jews, and an 1853 report claimed that although they were Jews, and "as [good] as any," very "little reliance is here placed in any of the descendants of the tribe." The credit reporter also observed that "they are in fair [credit] here, but Jews seldom remain + make good citizens." Shortly thereafter, a credit reporter claimed that the Lehman brothers were "Jews, but though Jews, are [considered] almost as good as 'white men.'" He maintained that they were "considered as [honorable] + trustworthy as it is possible for Jews to be," and were "an exception to the race, being [considered] honest."[66]

The credit reports on Lehman Brothers support J. P. Morgan's claim that trust was the fundamental basis of business. Clearly, some credit reporters ignored the Lehman's wealth and instead focused on their Jewishness, which, they believed, was a mark on their character and undermined their trustworthiness. Yet by utilizing a family network to establish a direct presence in New York, Lehman Brothers mitigated the impact of these prejudices, not only by working directly with Jewish creditors but also by establishing lines of credit with non-Jewish firms as well.[67]

Another Southern business that utilized family and ethnic networks was J. W. Seligman & Co. After stops in New York and Lancaster, Pennsylvania, four Seligman brothers set out for Mobile, Alabama, with a small amount of cash and $5,000 in merchandise that had already been paid for. When they arrived in Mobile, they found that they had too little capital to start a business in such a large city, and after searching for a better option in the interior, the brothers decided on Selma, Alabama. Once there, they set up a tent on a vacant lot and took turns peddling in different directions, scouring the surrounding region for additional opportunities. Their Southern operations soon found success, and they accumulated a "very considerable" amount of cash. After deciding that their business model could be successful, they rented a store in Selma, and by 1843 they had also opened stores in the Alabama towns of Greensboro, Eutaw, and Clinton.[68]

The Seligmans' Southern businesses were reliant upon Northern credit and goods, and to that end, two of the brothers traveled directly to New York to negotiate with suppliers and purchase goods. In the middle of 1842, James went to New York to purchase supplies. He paid cash for about half of his purchases, and for the other half he utilized credit. Ultimately, the Seligmans saw the importance of the New York market, and when they built sufficient capital, they decided to move their main operation to New York, where they opened J. Seligman & Bros. and imported goods from Europe.[69]

The move from Selma to New York was not the end of the Seligmans' family network connections. Brothers Jesse and Henry opened a branch in Watertown, New York, and it was there that Jesse Seligman and Ulysses S. Grant struck up a friendship that would last throughout their lives. Jesse and Joseph went west to San Francisco to join the gold rush, and Jesse also purchased merchandise for the company while overseas. In addition, the marriage of Babette Seligman to Max Stettheimer further developed the Seligmans' network. Stettheimer ran a clothing business in Natchez, Mississippi, and after the marriage, Stettheimer's relative Jacob joined the Seligman operation in New York. Stettheimer's connections stretched across the world, as he opened a clothing store in St. Louis, would later become a senior partner in Stettheimer & Bro., a dry goods importer in St. Louis, and he also became a partner in Seligman & Stettheimer of Frankfurt. Additionally, Jesse Seligman married Henriette Hellman, whose brothers Max and Theodore would later grow the Seligman enterprise in New Orleans as Seligman, Hellman & Co.[70]

Firms such as Lehman Brothers and J. W. Seligman & Co. figure prominently in the story of antebellum networks that emerged between North and South. They also figure prominently in the traditional narrative of American Jewish success in the late nineteenth century. Yet while these famous examples are easy to recognize, they represent but a handful of the thousands of Jewish businesses scattered throughout the country that followed similar, though less spectacular, trajectories. Although never reaching the upper crust of Jewish society, many of those smaller businesses were extremely successful in their own right, establishing direct connections with New York and then sharing that access with countless other smaller firms throughout the Gulf South. These firms have largely been forgotten, but they played an important role in the Jewish niche economy in the region.

While Goldsmith, Haber & Co. was one lesser-known firm, so, too, were those operated and financed by Isaias Meyer. Meyer was born around 1815 in Heuchelheim, Bavaria, and he arrived in America around the age of fourteen. His early business ventures were in Louisiana, and by the early 1850s he had settled in the thriving interior river port of Bayou Sara. There, he opened his own business and later played an important role in Charles Hoffman & Co., one of the town's most successful antebellum businesses. By 1853, his business interests had grown to include what would become Meyer, Weis & Co. of Natchez, Mississippi, and to directly access goods and credit in New York, Meyer also opened a wholesale dry goods store in the city. Meyer's New York store was the only New York dry goods store listed in the 1861 *Commercial Agency Record* as having branches in either Natchez or Bayou Sara. He also had a presence in New Orleans.[71]

Isaias Meyer's New York wholesale shop served as the lynchpin that connected his Southern business ventures to the goods and credit of New York. In New York, Meyer was "close + shrewd in his dealings" and was "good for his purchases." By the mid-1850s, he was "buying largely" and was "said to be in [good] standing + [credit]." His firm "made money," and its "[credit] is [good] with parties who know them." On the eve of the Civil War, he was "[making] money [very] fast," considered "first rate," and he had excellent credit. Meyer was successful and wealthy, with an estimated worth of $150,000.[72]

In the 1850s, as we have seen, Natchez offered financial opportunities for general merchants, and Isaias Meyer tapped into these opportunities through his financial interest in Meyer, Weis & Co. The roots of this firm emerged in New Orleans in the mid-1840s and was run primarily by Isaac Meyer (not to be confused with Isaias), Joseph Deutsch, and later Julius Weis, who had first arrived in New Orleans as "a poor young man," via "a sailing vessel, with a party of thirteen other young people from Rhine, Bavaria, Germany." Weis recalled that, upon arrival, "I did not have a cent. I had to borrow enough to get my baggage off the ship, and found a friend in Isaac Meyer, who was in partnership with a cousin of mine."[73]

While Meyer, Weis & Co.'s New Orleans branch was doing "considerable" business almost from the start, its partners turned their attention upriver to Natchez, where they opened what would become the firm's antebellum flagship branch. In 1847, one observer remarked of the Natchez branch that its proprietors always had "bags of money" and were "prob. rich." By the mid-1850s, "business [was] improving + change [was] only for the better," noted a credit reporter. They had "the confidence of the community" in 1860, had "just completed a most elegant" store, and everything was "flourishing."[74]

The firm had been importing most of its own goods for two decades prior to the Civil War, likely with the aid of Isaias Meyer's New York wholesale store or its house in New Orleans. But the partners of Meyer, Weis & Co. also had other business ventures in New York that gave them direct access to New York and international markets. Isaac Meyer spent time in Europe, where he purchased goods that were then imported to the New York store, which was under the direction of Joseph Deutsch. The primary business of that New York branch "consists of mostly buying for the Natchez" store, and their firm had the "full [confidence] of Houses who have sold" to them for many years," and they "generally have ready money." The ties between their Northern and Southern operations were so strong that one reporter noted at the start of the Civil War that the "dividend they may pay will be based upon the future secession in the [South]."[75]

In addition to Meyer, Weis & Co. of Natchez, Isaias Meyer had a second major outlet in Bayou Sara, Louisiana, through Charles Hoffman & Co., a large company about which one journalist wrote that few stores even in New Orleans could "surpass in value of [its] stock." Hoffman had immigrated to America and had begun as a "poor" peddler, "on foot with a pack," and he was in business by the late 1840s, by which time his firm was doing the most extensive business in the parish. As it grew, Charles Hoffman & Co. did so by way of its family network—Hoffman partnered with Isaias's nephew, and he also took on another of Isaias's nephews, Abraham Meyer. While the initial extent of Isaias Meyer and Charles Hoffman's business relationship is not clear, Hoffman and he had formed a close partnership by 1855, and Hoffman had joined Isaias Meyer's dry goods wholesale business in New York. The Bayou Sara branch sold drafts upon its house in New York, purchasing principally in New York while also trading in New Orleans. By the end of 1855 it was considered "the most solvent house in the parish" and "one of the best firms in this section of the country."[76]

Because of his stature in Bayou Sara and his access to the New York market, Isaias Meyer also developed economic relationships with other Bayou Sara businesses, not all of which were operated by Jews. For example, William George Schafer went to New York to meet Meyer in July 1860, traveling north on the Mississippi River and bringing with him his family and $790. He passed Natchez and Vicksburg, and on his journey he saw the Wolflin family, members of which also lived in Bayou Sara. He left his family along the way before arriving in New York nearly three weeks after his journey began. Once in New York, he went to purchase goods for his nephews, but he "was refused Louisiana money by the proprietress" because the "principle [sic] Banks failed." While he was unable to use his money for the gifts, he was able to make purchases for his business because of his Bayou Sara connections. Two days after his arrival he "went to the Office of Isaias Meyer," where he met with Isaias, A. Meyer, and A. Hirsch—of Bayou Sara—and Hirsch introduced him to Meyer & Sondheim, and shortly thereafter he "commenced making purchases." Over two weeks later he left the city, picking up his family along the way and returning to Bayou Sara via the river by the end of September.

Thus Isaias Meyer built an international network that gave his businesses access to both the European and New York markets. That network was based primarily on familial and ethnic ties, which, as we have seen, were predicated on trust. The primary partners, as well as clerks and subsidiary partners, were relatives and co-religionists, and some had emigrated from the same German towns. But this trust in the firm did not necessarily extend to credit reporters, as some reports were skeptical because the firm was run by Jews. The first "sentence" in an 1847 credit report entry about the business was a single word: "Jews." One credit reporter noted that they were "good men," but he also mentioned that "some think them good, others do not, [probably] because they are Jews." A later credit report cautioned that one "should not think any Jew safe for large amount." Nevertheless, Isaias Meyer and his partners were considered "among the better class of Israelites," and their firm was successful. This, no doubt, was in large part due to its direct connection with New York.[77]

While Isaias Meyer utilized his New York presence to bring Northern capital, credit, and goods to the South, his firms then shared goods and credit with businesses throughout the region. Meyer, Weis & Co. worked with a multitude of businesses in the Natchez area, and Charles Hoffman & Co. of Bayou Sara also provided goods and credit to local businesses—many of which were operated by fellow Jews, including Jacob Michael's dry goods store in Bayou Sara. Michael was Jewish and born in Prussia around 1815, and by the mid-1840s, he had opened for business in West Feliciana Parish. His initial business venture was unsuccessful, but by 1849 he had recommenced business and had taken in Caspar Michael, presumably a family member, as a clerk. He conducted an "extensive cash [business]," and he did some trading in New Orleans, and by 1852 his business had succeeded enough for him to purchase real estate.[78]

Michael's fortunes, however, soon soured. He lost $15,000 worth of goods to a fire in 1852, with only $5,000 of that insured. He resumed business, however, after that fire, but with his business mortgaged to Charles Hoffman for about $4,000. His business never really seemed to recover, and he purchased wherever he could get credit. In 1853, that credit was in New York, and the following year he planned to go to New York to make purchases. He also purchased goods from Charles Hoffman & Co., but only months after the purchase, Michael's business fell victim to Bayou Sara's great fire of 1855, and this time his property was uninsured. The *New Orleans Daily Picayune* first reported that "there was a most destructive conflagration at Bayou Sara last night. It is said that the whole town has been destroyed, but as yet we have no particulars." The initial report was accurate, and several days later the *Picayune* reported more thoroughly on the "disastrous fire," "by which the town of

Bayou Sara has been laid in ruins and her inhabitants deprived of their all." Though Bayou Sara did a large business in receiving, forwarding, and dry goods, the newspaper noted that "all of these establishments were entirely consumed with their contents." Jacob Michael's business did not survive the fire's aftermath, having failed by the end of the 1855. A credit reporter noted in 1858 that he proposed paying creditors 10 percent of what he owed them, but they seemed to want more favorable terms. Michael had also been in legal trouble. He was sued by his wife for a "[considerable] sum," but a credit reporter viewed it as a "swindling transaction, intended to cover up his property."[79]

While some businesses failed, Charles Hoffman & Co. survived and continued to grow. In less than two months, Bayou Sara was "fast being rebuilt in an improved style. Some of the largest and most commodious houses are now going up, and others have been contracted for." Though Charles Hoffman & Co. had been only partially insured, its losses were "supposed to be not [very] heavy." The firm had well-established credit networks connecting it to global Jewish firms, and with access to credit, the firm grew rapidly after the fire. By 1858 Hoffman operated two stores and owned two lots, upon one of which was his residence, and he also owned slaves. Heretofore his business had dealt solely in dry goods, but it now expanded its reach into groceries, hardware, and other items. The public, according to the Dun recorder, "has much confidence in this firm + it is regarded as the best House in this vicinity" and was considered the "largest [merchants] in our Parish."[80]

While Charles Hoffman & Co. established trust-based ethnic networks linking it to the goods and credit of New York and extended its ethnic network by extending credit to local Jewish businesses, it was once again not always trusted from the outside. A credit reporter's first entry for Bayou Sara's Charles Hoffman & Co. noted that it was a Jewish firm, and a New York credit reporter also noted that Meyer, Hoffman & Co. was run by "Israelites," and it was a "1st rate Israelite house" at that. Other Jewish-owned Bayou Sara firms were subject to similar assumptions. Jacob Michael was deemed a very "trickish + [probably] [unsafe] Jew." A. Levy & Co. was said to be run by "the most honest Jew in our town"— clearly implying that the honesty of Jews was hardly a given.[81]

For better or worse, Jewish firms trusted one another—particularly when family was involved. This trust stood behind the ethnic networks that linked partners within firms, that brought global merchandise and credit to Southern Jewish firms, and that provided goods and credit to scores of Jewish merchants scattered throughout the interior. These antebellum networks would be critically important in the postbellum years as cotton factors, who had dominated the cotton industry for decades, found new challenges from interior general store merchants. As operators of these stores, some of which had accumulated a significant amount of capital in the antebellum years, Jewish merchants were in the right place at the right time and on the path to postbellum success even before the first shots were fired at Fort Sumter in 1861.

2

The War Years

Slavery, America's "original sin," was at long last under assault. Abraham Lincoln was elected to the presidency in late 1860, and following a chorus of debates over slavery and states' rights, one Southern state after another seceded from the Union and joined together to form the Confederate States of America. But Lincoln had no intention of allowing a split in the Union, and when Confederates attacked Fort Sumter in the harbor of Charleston, South Carolina, in April 1861, what followed was a bloody civil war that left at least three-quarters of a million people dead.[1]

For merchants in the Gulf South, the war years were defined by two distinct economic periods. The first period began when the Union imposed a blockade on the Confederacy in the early stages of the war. This was an existential threat to merchants, directly threatening their livelihoods. Heretofore reliant on the very trade networks that the blockade targeted, merchants were now forced to find creative ways to survive. Some made a profit in clandestine smuggling and blockade-running, as global demand for cotton created abundant opportunities for this activity. Other merchants conducted business throughout the Confederacy, buying and selling whatever they could, wherever they could. Some survived by stockpiling cotton, others invested wisely and avoided Confederate currency, and some provisioned troops. In addition to these elements, a healthy dose of good fortune was often a prerequisite for survival as well.

While the second phase of the war continued to be defined by economic survival, it was also characterized by merchants returning to interior cotton towns and establishing or reestablishing their businesses and the networks that facilitated the North-South cotton trade. This shift began with the fall of New Orleans to the Union in 1862 but intensified the following year with Union victories at Vicksburg and Port Hudson. These military successes opened the full length of the Mississippi River for commerce, and global demand to restore the flow of cotton was extraordinary. But resumption of the cotton trade was not easy; plantations lay in shambles, the loss of life was staggering, and Confederates burned whatever cotton they could to keep it out of Union hands. But in an attempt to meet this demand, merchants found opportunity in interior cotton towns, leveraging networks to obtain cotton and credit and to provide an outlet for whatever cotton they could secure.

* * *

While rifles, muskets, and cannons were some of the traditional means of warfare in the battle fought over slavery and states' rights, the Union also turned to economic warfare—imposing a blockade upon the Confederacy with the intention of neutralizing trade. In New Orleans, "trade is at a standstill," noted one newspaper. "The importation of merchandise has almost entirely ceased; . . . everybody looks dubious and bewildered, not knowing what to expect or what may happen." The naval blockade greatly reduced the number of arrivals in New Orleans's port and severely curtailed the number of river steamboats, preventing necessary supplies from reaching the city. Federal officials hoped that by prohibiting the export of Southern cotton and the import of goods, they could stifle any attempts by the Confederacy to exchange its largest cash crop for goods that might aid its war effort. Ultimately, through its Anaconda Plan, the Union aimed to control trade and wrest control of Southern ports and the Mississippi River, the main thoroughfare that brought cotton and other produce from the interior to New Orleans.[2]

For merchants, who relied on trade networks between the North and the South, the blockade was catastrophic, striking at the very heart of their livelihood. Julius Weis recalled that "when the war broke out," his firm "had about $100,000 on our books, and a large stock of goods on hand, on which we owed considerable money in New York." However, with a Union blockade in place between North and South, "business was demoralized," and the firm "could not remit for payments when they became due." His partners, who operated the New York branch of the firm that bought goods for the Natchez store, were forced to sell their dwellings and close the store to cover a $75,000 debt. One partner went to Europe and another returned to Natchez.[3]

Similarly, the New York branch of Lehman Brothers had "sent most of their goods to Montgomery" before business was "entirely interrupted"

by the crisis. The firm was soon reported as being "behind" in its payments, and without a Southern outlet for its goods, it was soon "buying
nothing," and its New York office was "most of the time closed." Emanuel
Lehman left the city and was "traveling to solicit orders" to maintain
some semblance of business.[4]

Despite the blockade, demand remained high for the activity that
merchants and factors had conducted in the antebellum years. Both had
previously brought goods into the South along their trade networks,
and with a blockade in place, the Confederacy faced severe shortages in
staple and luxury goods. Prices rose to extraordinary levels. Merchants
and factors also purchased cotton for shipment across the globe, and in
regions that had been dependent upon Southern cotton, its dearth was
catastrophic. On the eve of the war, for example, 77 percent of the 800
million pounds of cotton that Britain used came from the United States.
Similarly, 90 percent of cotton used by France, and 92 percent of cotton
used by Russia, was also Southern cotton. With a blockade in place,
Britain's import of Southern cotton tumbled by 96 percent, and once it
became clear that the war would not end quickly, cotton prices quadru-
pled, and production slowed. As a result, one-quarter of the population
was unemployed in Lancashire, and riots broke out in several British
towns with cotton-based economies that were beset by high unemployment. France, Russia, and the German lands were similarly crippled by
the halt in Southern cotton exports. Without Southern cotton, factories
closed permanently or curtailed the number of days per week that they
operated.[5]

Many in the South believed that cotton would either prevent or win
the war for the Confederacy. New Orleans's merchants understood the
situation in Europe and in factories across the globe, and they initially
believed that the South could leverage their cotton to stave off the impending conflict. But when this did not happen, and once the war began,
many in the South nevertheless assumed that Europe's dependence on
American cotton would mean that Europeans would intervene on behalf
of the South.[6]

The Union, of course, hoped that European powers would not support the Confederacy, and while some advocated such support, Europeans instead attempted to increase cotton production across the globe to
make up for the lack of Southern cotton. This plan was also encouraged

by Union Secretary of State William H. Seward. Although European cotton merchants and manufacturers lamented the low quality of some of that cotton, these alternate sources nonetheless allowed the European industry to survive while also reducing the Confederacy's leverage.[7]

Although the blockade was imposed by the Union, demand for Southern cotton also remained high in the North, where the cessation of legal cotton imports also had a devastating impact. Pressures created by the cotton famine were so strong that many believed that New York's financial interest in the South would prevent a conflict. Northern loans, for example, were often backed by slave collateral. Moreover, New York's garment industry produced 40 percent of the clothing for the nation and was deeply reliant upon Southern cotton. The economic interests between New York and the South were deeply intertwined.[8]

With high demand for cotton around the globe, as well as the strong demand for staples and other goods in the South, opportunities abounded for clandestine smuggling and blockade-running. For many whose livelihoods had been otherwise interrupted, the staggering profits to be had were too tempting to ignore. For example, a smuggler could purchase a bale of cotton in the South for approximately $100, and if he could sneak it through the blockade, he could then sell the cotton for as much as $500 in the North. Taking those proceeds he could then purchase foodstuffs and other such goods in the North, and, if successful in smuggling them back into the Confederacy, could sell those goods at significant markups because of their scarcity in the South. With legal trade networks severed by the blockade, merchants, whose livelihoods had been entirely upended, determined that the significant rewards outweighed the many risks. Smuggling allowed merchants to earn capital, despite the embargo on trade and the disruption of war.[9]

While the bulk of smuggling and blockade-running occurred directly between Europe and the Confederacy, often via Nassau, some smuggled on a smaller scale at Texas's border with Mexico. There, merchants often traded goods for cotton, which would then be shipped to Europe or to the North. Other illicit trade occurred between Union and Confederate lines, and some who participated in this latter trade were Jewish merchants, who had a history of smuggling that predated their arrival in America. One of those Jewish merchants who turned to smuggling was Julius Weis, who purchased twenty ounces of quinine for $1.25 per ounce in Union-held territory and, once back in Natchez, sold it for $10 per ounce. He also purchased a stock of goods at auction that had been smuggled by blockade-runners, and he took those goods to Jackson, where he opened a store.[10]

In nearby Natchez, merchant Henry Frank acquired permits for his wife and daughter to pass by Union guards, as "the 'soldier boys' had written home that they needed boots, shoes, socks, shirts, trousers, everything, it seemed." The plan was for friends living in the countryside to "meet them and forward the clothes. Fortunately," recalled a relative, "the women in those days wore great hoop skirts, and under these, around their waists, Mother, Emma and Carrie hung all the needed articles." They then were "driven to the city limits, where the passes had to be examined. With fear and trembling," according to family lore, "Emma handed the guard the papers. Imagine her delight when she noticed that he was trying to read them upside down! 'Any contraband goods?' and all being fair in love and war, they answered 'No.' 'Drive on then and have a nice day with your friends,' was the pleasant rejoinder of the ignorant unsuspecting guard."[11]

Aaron Hirsch of Batesville, Arkansas, was another Jewish merchant who smuggled during the war. Hirsch recalled that "medicine was very much needed, and having none, I took a few bales of cotton, secured permission to pass the Confederate lines, went by land some 120 miles with my negroes, sold the cotton in Memphis, receiving for same quinine and gold." However, on his return, he was forbidden from crossing the Mississippi River into Arkansas with the gold and quinine. He then found an old acquaintance who made "an old flannel undershirt for my negro and sewed all the gold I had in this shirt." After waiting two or three days for a pass to leave Memphis, the pair "got through the lines all right."[12]

Not all smugglers were as successful. Heyman Herzberg claimed to have joined "a couple of men who had already made money as blockade-runners and were preparing to go north once more." However, while attempting to smuggle goods into the north, he was arrested, and though he did make it to Philadelphia, he lost money in the misadventure. He was somewhat more successful on his return trip, smuggling a small amount of goods back into the South.[13]

While merchants could earn money through smuggling and blockade-running, they could also do so through legal trade within the

Confederacy—wherever and whenever circumstances allowed. For example, Vicksburg Jewish merchant Levi Lowenberg fled his city around 1861, and because he was exempted from military service owing to his clergy status, he was able to set up a small store about four or five miles outside of town. There, Lowenberg lived in "a large dwelling with four rooms" and had a "little sale room in the dwelling" where he "kept articles for retail." He sold coffee, flour, sugar, molasses, and bacon, which "were extremely scarce in the Confederacy, and certainly were exhausted in the vicinity of Vicksburg before June, 1863." This, according to one contemporary, was "the nearest place outside of Vicksburg where we people could go to trade."[14]

For merchants like Levi Lowenberg, the gamble to avoid Confederate currency, which collapsed in value after the war, turned out to be wise. New Orleans banks adopted Confederate currency, but those who were able to avoid Confederate dollars certainly exited the conflict in much better shape than those who could not. Lowenberg received flour in Jacksonport, Arkansas, "for fees in place of Confederate money, which I refused to receive." He also acquired sugar, coffee, bacon, and molasses in Louisiana "in the same way," as well as some goods that he had earned "for service as a rabbi in performing circumcision." Yet there were times during the war when he was "obliged to take" Confederate currency, though he claimed to not have any Confederate bonds or securities.[15] Similarly, W. G. Schafer invested $700 in a New Orleans coffee house with fellow Bayou Sara resident A. Szabo, later buying out Szabo's interest with $1,700 in borrowed U.S. treasury notes. He then sold the coffee house for $3,000 in U.S. treasury notes cash and returned to Bayou Sara, prepared to resume his mercantile activities.[16]

Not everybody was able to avoid Confederate dollars. While M. Bodenheim was speculating in goods throughout the South, he claimed at one point to have had "nothing but Confederate money." But while he made 50–75 percent profit on the goods he acquired and sold in the South, it was apparently in a currency that would be virtually worthless at the end of the conflict. Similarly, Charles Lehman of Vicksburg was also speculating for comparable profit margins in sugar, dry goods, "and any thing that we could get," but he also claimed to have had "nothing but Confederate money."[17]

Julius Weis was successful by trading throughout the Confederacy and for the most part avoiding Confederate dollars. For example, he took a stock of clothing to Memphis, where he sold it to Confederate soldiers for Confederate dollars. By using the money to purchase a tract of land, and then selling that land for the same amount of U.S. dollars after the war, Weis claimed to have avoided the aftershocks associated with the collapse of Confederate currency. Similarly, Weis warehoused sugar that he later shipped to Georgia and sold for Confederate dollars. He invested most of those Confederate dollars in foreign exchange that he sent to Lazard Frères in Paris, but he also purchased a slave with the proceeds of the sugar sale.[18]

While merchants were, in hindsight, wise to avoid Confederate dollars, they could also be rewarded if they accepted cotton as payment. This was the case for Abraham Levy and Emanuel Meyer. Levy and his siblings had come to America from the German lands, and once in America, Abraham became the family patriarch. In Bayou Sara he joined the firm of his mother's relative, L. Bach & Co., and he had taken over the firm by 1853. He worked with family members in the Bayou Sara store, and part of Levy's success was due to a family network of stores throughout the region and the country. The firm conducted trade in New Orleans and was also affiliated with Leopold Bach's short-lived business in New York. Meanwhile, Abraham's brother Samuel operated a store in Rodney, Mississippi, until his death from yellow fever around 1855, and his brother Daniel operated a store in Williamsport, Louisiana.[19]

Prior to the war, Abraham Levy sent merchandise to his nephew Emanuel Meyer in nearby Clinton. That continued after the outbreak of the conflict as Meyer peddled and sold the goods that Levy had provided him. He often accepted payment for those goods in cotton, despite the difficulties in legally bringing it to market, and many of these transactions were small. One planter, for example, paid a portion of his bill with 3 bales of cotton, valued at $120.17. In 1862, Levy endorsed notes for Meyer from New Orleans, and Levy closed his Bayou Sara store during the conflict, instead focusing on backing Meyer.[20]

While Southern merchants did whatever they could to find opportunities while trade networks were disrupted, some Northern merchants found opportunity in the South by serving the Union Army as sutlers. Sutlers followed behind military units, ostensibly improving the quality of life of troops by selling them goods such as tobacco, liquor, clothes, and foodstuffs. The concept of a sutler was not new to the Civil War; during the period of Alexander the Great, "camp followers," as they were then known, followed military units and sold similar goods. As European nation-states emerged, the profession was incorporated into the military structure, and it was officially recognized in Britain in 1717. In America, the secretary of war and other army leaders officially brought sutlers under military regulations in 1822. Jews had been permitted to partake in this profession in Europe, and they were also allowed to serve as sutlers in America. One Civil War officer noted that when a sutler's wagon was unloaded, it "was an important event because sutler's goods had been scarce to be obtained even by officers."[21]

Figure 2.1. "Sutler's Tent." Image courtesy of the Library of Congress (LC-B8171–2448).

Figure 2.2. "Caricature of Jewish Sutler." Image courtesy of the Jacob Rader Marcus Center of the American Jewish Archives, Cincinnati, Ohio (PC-4585).

Contemporaries commented that sutlers were far more common for the Union than the Confederacy, and some Jews who had been peddlers or merchants prior to the war served as sutlers. Yet while Northern sutlers had been part of the Union Army, some stayed in the South after the war, and many were welcomed there with open arms. This was the case with Henry Frank and Isaac Lowenburg, both of whom became well-respected postbellum merchants in Natchez, and Lowenburg was also twice elected mayor of the city. Frank and Lowenburg, recalled a relative, "were in the commissary department of the Union Army." They visited John Mayer, president of the local congregation, who "invited them to attend the services during the Holy Days . . . upstairs in the old engine house on North Union Street." Although they were with the Union Army, Mayer "invited these new acquaintances to visit his family, and, being cordially received, they became frequent visitors," and political allegiances were cast aside—at least as much as possible. "Many were the heated discussions between these 'Yankees' and our rebel family, until Mother forbade political wrangling, but encouraged social affinity, prompted by her usual tact and good sense, to say nothing of her clever foresight, for two of these hated 'Yankees' became loved and loving sons to our dear parents," each marrying a daughter of John Mayer.[22]

Thus, for merchants, the first phase of the war was defined by creative modes of survival in a time of economic disruption. This need for creativity continued into the second phase. But the second phase was also defined by the resumption of the legal North-South cotton trade, the arrival or return of merchants to interior towns, and the establishment or reestablishment of the networks that facilitated the cotton trade. The transition into the second phase began with the fall of New Orleans to Union troops in the spring of 1862, but it was not firmly ensconced until after the fall of Vicksburg and Port Hudson in 1863.

Prior to the war, New Orleans' strategic value was in large part centered on its port—one of the most important in the United States—which shipped agricultural products such as cotton from the Lower Mississippi Valley to places around the globe. The Crescent City also played a major role as a regional center of finance, supporting much of the activity in the surrounding region. Both the Confederacy and the Union recognized the strategic importance of the Crescent City, and in 1862, federal gunboats moved upriver in a nighttime raid past Confederate fortifications and soon took the city. With New Orleans in Union hands, Secretary of State Seward and Secretary of the Treasury Salmon P. Chase heralded the Union's occupation as a means to restore the flow of cotton without the Confederacy profiting from the trade.[23]

However, Confederates scoffed at the Union's goal of profiting from Southern cotton; with federal guns trained on their city, New Orleanians refused to surrender any mercantile commodities of value. New Orleans's citizens burned 15,000 bales of cotton, as well as sugar and tobacco warehouses, steamboats, and ships, as the Union was taking their city, lest it fall into Union hands. "The air was thick with the smoke of burning cotton; and other property," detailed one account of the battle. With commodities aflame, New Orleans surrendered, and by the beginning of May 1862, the Crescent City was in Union hands.[24]

Some Union officials heralded the Union's occupation of New Orleans as a means to restore the flow of cotton, and the Union pushed to restore commerce over Confederates' objections. Secretary Chase instituted an intricate permit system, whereby those with permits could enter this lucrative trade. Some Southerners who lived in areas captured by the Union and who were deemed loyal to the Union could receive a permit to trade in cotton, and permits to conduct business across Union lines were coveted because of the opportunity for substantial profits. Cotton prices rose dramatically, from $45.50 per bale in the 1861–1862 season, to $231.32 in 1862–1863, and then again to $356.20 in 1863–1864. This, compared to the sixteen-dollar monthly salary at the end of the war for Union troops, offered tremendous incentive to trade in cotton.[25]

Not surprisingly, with such high profit margins, this system was rife for abuse by speculators, government officials, soldiers, and commanders. Trade permits were theoretically issued to the merchants most loyal to the Union, but bribes, kickbacks, or other underhanded tactics were frequently prerequisites to obtaining them. One official noted that "every colonel, captain, or quartermaster is in secret partnership with some operator in cotton; every soldier dreams of adding a bale of cotton to his monthly pay." He claimed that "soldiers on picket are bribed, officers are bribed. . . . Honesty is the exception and peculation [embezzlement] the rule wherever the army is brought into contact with trade."[26]

While restoring the flow of trade was the ultimate Union goal, the system was beset by tepid support from War Department officials. Union generals in the midst of battle were not always welcoming or encouraging of trade across Union-Confederate lines. With Benjamin Butler in charge of New Orleans, obstruction from the War Department, a kickback scheme with his brother, and his disdain for the New Orleans mercantile community all prevented the resumption of the cotton trade in the ways in which the Union had envisioned. Once Nathaniel Banks took control of New Orleans from Butler, he worked with Isachar Zacharie, a Jewish confidant of Abraham Lincoln, who was likely part of a plan that would have purchased cotton directly from Southern growers in exchange for Northern goods. Zacharie faced accusations that he himself was profiting from cotton speculation.[27]

Perhaps the most famous official who was not embracing of trade across Union-Confederate lines was Ulysses S. Grant. He knew that those who passed from Confederate lands into Union-held territories passed on classified military secrets such as troop positions, and he assumed that those moving into the Confederacy from his territory did the same. He also believed that trade with the enemy, legal or illegal, further hindered the war effort if Confederates acquired goods such as food, weapons, or other supplies that could prolong the war. He thus called cotton traders "a curse to the Army," and Grant was not alone in his outspokenness. General William T. Sherman claimed that the Union could not "carry on war and trade with a people at the same time." Yet Grant realized that part of his mission was to open the area for commerce, noting that "instructions from Washington" were "to encourage getting Cotton out of the country."[28]

Nonetheless, Grant's opposition to cotton traders was increasingly focused upon Jewish merchants—an obsession fueled in part by his frustration over his father's attempted kickback scheme with a group of Cincinnati Jewish merchants. Grant ordered one commander to "examine all baggage of all speculators coming South" and to turn away anyone carrying gold. Moreover, he also said that Jews, whom he called "a nuisance," should "receive special attention." Grant then issued a call to "refuse all permits to come south of Jackson for the present" and noted particularly that "the Isrealites [sic] especially should be kept out." He declared that "no Jews are to be permitted to travel on the Rail Road southward from any point . . . they are such an intolerable nuisance that the Department must be purged for [sic] them." Shortly thereafter Grant wrote to Sherman, telling him that "in consequence of the total disregard and evasion of orders by the Jews my policy is to exclude them so far as practicable from the Dept." Ultimately Grant issued General Order no. 11, expelling "Jews as a class" from his department—an order that was swiftly overturned by President Lincoln.[29]

Without the full embrace of trade between Union and Confederate lines, and with New Orleans now isolated from the cotton-growing regions alongside the Mississippi River, "that stopped all the business," recalled James Conklin, who lived in the region. "Supplies from N. Orleans are entirely cut off," observed Bayou Sara's W. G. Schafer, causing a spike in prices when goods could be obtained at all. Flour was selling for $40 per barrel but could "hardly be had." Lard, selling at fifty cents per pound, was "very scarce," and so, too, were cigars, which were only available from "home manufacture." In terms of liquor, there was "none for sale," nor was there any more coffee. There was also a great deal of uncertainty for merchants. After the fall of New Orleans, Julius Weis traveled to the Crescent City to withdraw about $7,000 held by the Citizens Bank, fearing that it might have been confiscated had he waited. M. Bodenheim claimed that his firm had between $30,000 and $40,000 worth of dry goods, and "when Farragut came here we moved them to Jackson," he recalled.[30]

Though legal trade was beginning to resume, merchants who were cut off from New Orleans still faced difficulties and had to get creative to eke out a living. For merchants in Clinton such as Emanuel Meyer, the suspension of the rail link to the Crescent City via Port Hudson and Bayou Sara brought commerce to a near standstill. Business was slow for Meyer, and he peddled while also selling from a store. His account books stopped for a period in 1863, and the handful of Clinton's Jewish firms that remained traded among themselves in an attempt to fill their orders; Meyer's partner, for example, purchased goods from the Clinton firm of Lazarus and Leon Bloom. Yet business did not end completely, as Meyer purchased 131 bales of cotton between April and June 1863. Other merchants continued to buy and sell whatever and wherever they could. Together with a partner, W. G. Schafer purchased a stock of dry goods and rum in Plaquemine, Louisiana, loaded the goods onto a wagon, and over the course of several days managed to haul the goods to the ferry. He then exchanged most of those goods for tobacco, some of which he sold in his store. Schafer soon entered a short-lived partnership, purchasing $5,500 worth of salt, lard, and whiskey.[31]

While legal trade had begun to resume with the capture of New Orleans, it was not until the fall of Vicksburg and Port Hudson, which brought the full length of the Mississippi River under Union control, that the resumption of trade intensified. In the spring of 1863, General Nathaniel Banks, who had been placed in charge of New Orleans, moved his troops upriver to secure the Mississippi River, and his military operations extended into the countryside. Meanwhile, as Union troops under Banks's direction continued to move upriver from the south, Union General Ulysses S. Grant concurrently moved downriver from the north. With his bloody victory at Vicksburg in July 1863, coupled with Banks's victory downriver at Port Hudson, the full length of the Mississippi River came under Union control. Steamboat traffic resumed, and one commander gave "orders to the vessels in the district not to interfere with the trade or travel in the river. If the army authorities give passes, they are to be considered sufficient." This meant that cotton could now flow from the interior, and the world was eagerly awaiting it. The British ambassador to Washington reported telling Seward that "we had waited with the greatest patience while the military operations were going on upon the Mississippi, but that now the River was open, and the time has come at which we had been promised an ample supply."[32]

But though Seward and other officials hoped for a quick resumption of trade, the world would have to remain patient, as there were several challenges to the immediate resumption of cotton-based commerce. One of those challenges was the steadfast refusal of Confederates to

Figure 2.3. "The Levee at Vicksburg Miss., February, 1864." Image courtesy of the Library of Congress (LC-USZ61–1597).

Figure 2.4. "Main Street, Little Rock, Arkansas, 1860–65." Image courtesy of the Jacob Rader Marcus Center of the American Jewish Archives, Cincinnati, Ohio (PC-2688).

allow cotton to fall into Union hands. This had been true for much of the war—some New Orleans cotton factors had asked planters "not to ship any portion of their crops of Cotton to this city, or to remove it from their plantations, until the blockade is fully and entirely abandoned, of which due notice will be given." Instead, observed one contemporary, cotton should be "stored far away from any water-course, road, or railway, and never more than twenty-five bales in one place."[33]

The most spectacular way that Confederates prevented cotton from falling into Union hands, thus hindering the quick resumption of the cotton trade, was to burn it. Just as New Orleans residents had burned cotton to keep it out of Union hands after their city had been taken by the Union, merchants who had been paid in cotton in the early years of the war, or had otherwise saved it, found themselves the targets of conflagration. Julius Weis recalled that "during the war, our firm had succeeded in collecting some of their outstanding debts in cotton, which we had stored away in the country, on a plantation." Selling his stockpiled bounty, "when cotton went to fabulous prices," could have netted a fortune, but when Confederate troops discovered the approximately 460 bales that Weis had hidden, "they managed to set fire to it and burned it all up," keeping it out of Union hands.[34]

In 1862, Mayer Lehman had entered a partnership with a Montgomery cotton agent named John Wesley Durr, and Lehman, Durr & Co. purchased a cotton warehouse where they could warehouse cotton until prices were right. However, Lehman Brothers' warehoused cotton was burned, and one Dun recorder estimated that Lehman Brothers lost at least $250,000 during the war, although that figure may have been significantly higher.[35]

These were not isolated incidents. One Confederate official was stationed near the river in Bayou Sara "for the purpose of preventing cotton coming in, and . . . his orders were to burn it if found on the way to the enemy and likely to get into his hands." In one incident, the commander of the second district noted that "9 bales of cotton were brought in by a Jew to the river bank, to the south of town and nearly abreast of this vessel. . . . The next morning, at 3:30, it was burned." Shortly thereafter, 15 bales were brought to the river's edge, but while an empty coal barge was being prepared to pick up the cotton, "the rebels discovered the cotton and set it on fire." W. G. Schafer noted that he "heard that Mr. Mann's Cotton was burnt" in 1863, and he reported the following year that 26 bales of cotton were burned at the landing. Two days later, he claimed, thirty-three Confederate soldiers came to town and burned 5 bales.[36]

While the burning of cotton challenged Union efforts to restore the flow of trade and cotton, there were other significant dynamics that prevented the quick resumption of the cotton trade. An estimated 22.6 percent of white men who were born in the South and who were between the ages of twenty and twenty-four in 1860 died during the war. Recent estimates suggest that one in ten white men who were of military age in 1860 died as a consequence of the war, and 200,000 white women were left as widows. Such widespread death affected the labor and production chain from growers to factors and merchants, and it slowed the resumption of the Lower Mississippi Valley's cotton trade.[37]

Charles Toorain, whom J. W. Dorr called one of the "principal merchants" of Bayou Sara prior to the war, was one of those who did not survive to resume his dry goods and grocery store. He had served the Confederacy in Louisiana's Fourth Infantry, and he was memorialized as "fighting at the head of his company. He was the bravest of the brave, and in his death our country has sustained a serious loss." Toorain's estate was insolvent after the war, and his death reminds us how the bloody battle and loss of life on its own reshaped the mercantile map.[38]

In addition to the loss of life, entire towns were destroyed, disrupting the flow of cotton and goods. Greenville, Mississippi, for example, was burned to the ground during the war. Farm buildings, warehouses, and gins were destroyed, and railroad infrastructure was heavily damaged. At war's end, one estimate suggested that Greenville's population was reduced to fewer than 500. After the war, the town of Greenville was rebuilt about four miles upriver, on higher ground that would ostensibly protect against flooding.[39]

Vicksburg, the site of Grant's bloody victory, was also in shambles, and Bayou Sara and St. Francisville were also heavily damaged. According to one account, "There was no confederate force at St. Francisville that day to defend the town. The lovely old place lay passive and took its shelling. . . . Shells riddled the old courthouse, riddled Grace Church, shattered the beautiful stained-glass window above the altar." W. G. Schafer reported that sixty-seven houses had been destroyed in the bombardment, including those of Whiteman Bros; Meyer, Hoffman & Co.; Charles Hoffman; and A. Levy; as well as the West Feliciana rail depot. But Natchez escaped relatively unscathed, in part because the Confederacy chose to fortify Vicksburg instead. Natchez may also have been spared because of its significant number of Union sympathizers, which possibly dissuaded Union troops from sacking the town.[40]

While destruction in the towns that marketed cotton certainly slowed the resumption of trade, so, too, did the devastation on the plantations themselves. "The plantations that at the advent of this army were like smiling gardens of Paradise, were left almost a wilderness," recalled Julia Nutt of Natchez. "I visited the plantations soon afterwards and saw it all. The gin houses were burnt; houses torn to pieces; fencing burnt; all farming implements gone; all stock; household articles and everything on the premises that was of any value or consideration." Those who returned from the war often found "their homesteads destroyed, their farms devastated, their families in distress." Even if plantations were ready for immediate planting, the river was not opened to commerce until after the prime cotton planting season.[41]

While damage to towns and plantations was significant, damage to the infrastructure that connected cotton towns to markets such as New Orleans was also substantial. Prior to the war, Louisiana's infrastructure was hardly a model of efficiency, but years of war and neglect brought the problems to an entirely new level. Very few roads were maintained, and floods washed away bridges, but roads weren't the only problem. Railroads such as the West Feliciana Railroad were impassible after the conflict, and Vicksburg's rail service was interrupted by the destruction of the Big Black River bridge, twelve miles east of town, during the 1863 campaign. Even after the bridge was replaced, a standard joke was of an "accident" which took place on the railroad—that a train once ran on time and on schedule from Vicksburg to Jackson. And while rivers were still for the most part navigable, the number of steamboats available had been significantly reduced. Moreover, breaches in river levees had not been repaired during the conflict, and following the war new damages outpaced the rate of repair.[42]

Looting was also a problem. "Before I could dispose of all of the goods, Grant came through on his way to Vicksburg," Julius Weis recalled, "and I was compelled to leave my store in charge of some one else, and when I returned there was very little of value left, most of the goods having been stolen."[43]

All of these factors meant that the Lower Mississippi Valley was unable to produce and ship cotton as fast as Seward and others had hoped. Yet commerce did slowly resume, and the cotton industry began to rebuild. Just as they had done in the early years of the war, merchants found economic opportunities wherever they could. Lehman Brothers operated in Montgomery until 1862, when it welcomed new partners. Lehman Brothers then moved some of its Southern operation from Montgomery to the Crescent City where the brothers created Lehman, Newgass & Co. with Mayer's wife's brother, Benjamin Newgass, who had previously been in the tobacco business in Louisville, Kentucky. This firm sold wholesale merchandise and also maintained a presence in the cotton industry.[44]

Lehman Brothers also found opportunity directly from Alabama's governor, who in 1864 sought to provide imprisoned soldiers with clothes, blankets, and other provisions and hoped to pay for these goods with cotton. "I have appointed Mr. Meyer [sic] Lehman as the agent of the State, under this act," wrote Governor T. H. Watts to Jefferson Davis. "He is a business man of established character and one of the best Southern patriots . . . and is thoroughly identified with us." In order to trade the cotton for goods, wrote Governor Watts, "It will be necessary for him to go through the lines. I ask that he be furnished with proper passports and indorsed by you as the agent of the State of Alabama." Permission was apparently granted, and Lehman then wrote to Ulysses S. Grant, advising him that Alabama had appropriated $500,000 for the amelioration of the condition of Alabama prisoners held by the Union. He advised Grant that the Confederate government had granted permission "to ship cotton to the amount of this appropriation" and asked for "permission to pass it through the blockade," hoping that a U.S. vessel would "be permitted to carry this cotton to the Port of New York, to be there sold and the proceeds applied" to the cost of the goods for the prisoners.[45]

Not everybody was lucky enough to secure state contracts. For other merchants, opportunity awaited in interior cotton towns. Some merchants who opened for business in the river towns had not lived there prior to the conflict. Isaac Lowenburg, for example, had arrived in America around 1858 and worked as a sutler during the war, following General Grant and provisioning troops. When Grant's troops entered Natchez in 1863, Lowenburg followed them into the town, and he set out his own shingle in Natchez by the end of 1863. Lowenburg sold groceries and dry goods while operating a cotton factorage business, and his customers initially included Union soldiers, freed blacks, and those planters and townspeople who remained during the war. Lowenburg also had acquired permits to ship cotton and obtain goods.[46]

While some newcomers arrived, many of those who had fled interior port cities during the war returned. In Vicksburg, Charles Pine, who had been injured while serving, was sent to Mexico during the war to buy clothing for soldiers. At some point in early 1864 he returned to Vicksburg, where he stayed until the end of the war. Also returning to Vicksburg was Levi Lowenberg, who made his way back to the city about three weeks after its surrender, and he was soon "dealing in cotton, sugar, etc." But not everybody returned immediately. M. Bodenheim recalled that, "when Grant came there," rather than returning, "we removed to Mobile and commenced speculating there with sugar, dry goods and anything that we could get." He insisted that he "was not in blockade running" but, rather, "was just speculating right here in the South," and he apparently did not return to Vicksburg until 1865. In Natchez, Abraham Isaacs, who had come to Natchez immediately before the war, entered the dry goods and grocery business on his own in 1863.[47]

Because R.G. Dun reporters did not generally report on businesses until after the conflict ended in 1865, it is difficult to quantify exactly when merchants returned to their antebellum towns. But, by comparing 1860 Dun information with that of 1866, Dun reports can nonetheless provide guidance. For example, in Shreveport, Louisiana, Dun agents in 1860 counted forty-four businesses in the cotton economy, approximately sixteen of which were operated by Jews. By the time Dun records resumed in 1866, twenty-five of those cotton economy businesses were still operational, and this included approximately eight Jewish firms. Among them was A. Winter's dry goods store, which was in Shreveport by 1851. Winter soon took in a partner and operated as Winter & Weinstock, and his partner provided a direct connection to New York via Faber & Weinstock, but they dissolved the partnership prior to the war. After the conflict, Winter resumed business in Shreveport, having "saved his money slowly + surely." He emerged from the war "in debt to some extent," which by one estimate was "several thousand [dollars] at the close of the war." But though his sales were sluggish, a Dun agent believed that he should be able to repay those debts, though "with a little delay."[48]

Another Shreveport Jewish firm that reopened after the war was that of the brothers Edward and Benjamin Jacobs, "young men" of good business habits, but "they belong to that tribe we cannot recommend." Around the outbreak of war, Dun recorders noted that the firm conducted a "heavy business," and the firm's strength led recorders to believe that the business would "be affected but little by the hard times. They will be able to pay all their debts." That belief was correct, as they remained in business during the war, and recorders noted immediately after the conflict that E & B Jacobs kept "a large stock" and that the firm was likely conducting "the largest [business] in the city."

While Dun agents found that just over half of Shreveport's cotton economy businesses had resumed operations by 1866, the continuity in Bayou Sara was even more pronounced, where about three-quarters of the cotton economy businesses had resumed by 1866. Even further, virtually all the Jewish businesses had resumed by 1866, highlighting particularly the continuity of Jewish economic life from the antebellum to postbellum years. The only Jewish firm that did not return was that of Charles Hoffman and Isaias Meyer, although it was not because of failure. Isaias Meyer had an estimated fortune of $200,000 by the eve of the conflict, and shortly after the outbreak of war he reported that his Bayou Sara partnership with Charles Hoffman was in liquidation. By war's end, it had indeed dissolved, and Meyer also appears to have pulled out of Meyer, Deutsch & Weis of Natchez. But he did not founder as a businessman, and he retained his office in New York. He invested money in New York City real estate and transferred what appears to be ten properties to Isaac Meyer, an antebellum business partner, in 1861. These "RE conveyances by Isaias Meyer to Isaac Meyer" were "in consideration of $100,000." All of this meant that he was still wealthy in 1864 and could "buy all he wants." Meyer also formed a short-lived partnership in Bayou Sara after the war.[49]

The remainder of the Jewish-owned firms did return; among them was Julius Freyhan & Co., which had been very small prior to the conflict. Starting in 1862 Freyhan had served the Confederacy as a noncombatant musician, but according to his records, he deserted while on a march in Summer 1863. Shortly thereafter he was captured by the Union near Jackson, and he apparently spent the remainder of the war in prison. After the war, and without a large nest egg—in fact, there was a judgment in place against him for about $240—Freyhan apparently started anew as a clerk, either in Jackson or in Bayou Sara, before opening a "little country store" that would quickly become the best in West Feliciana Parish.[50]

Freyhan's firm was joined by several other Jewish businesses that had resumed operations by 1866. On the eve of the conflict, Moses Mann had an estimated worth of $5,000 and, according to the opinion of a credit reporter, "has not the confidence of the Country." Immediately following the war, Mann was conducting a small business, apparently on his own, and he would soon add partners and grow rapidly. Prior to the war Abram Wolf operated a general store that was involved in forwarding and commission, and he had "no means except [a small] country store." Following the conflict, the firm appears to have reemerged, but in

the name of his brother Gustave. Charles Wolflin also resumed operation of his dry goods and grocery store after the war. In the antebellum
years he had conducted "a [small] but apparently a [safe] [business],"
and he owned slaves and also kept a large beer saloon. By 1865 he had
"resumed doing [a small] business." Another seemingly Jewish firm that
resumed business was that of C. P. Whiteman & Co., which "lost their
books + every thing else during the war" but immediately after the conflict was "doing well."[51]

Also among the firms that returned to Bayou Sara was A. Levy & Co.,
which in 1866 was deemed the "No. 1 house" in Bayou Sara. On the eve
of the war, Levy's firm was termed one of the "principal merchants of the
place" by J. W. Dorr, and as we have seen, Abraham Levy made money
speculating in cotton in Clinton during the war. By 1866, Dun recorders
observed that A. Levy & Co. was conducting "a large business," and Levy
was "said to be the most honest Jew in our town." In 1868, Levy was "said
to be the wealthiest man in the place."[52]

As trade resumed after the fall of Vicksburg and Port Hudson, merchants leveraged economic networks, which functioned in much the
same manner as they had in the antebellum years. Abraham Levy and
Emanuel Meyer had received cotton as payment during the period that
Clinton had been cut off from New Orleans. They sold that cotton in
New Orleans to Kahn & Adler—a firm operated by merchants who had
once lived in Clinton. Levy became the patriarch of a family network
that connected interior towns to New Orleans and New York.[53]

Goldsmith, Haber & Co. also traded successfully once legal commerce opened between North and South. Ferdinand Goldsmith had
invested $500 in sugar, storing it in his uncle Manuel's New Orleans
store. After the Crescent City was captured by the Union, he received a
permit to sell that sugar in New York and netted $2,500 in the transaction.
He then sent money to his uncle Isaac Haber, and he purchased ten cases
of dry goods, which he sold at a significant profit after paying exchange
fees in New York. Goldsmith then entered the jobbing and wholesale
business, and he remained in the cotton business after the war.[54]

Julius Weis also epitomizes the ways in which, after the fall of Vicksburg, networks provided business opportunities for merchants. After
Weis "once more entered into regular business," he sensed opportunity
in the Crescent City, and in 1864 he relocated to New Orleans. There, he

opened a dry goods store in rented quarters and "did fairly well from the first," he recalled. He "sold cotton in the rear of the store and dry goods in the front," and this was his "first experience in the cotton commission business." His operation proved to be quite successful, as he "made considerable money." "We did very well until peace was declared," he recalled.[55]

Part of Weis's success was his ability to reconstruct the networks that had linked him to nearby cotton farmers. Cotton was increasing in price, he recalled, and "a great many of my old friends among the farmers in Jefferson and Claiborne Counties, who had saved some cotton from the wreck of the war, soon began to ship cotton to me in a small way." These shipments, he believed, were "partly because they had confidence in me, and because some were indebted to their old commission merchants."[56]

But he also reestablished the networks that connected him to financing sources—particularly in New York. Once "communication was again open with New York," Weis recalled, his firm repaid its "old indebtedness to Northern merchants in full, with interest." When he purchased cotton in New Orleans he did so with an eye toward shipping it to New York, and used the proceeds of his cotton sales to pay for goods that he could sell in his store. This arrangement proved to be quite lucrative. Weis recalled that early one season cotton was selling for 75 cents per pound, but the price rose to $1.00 by summer. "Naturally by this operation I made considerable money," Weis later noted, "as cotton advanced in price while in transit." Weis continued these transactions for three months, clearing $30,000, but his luck soon ran out. He purchased 200 bales of cotton for $1.75 per pound and decided to forgo the opportunity to sell in New York at $1.85 per pound because, "as cotton was continually increasing in value, on account of its scarcity, my partners, Mr. Mayer [sic] and Mr. Deutsch, expected it to go to $2.00 per pound and therefore held the cotton." However, before they could sell, "Gen. Sherman made his great raid through Georgia, thus breaking the backbone of the Southern Confederacy, and cotton began to decline rapidly," and they ultimately lost $26,000 in the transaction when the cotton was finally sold.[57]

Weis's assertions were corroborated by Dun recorders who claimed that the firm had made a profit speculating in cotton during the war. While it had owed $75,000 in 1862, it had already repaid those debts by 1864 and had $100,000 left over. It was doing a "good jobbing [business]," and was "in 1st rate [credit]." By the close of the war it was doing a good wholesale business, "steadily improving and recovering [the] position" it had held prior to the war.[58]

Other speculators buying cotton in the South also understood the need to sell at the right time. One Union commander around Bayou Sara observed that there was little cotton being shipped from the west bank of the Mississippi River, "owing, I think, to the low prices. There has been a large quantity purchased by speculators and payments made on it, but the low prices now make them rather willing to lose the payments already made than to complete the bargain." He also claimed that he had "conversed with several intelligent planters, who say that no quantity of cotton will be sold before it is a dollar per pound. This price will enable them to realize about 35 cents per pound, after paying the transportation in the rebel country."[59]

By April 1865, the war was winding down, and Confederate forces began to surrender in significant numbers. Jefferson Davis was captured on May 10, symbolically handing the Confederacy defeat and restoring the Union. Slavery had been abolished, and the cotton industry would change markedly in the postbellum years, increasing its reliance on interior merchants. Those who had saved capital had a sound financial base for the postbellum years, and those who had entered the postbellum years with trade and credit networks were equipped to survive the vicissitudes of the postbellum economy.[60]

3

Timing Is Everything

In the postbellum years, a myriad of structural forces aligned to position interior general store merchants at the forefront of the cotton economy. The telegraph brought up-to-the-minute cotton prices to interior markets, facilitating cotton sales closer to the point of production and bypassing the need for factors in port cities. New compression equipment made it more efficient to prepare cotton for transport directly from interior towns, usurping another prime function of the antebellum cotton factor. Rapid expansion of railroad lines meant that cotton could now be shipped overland, directly from interior markets to New York and other cities, and it also fostered the development of new cotton market towns. Within those interior towns, the collapse of Southern banks and Confederate currency meant that traditional financing structures could no longer provide the credit necessary for the cotton economy. Instead, the burden fell to interior general store owners, with capital saved from the war years or with credit networks to financial centers such as New York. Jewish merchants, who had been concentrated in this niche at the margins of the antebellum cotton economy, became the lifeblood of the Southern economy as the changes of the postbellum years brought their niche into the mainstream.

But despite the structural changes that positioned Jewish merchants for success in their niche economy, that success was neither guaranteed nor linear, and it was closely linked to the vicissitudes of the postbellum economy. Three distinct periods shaped mercantile life after the war, and the ebbs and flows of these eras very much dictated both when and how businesses could succeed. First, 1866–1867 was defined by floods, crop failures, disease outbreaks, and depressed prices. Firms that had saved capital from the war often relied on these capital reserves to survive, but new firms did not have that luxury. But in some of the region's most important cotton towns, these new firms were predominantly operated by non-Jews, who were in the wrong place at the wrong time, quickly extinguishing the burst of non-Jewish mercantile activity that these merchants hoped would be their ticket to the bourgeoning industry. But the fortunes of the region soon ticked upward, as a stronger economy defined a second period that lasted from 1868 to 1873. New businesses that emerged during this time generally found greater success than those that had opened during the previous years' economic downturn, and Jewish merchants, who opened new businesses in the region in greater numbers during this period, were in the right place at the right time. They worked directly with freedmen, which made good business sense, broadening their customer base. But the Panic of 1873 ushered in the third period, 1873–1879, which was accompanied in the ensuing years by yellow fever outbreaks, flooding, violence, and political and legal instability, among other challenges—all of which made these years particularly difficult for businesses. To survive these down years, merchants, Jewish and non-Jewish, once again relied on ingenuity, capital reserves, and credit networks.

* * *

While the factorage system, which relied on sales in port cities, characterized cotton marketing in the antebellum years, the postbellum years saw a major shift; *Bradstreet's* observed that cotton buying in the interior had become "general throughout the South about the year 1875." This shift paralleled a global shift to the interior that was also occurring in other cotton-growing regions of the world, including Egypt and India. Improved communication technology after the war was one reason that precipitated this move from port cities, as interior merchants now had the same access to international cotton prices as did cotton factors in larger cities. The telegraph, transatlantic cable, and then the telephone meant that cotton merchants would know international cotton prices almost immediately, and as telegraph lines followed railroad tracks, that knowledge became available to those in inland towns as well. Thus the New Orleans factor's expertise in selling the cotton at the best time and highest price became superfluous—the interior merchant could do it without assistance.[1]

Moreover, as communication technology was pushing interior towns toward self-sufficiency, new compression equipment was doing the same. One periodical noted that "new compresses of great power in towns which formerly sent their cotton half pressed to the ports" played a significant role in the growing trend toward inland purchasing. With the older equipment, only about 22 bales could be loaded onto a rail car. However, with improved interior compression, that number rose to about 47 bales per car, more than doubling capacity and significantly reducing transportation costs.[2]

These changes increased the importance of towns such as those along Mississippi River tributaries. Yazoo City, Mississippi, along the Yazoo River, and Camden, Arkansas, along the Ouachita River, were two of the many towns to benefit from this move to the interior. So, too, did towns along the Red River, including the Louisiana towns of Natchitoches, Alexandria, and Shreveport. One observer noted that, by the end of 1865, "steamers were entering the Red [River] loaded with plows and other plantation supplies." Shreveport's Columbia Cotton Compress, for example, made the transport of cotton from Shreveport more profitable. The facility took in cotton that had already been ginned and baled, and it was stacked and stored in a central compound. The cotton was then further compressed, and now taking up less space, it was far more efficient to transport. The compress was at the mouth of Cross Bayou, and with easy water access, cotton could be shipped easily by steamboat via the Red and Mississippi Rivers to New Orleans.[3]

While interior port towns along the Mississippi's tributaries were central to the postbellum cotton industry, so, too, were the interior port towns of Vicksburg and the Bends. Although a *New York Times* correspondent described Bayou Sara as "the remnant of a once flourishing town on the Mississippi," he still noted that, despite its decline, "Bayou Sara was too good a business point to be abandoned." Offering river access to New Orleans to move vast quantities of cotton, the town remained "the entrepot for the surrounding country for forty miles back."[4]

Vicksburg, which had long been reliant upon the Mississippi River to ship its cotton to New Orleans, also had a central role. The city was positioned prominently at the Yazoo River's junction with the Mississippi River, and steamboat traffic from the Yazoo River brought cotton from the Mississippi Delta, which quickly stacked up along Vicksburg's levee. One observer noted that one particular ship could load 1,000 bales in

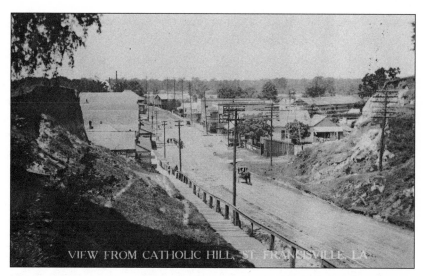

Figure 3.1. "View from Catholic Hill, St. Francisville, LA, toward Bayou Sara." Image courtesy of the Louisiana State University Special Collections, Elizabeth Dart Collection (121:9, box 3).

Figure 3.2. "Preparing Cotton in Bayou Sara." Image courtesy of the Louisiana State University Special Collections, Elizabeth Dart Collection (121:9, box 14, folder 1).

a day "and not even make a dent in the supply." Edward King similarly described how "thousands of bales and barrels roll and tumble down the gangways which communicate with the boats, and the shouting is terrific." Cotton could then be shipped down the Mississippi River to New Orleans.[5]

The other cotton market towns in Vicksburg and the Bends also remained central to the cotton industry after the Civil War, and compresses that increased efficiency were key to their success. Greenville, Mississippi, was destroyed during the war but rebuilt four miles upriver, and its cotton compress was one of the strongest businesses in that town. Port Gibson was home to "one of the handsomest cotton factory buildings to be seen anywhere." Natchez, Mississippi, according to Mayor Isaac Lowenburg, featured two cotton compresses, two cottonseed oil mills, and foundries, while more were projected or under construction.[6]

While the cotton industry's move to the interior was due in part to the telegraph and new compression equipment, the railroad also played a key role in this shift. Prior to the war, cotton in the region had primarily been shipped via river to New Orleans, where it was then sent by ships to points in the northeast and around the globe. However, overland cotton shipments by rail rose steadily in the postbellum years at the expense of New Orleans's receipts. By 1877, the U.S. internal commerce report declared that cotton was now "transported by direct consignment from the point of production to the factory," making cotton marketing cheaper as "the incidental expenses of commissions, warehousing, handling, &c., are saved." Merchants with the requisite networks could now send cotton directly to their contacts in the northeast and to other cities throughout the United States, cutting out fees that factors or other port city intermediaries may have charged.[7]

The railroad came to cities and towns that had previously relied solely on rivers. Shreveport welcomed the Southern Pacific Railroad, later known as the Texas Pacific, and a rail spur connected Shreveport's cotton compress to the major rail lines running through the city, allowing for overland transport throughout the country. The city was fast becoming a rail hub by the 1880s, and by 1887, Shreveport was connected by rail to Dallas in the west and to the Mississippi River to the east. Rail through Vicksburg, however, was not entirely reliable. Natchez was finally connected by rail to the rest of the country in 1882, and a narrow

Figure 3.3. "Cotton Scene in Houston and Texas Central Railway Yards." Image courtesy of the Library of Congress (LC-USZ62–29471).

gauge railroad came to Greenville in 1877, offering connection to the Illinois Central Railroad that ran between Memphis and New Orleans. The railroad between Memphis and New Orleans ran approximately forty miles from Bayou Sara, so that town remained tied to the Mississippi River, relying instead upon the West Feliciana Railroad, which acted essentially as a Mississippi River tributary, bringing interior cotton to the town for river shipment.[8]

While railroads came to river towns that had previously been cotton markets, interior railroads that cut through areas where river transportation was impossible meant that new areas and towns were now economically viable locations for producing and marketing cotton. Previously, poor roads had meant that it had been nearly impossible to produce and market cotton on fertile interior land if it did not have nearby river access. "The great difficulty of the United States is country roads, and the want of stone and rock," declared Robert Somers on his 1871–1872 tour, who also observed "the constant tendency to drop into ruts and puddles both wide and deep wherever wheeled vehicles can pretend to go." These poor roads prevented towns from benefiting from their proximity to rich cotton soils. For example, one group became so frustrated with the roads to Vicksburg that they petitioned the Warren County board of police, telling them that they were "desirous of hauling their cotton and produce to Vicksburg for sale and shipment but have found great difficulty in getting to and from said City owing to the almost impassable condition of the roads &c."[9]

The railroad changed this. "It is only by the iron track, liberally distributed," Somers noted, "that the produce of the Southern States can hope to get to market." He described how railroad cars were "choked with cotton bales; the freight trains, one a day, are long and heavy, and the rolling stock inadequate to the occasion." Along these new railroad lines, Somers noted, were "fertile tracts, yielding heavy crops of cotton on a soil that is inexhaustible." All of these advances, he noted "pass through wide interior regions of country, thinly peopled indeed, but settled and in working order, and capable of much development."[10]

As the railroad opened new land to farming, it also led to the rapid rise of interior market towns, many of which grew up alongside their rail lines or junctions. Such was the case for Selma, Alabama, which was situated on the Alabama River and had also been home to the Seligmans' business ventures in the antebellum years. The rhythms of postbellum Selma were defined largely by the cotton cycle. Robert Somers observed that, when the cotton from surrounding fields was ready to pick and bring to market, "tough and weather-worn men . . . come riding through the depôts inquiring eagerly for hands to come and pick their stands of cotton, or drive their teams with the bales already made." The town, he observed, was an "extensive cotton mart" where farmers could sell their crops, and there were "several large yards for storing cotton." The cotton would then be loaded onto steamboats, which "call twice or thrice a week and carry down considerable cargoes of cotton to Mobile" via the Alabama River, which, he noted, winds past the town "in rather beautiful curves under deep banks of reddish sand."[11]

While it was a river town, Selma was also "struggling hard to become, and has become to some extent, an important inland railway centre." Somers believed that the amount of cotton coming through Selma was far greater than the local plantations were producing, so he surmised that some of that cotton was arriving from interior towns along the railroad. "The railway must be helping Selma," he concluded, but he feared that the town would be unable to compete with Montgomery, which held similar advantages.[12]

Other towns that grew as a result of the railroad included Opelika, Alabama, whose location in the Black Belt and along railroad lines made it an attractive town for Jewish merchants such as Isidor and Herman Weil. The Weil brothers arrived in Opelika after the war, first joining the business of three uncles, before taking over the Opelika business. Weil Brothers was located downtown, overlooking the railroad tracks and warehouses, and it consisted of a general merchandise store downstairs and a cotton brokerage firm upstairs. Like other cotton businesses, Weil Bros. advanced merchandise from its department store and collected cotton after the harvest as payment for those debts. Before long the firm was buying cotton directly from farmers and paying them in cash. But with low margins, the brothers' success would ultimately depend upon volume and on rapidly moving cotton. Given the desire to avoid warehousing and financing charges, Weil Bros. opened a buying office elsewhere and eventually created a network that included Eufaula, Dothan, Selma, Mobile, Decatur, and Montgomery.[13]

Another emergent railroad town in which Jewish merchants thrived was Meridian, Mississippi, which grew in large measure because of its location at a major rail junction. Meridian was established in 1860, but most of the city was destroyed during the Civil War battle of Meridian in 1864. "More than 10,000 U.S. troops have been ordered to destroy all rail approaches, bridges and trestles leading into the city," reported the *Civil War Chronicle*. At the end of the operation, General William T. Sherman declared that his troops had "destroyed the only remaining railroads in the state" and that "Meridian with its depots, store-houses, arsenal, hospitals, offices, hotels, and cantonments no longer exists." The city began to rebuild, and the railroads were soon repaired, but when Edward King visited Meridian between 1873 and 1874, he called it "a new town in the woods." Similarly, Robert Somers called Meridian "a lump of a town, sprawling over sandy mounds in a wide open bosom of the forest." But, he noted, "the construction of the Alabama and Chattanooga" Railroad "naturally brought a deal of labour, money, and traffic about the little town, and helped it over its early stages." Soon, he observed,

Meridian was "growing up rapidly, and several large brick warehouses have been recently erected on lines intended to be developed one day into streets." And, he described, "a long row of stores faces the railway, with ample space between for all manner of open-air business." The city grew remarkably quickly because of the railroad—by 1890 it was one of the largest cities in Mississippi.[14]

Meridian was estimated to have the fourth largest Jewish population in Mississippi in 1878, and many of the town's businesses were operated by Jewish merchants who thrived in this postbellum railroad town. This included Baum & Co., operated by Joseph and Leon Baum—both Jewish "men of capital," who purchased significant quantities of cotton from farmers. By 1879, their Meridian store was the "largest [business] here," eventually growing to encompass a city block. In addition to their Meridian branch, which was attended to by Joseph, the firm also had a

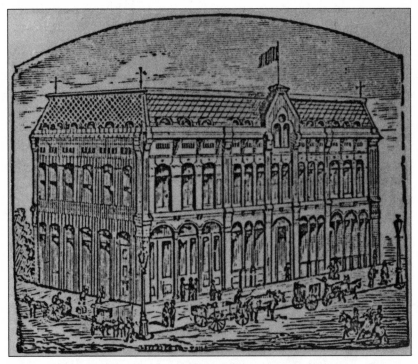

Figure 3.4. "Architect's Sketch of Baum Block, Meridian, Mississippi." Image courtesy of the Jacob Rader Marcus Center of the American Jewish Archives, Cincinnati, Ohio (MSS 601, box 5, folder 2).

branch in Philadelphia, where Leon lived, and they conducted a "heavy" business. They also had a branch in Corinth, Mississippi.[15]

Moving northeast, the growth of the Alabama Great Southern Railroad from Meridian to Chattanooga, Tennessee, illustrates clearly how the railroad quite literally made the towns alongside its tracks. This railroad ran through Eutaw, Tuscaloosa, Gadsden, and Birmingham and was not chartered until 1877. At that time, these towns were fairly small. In 1880, Birmingham's population was just over 3,000 people, but that grew to over 26,000 just ten years later. Mercantile growth was similarly impressive. Dun recorders noted just under 100 businesses in 1880, and that number had increased at least eightfold by 1890. The growth of Jewish businesses was also exceedingly robust, and the vast majority of new businesses along the railroad were in Birmingham.[16]

While towns such as Selma, Opelika, Meridian, and Birmingham owed their success to the railroads, they were not alone. Mercantile life grew along the Tennessee & Virginia Railroad in northern Alabama, including Tuscumbia, Decatur, and Huntsville. The same is true for a

Figure 3.5. "Commercial Street with Wagons Laden with Cotton Bales, Gainesville." Image courtesy of the Library of Congress (LC-USZ62–16565).

Figure 3.6. "Cotton Market in Montgomery." Produced courtesy of the American Museum in Britain, Bath (NA 045).

line of towns in Louisiana and Mississippi, stretching north from New Orleans along the Illinois Central Railroad, and inclusive of Brookhaven, Canton, Hazelhurst, Sardis, Oxford, Holly Springs, and Jackson. Jewish merchants played a key role in the development of these towns.[17]

Thus the growth of the railroad, improved communication, and new compression equipment meant that interior towns were fast becoming the heart of the cotton industry. While this was good news for merchants in these towns, it was even better news for dry goods and general store owners. Changes to the financing of the cotton industry meant that general stores in those towns—those stores that had access to credit— supplanted antebellum cotton factors and became the most important institutions in the region's economy.[18]

Credit, as it had been in the antebellum years, remained essential to cotton farming and production, as farmers would borrow money for supplies, foodstuffs, and luxury goods, and they would repay their debts after harvest. But many farmers, unable to sell cotton during the war, had fallen into debt, and many merchants were also behind in their payments. But as merchants and farmers tried to crawl out from under that debt, many were stymied by the collapse of the South's banking structure. Prior to the war, the eleven Southern states had 15 percent of the nation's banks, and capitalization of Southern banks was nearly twice the national average. After the war, however, these states had only 2 percent of the nation's banks despite housing a quarter of the nation's population. Much of this decline was due to legislation, as the National Banking Act prevented banks from holding real estate under mortgage and prohibited them from holding the title and possession of real estate to secure debts for longer than five years. Additionally, Congress passed a 10 percent tax on the notes issued by non-national banks, virtually eliminating the issuing of notes by state banks nationwide. The South was particularly hard hit by these measures, as it had relied more heavily on this form of credit than had the rest of the country. Widespread illiteracy, geographical dispersion, and lack of collateral also discouraged lending from banks and prevented Southern banks from meeting the needs of Southerners after the war.[19]

Reflective of these changes is the Bayou Sara banking house of Robinson Mumford. Mumford was quite successful before the war, worth an estimated $120,000, and he had a "[considerable amount] of money loaned at interest." Mumford's Bank of Exchange and Deposit, according to journalist J. W. Dorr, who visited New Orleans before the war, was "a prominent object in the town, occupying a very handsome building." The last Dun reference to his business was in early 1861, and a report in 1865 noted that Mumford had "not resumed business" and had "much difficulty in collecting Bills Receivable." Although his name later appeared on the ledger books of one Bayou Sara business, Dun recorders in the war's immediate aftermath nevertheless claimed that Mumford had "retired from [business]."[20]

Mumford's bank and its inability to survive reflects and illustrates the fundamentally different economic landscape in which cotton merchants operated in the postbellum years. Farmers and merchants throughout the Gulf South were desperate for credit to jumpstart a sputtering economy, but there were "no banking funds visible in such places as Selma adequate to the amount of trade," as Robert Somers observed. Without available credit from traditional banking structures, interior general stores became the lynchpin to the region's economic recovery. Some of these stores could offer credit to their customers because their proprietors had made money during the war—through cotton speculation or by selling goods whenever and wherever they could.[21]

Other stores could offer credit because their owners could leverage economic networks with New York. Somers noticed this, observing that "the volume of business in cotton and other merchandise is transacted by credits established in New York, which are only banking in another form." But the resumption of credit networks was no sure bet. "Manifold new investment opportunities had opened up by 1865," argues Sven Beckert, "from western railroads and mines to industrial enterprises in the North." Faced with a plethora of new options, many Northern investors turned to other opportunities such as the railroad, Minnesota timberland, iron and copper mines in Michigan, and coal and oil in Pennsylvania. On top of this, the South's general political instability provided another factor as to why investment in the Southern cotton industry was limited. But at least initially, many New York merchants retained their economic connections to the South.[22]

Jewish merchants were particularly well poised to leverage these structural forces. Several of the nation's largest Jewish financial houses had escaped the war in a strong position and were prepared to invest in the Southern market, reconstructing the same ethnic networks that had emerged in the antebellum years. Lehman Brothers, for example, had speculated in cotton and had made a fortune in the waning years of the war, and much of its postbellum investment was in Southern cotton. Lehman Brothers worked closely with J. W. Seligman & Co. to bring global capital to scores of cotton businesses throughout the Gulf South. While Gentiles operated many of the businesses with which these firms worked, Jews operated a great number of them. In much the same way as ethnic trust networks emerged in the antebellum years, these networks blossomed in the new postbellum milieu. Once on the margins of the antebellum cotton industry, Jewish merchants now concentrated in a niche economy that quickly became the mainstream.

While this niche economy positioned Jewish merchants for success in the postbellum cotton industry, success was neither guaranteed nor linear, and it was dictated largely by structural factors outside of their control. Immediately after the war, cotton prices rose to extraordinary levels, drawing newcomers—Jewish and non-Jewish—to the Lower

Mississippi Valley in search of profits. One contemporary noted that the price of "cotton is so high that merchants are anxious to advance [money] to put in a crop."[23]

Those merchants, however, who extended themselves with the belief that 1865 portended the future, were sorely mistaken. Supplies of stockpiled cotton dwindled. One merchant mused that "after these lots are shipped we do not know of much more that we can control & there will soon be a large falling off" in cotton shipments. Even the initial capital infusion from postwar investment was nowhere near enough to rebuild. Little remained of the proceeds of the 1865 crop after transportation charges, commissions, and interest that had been assessed on debts that had been outstanding over the course of the war.[24]

Despite the high hopes that 1865 initially instilled, the period between 1866 and 1867 wreaked financial havoc on those in the cotton industry. By late May 1866, eight parishes along the Mississippi River had flooded, in large part because of levee breaches, and continued rains pushed the Red River to also overflow its banks—Alexandria, Louisiana, for example, was said to be under three to six feet of water. In Bayou Sara, W. G. Schafer reported in April that the town saw "several heavy rains for the last ten days," which "made it impossible to pass along the streets in town." As waters receded throughout the region in early June, farmers replanted their cotton, hoping to reap at least a small harvest. Yet by the end of July, adding insult to injury, caterpillars devoured much of the remaining crop. When all was said and done, in 1866 Louisiana farmers planted over 1 million acres but harvested only 131,000 bales of cotton. Cotton prices dropped almost 40 percent in the first four months of 1866.[25]

With farmers and merchants still reeling from the disastrous season of 1866, the crop season of 1867 did little to soften the blow. Farmers planted fewer acres, so even if crops had turned out well, production would have suffered. But again, the mighty Mississippi flooded its banks in the spring. W. G. Schafer noted on March 21 that the river was high at Bayou Sara and that "water in Town [is] increasing fast in Ditches." Two days later the water was "beginning to run over Principal Street," and five days later the water was "about 10 inches over the Market House ground." It was not until a month later that Schafer noted that the river was finally "on a decline." As a member of the Levee Committee, Schafer had the railroad levee cut, and water began to flow out at the rate of one inch every twenty-four hours. Within a week, that rate had increased to about two inches per day, and it was not until two weeks later that water began to leave Principal Street. Yet Mother Nature intervened, and heavy rains for the next two weeks, coupled with the slow falling of the river, meant that Principal Street remained "partly under Water and impassable." However, after three rain-free days, he reported that the streets were "drying fast" and that repairs had commenced on Sun Street. Throughout the month of June, Schafer worked to appropriate funds for the repair of Principal and Sun Streets and hauled soil to raise Principal Street "20 inches on Water level." That work continued for much of June before life apparently settled back to normal.[26]

While flooding was difficult on the town, it also damaged crops in the surrounding countryside. But to again add insult to injury, crop infestation followed floods as it had the previous year, destroying much of the cotton that had survived the deluge. In addition, cotton prices plunged as the salvaged cotton came to market, and even more, a yellow fever outbreak struck in September. Farmers and merchants who hoped that a strong crop would erase their 1866 losses were to be disappointed and spiraled deeper into debt. In early 1868, the New Orleans Daily-Picayune observed the "once fertile and happy land" of West Feliciana Parish and asked, "What meaneth these desolated fields lying idle as far as the eye can reach?" The reporter spoke of a decrease in labor and agricultural productivity, adding "O, how are the mighty fallen." In 1868, he noted, "Not half as much land is in cultivation in this parish as there was last season."[27]

All of this created an extremely challenging business environment for those in the cotton economy. The "prosperity of all merchants here depends entirely upon the crops this season," observed one Dun recorder, foreshadowing an anxiety that would continue for years. As farmers could not produce enough cotton to repay their debts to their merchants, merchants who were counting on repayment from farmers also fell into debt with their financial backers. In order to survive the downturn, merchants needed either stockpiled cash from the war or creditors who trusted them enough to let them work through their debts.[28]

Many of those who survived the war seem to have weathered the 1866–1867 downturn, either from capital in reserve from the war or from their profits from 1865. From summer 1865 to spring 1866, E & B Jacobs of Shreveport conducted merchandise sales of $382,459, which provided a cushion when the economic situation soured. In 1866 the firm kept a "large stock," had a "large" amount of capital, were worth "at least" $100,000 and "[probably] much more," and appeared to be doing "the largest [business] in the city." The firm survived the downturn of 1866–1867, and by 1868 their estimated worth had grown to $150,000.[29]

In Montgomery, Alabama, Jacob Abrahams & Bro. had "a good country trade" prior to the war and in early 1866 was said to have "made money fast" and was "[considered good] for all bills." In 1868 it was still "one of the most substantial Jew firms" and owned real estate. Shortly thereafter a recorder claimed that it did "a considerable [commission] business in cotton, advancing to planters, &c." and had the "confidence of all."[30]

Isaias Meyer invested in Bodenheim, Meyer & Co., which survived the downturn largely because the firm had a significant amount of capital when it opened. Meyer, a Dun agent claimed, was a "man of [considerable wealth]," and Henry Bodenheim, his partner, had previously been in the dry goods business in Vicksburg and New Orleans and was also "said to have [considerable] means." Bodenheim had made money during the war, resided in New York in 1866 while a cousin ran the Vicksburg store, and had an estimated worth of between $100,000 and $150,000 shortly after the conflict. In the year after the war, H. Bodenheim & Co. reported sales of $200,000, all of which they claimed was in cash, and Dun agents estimated that the firm's capital in 1867 was $80,000, and that increased to $100,000 shortly thereafter.[31]

Yet by 1868, business had slowed, and the downturn had affected their bottom line. They had "done a southern [business] which has not turned out as well as they anticipated," observed a credit reporter, and they were "a little slow" in paying. The situation was not a crisis because they had avoided "any heavy losses," and still had "abundant means." The partners were "abundantly solvent and good for all their indebtedness" and could "undoubtedly pay for what they purchase." But because trade was "at a stand still," the members of the firm were nevertheless talking about going out of business. By 1869, they were still not profitable, and by 1870 they were worth a "[considerable amount] but are not making any money now." While the firm recovered slowly, it nonetheless did recover.

Bodenheim, Meyer & Co. was also involved with Isaias's nephew Gabe Meyer's business in Pine Bluff, Arkansas, which also survived the 1866–1867 downturn.[32]

One of Isaias Meyer's antebellum business partners, Julius Weis, also survived the downturn because of capital reserves. Weis, as we have seen, had established a cotton commission and factorage office in New Orleans as part of the Meyer, Weis & Co. conglomerate, and the firm had "made a large amount during and after the war." In 1866, Meyer, Weis & Co. was deemed a "good firm," and Weis's cotton commission business processed 5,000 bales of cotton. Although that number doubled in 1867, the firm was nonetheless deeply affected by the economic malaise, as, Weis recalled, "it was a very disastrous year, and we lost considerable money on parties to whom we had made advances, on account of the short crop." A Dun recorder corroborated this, noting that they had probably "lost heavy." Part of the firm's trouble was that the prices of supplies dropped alongside the failure of cotton. "We had a large stock of such goods on hand," Weis recalled, and as a result, "we sustained a very severe loss, having purchased them at high figures." For example, he noted an example of sheeting that plummeted from 42 cents per yard to 4.5 cents.[33]

Weis had successfully speculated in cotton during the war, and it seems likely that his cash reserves sustained him through the downturn, as his firm was still "first rate" in 1868. The commission business in 1868–1869 had received 30,000 bales of cotton, and this total continued to rise each year. The firm was worth an estimated $250,000 by spring of 1868, and focusing on cotton, it was worth an estimated $300,000–$400,000 by late 1869. The New Orleans branch soon became one of the largest cotton houses in the city, and by 1871 its worth was estimated between $600,000 and $800,000, although some believed that this estimate was high.[34]

Moses Mann was another antebellum merchant who survived both the war and the 1866–1867 downturn. Immediately following the war, Mann was conducting a small business on his own. He soon added a partner, Joseph Kraine, and the firm grew rapidly. By early 1868, the firm was "doing a large business," and while Mann had been active during the war, some of the cash reserves that let him survive the downturn may have come from his choice to sell "principally for cash," which likely limited his exposure to merchants who could not repay their debts because of poor crops. A Dun recorder noted that in 1868 his business was "the strongest house here," and Mann was "said to be very wealthy," with one estimate suggesting that he was worth $100,000. Mann also had enough capital by the end of 1867 to finance his brother-in-law Leo Meyer's ill-fated business.[35]

But Jewish merchants held no monopoly on survival during these years—some Jewish businesses failed, and some non-Jewish businesses succeeded. As for the latter, Hatch & Irvine was a West Feliciana Parish partnership between J. F. Irvine and W. D. Hatch that began in 1860. Hatch likely made money during the war, as in 1866 he was deemed the "wealthiest merchant in the Parish," while carrying on the business by himself. "But having furnished supplies very liberally he is now pressed for money," a Dun agent observed in 1868. Nonetheless, it was assumed that "when the crops come in he will pay promptly." By 1869 he was again advancing "heavily in plantation supplies," and he also owned a steam gin and press. In 1870 he was deemed a "successful speculator" who was "doing the largest commission business in the Parish."[36]

While some businesses survived the downturn with capital saved from the war, other businesses that had escaped the war with capital failed. W. G. Schafer rode out the final years of the war in New Orleans, and after making money by selling a coffeehouse for a tidy profit, he returned to Bayou Sara. There, he resumed his life and mercantile activities, renting out house lots and a stable, hiring a servant, and purchasing an adjacent lot in a cash transaction. His business was operational by the end of 1866, and while initially he was conducting a "good" business, he was soon "declining" and "slow to pay." In March 1868 one of his employees left him "on a/c of the decrease in Business," and by the end of 1868 he had closed his store, entering a partnership in New Orleans.[37]

Though it wasn't a guarantee of success, capital helped businesses survive the 1866–1867 downturn. But the uphill climb was even steeper for businesses without capital—particularly new businesses. As a result, vast numbers of businesses that opened their doors during these years were extremely short-lived—even those operated by individuals with previous mercantile experience. And in some of the most important towns in the Gulf South, the majority of businesses that opened their doors during these years—and thus faced an extremely high bar for success—were operated by non-Jews.[38]

Bayou Sara fits the pattern in which new businesses were predominantly short-lived and overwhelmingly operated by non-Jews. This included Leake & Stewart, a partnership between antebellum merchant John Leake, and Henry Stewart, who apparently furnished the bulk of the capital for the venture. In 1866 the firm was deemed "the best," and Leake was known as "the most popular merchant in the Parish." Yet despite their apparent early success, the firm had abruptly closed by 1868.[39]

Carlos Wilcox arrived after the war and operated a small, short-lived dry goods and grocery store in St. Francisville. A Dun recorder noted that he was "not good nor honest. Watch him," and Wilcox "sold out" and was "worth nothing" by the start of 1867. John T. Tice had opened a "small business" by 1866 but appears to have left the area within a year, and he died shortly thereafter. His widow, however, continued the business for a few years. A. J. Bogel had been in Bayou Sara during the conflict, and he had "made money by speculating in cotton + furnishing supplies." Though he was "doing very well" in 1867, he was out of business by 1868.[40]

These firms were far from alone. The mercantile establishment of Norwood & Payor was open for business in 1866 and was "said to be wealthy" and "doing well." Yet by early 1868, it was doing "no" business and its proprietors "have no money." W. L. Bell operated a "reliable" small business in 1866, but by 1868 was considered "hopelessly insolvent." Bell was rumored to have a drinking problem, spending "all he can get for whiskey." He was soon sold out by the sheriff and by the beginning of 1870 was broke and had left town.[41]

There were exceptions to the lack of longevity for firms that opened during the downturn. For example, Charles Farrelly was new to town in 1866, and he opened what a Dun recorder deemed a "very small" business. A Dun agent questioned his honesty, noting that, while he was postmaster, several people were receiving their letters already opened. Farrelly fell victim to yellow fever in 1867, and his brother William took over the business, but by 1870 William had died as well. A brother, Bernard Farrelly, appears to have taken over the store, and he also served as postmaster in 1870. The firm continued until around 1890.[42]

Another exception was Emile Weber's firm, which opened during the downturn and lasted until 1874. Weber had resources on which to draw that helped him to survive the lean years, apparently having weathered the challenges of 1866 and 1867 with the aid of his brother and mother, who had been in business in nearby Donaldsonville, Louisiana. Weber survived, and by 1868 he was "doing very well." He was soon conducting "considerable" business and owned "considerable" real estate. He had a "large store" and good business capacity, and he was considered "reliable." His store lasted until a fire occurred in early 1873, and by then Weber was a state senator, having previously been elected sheriff.[43]

While the majority of businesses that opened in Bayou Sara in this period were operated by non-Jews, there were a handful of Jewish-owned businesses that opened their doors as well. Most of them were the short-lived ventures of Moses Mann and Isaias Meyer, two merchants who had had antebellum business interests in Bayou Sara. But the firm of Picard & Weil also opened its doors in 1866, weathered the downturn, and in the ensuing decades became one of the strongest businesses in town.[44]

Thus in Bayou Sara, very few businesses that hung out their shingles during the 1866–1867 downturn found the success their proprietors had hoped for. But in terms of the Jewish role in Bayou Sara's mercantile life, it is striking that an influx of non-Jews arrived at precisely the time that business had slowed to a crawl. These businesses were in the wrong place at the wrong time and struggled mightily because of it. Upriver in Greenville, we see a similar pattern. Several non-Jews opened stores during the downturn; most did not last very long. And like Bayou Sara, Greenville featured a handful of Jewish-owned businesses that opened during the downturn yet survived. Unlike S. Alexander's dry goods and grocery store, which did not survive past 1867, Moses Seelig's general store lasted until 1874, when it entered bankruptcy and then was struck by fire. The general store of William Marshall & Co. opened for business in Greenville in late 1866 or early 1867, and the firm lasted until Marshall's death in the mid-1870s.[45]

In Natchez, Henry Frank arrived during the war as a sutler, and in 1866 he "purchased too large a stock for the market." But by 1867 he had "pretty well recovered" and was at that time doing "the largest dry goods [business] in this place and seems to be permanently established." He was soon paying "promptly as his bills mature," his sales were large, and he was deemed to be "out of his old troubles."[46]

Finally, if we turn our gaze to Shreveport, Dun recorders counted forty cotton economy businesses in 1866, around a quarter of which were operated by Jews. Many of them, however, may have settled in Shreveport during the latter years of the war, perhaps accounting for the higher percentage of Jews than elsewhere. Data for 1867 more closely resembles the patterns in Bayou Sara and Greenville. Dun agents recorded fifteen new businesses in Shreveport in 1867, and only one-third lasted for more than two years. Only four of the new businesses seem to have been operated by Jews, and only one of the four lasted more than two years—Simon Herold, who was operational by mid-1865, remained in business until the start of the twentieth century.[47]

Thus the 1866–1867 downturn is important for understanding how structural factors affected mercantile success more broadly. Businesses that survived these years often did so because of capital reserves they had built up during the war or in its immediate aftermath. But the period is also important to understanding Jewish mercantile life specifically. While Jewish and non-Jewish firms that saved money during the war used those profits to survive the lean years, new businesses did not have that same security blanket. And for some of the key towns in the Gulf South, new Jewish businesses fared better for a simple reason—few of them opened. While these towns are clearly too small a sample size to draw sweeping conclusions for the entire South, they do suggest that this burst of non-Jewish mercantile life occurred precisely at the wrong time, as two catastrophic crop seasons placed a strain on the region's cotton economy.

Following the disastrous crop years of 1866–1867, the outlook for Southern merchants brightened. Cotton prices doubled between late 1867 and spring 1868, and increased production ushered in a period of prosperity that would last through the summer of 1873. Better crop yields, a strong economy, and advantageous laws passed partly in response to the economic challenges of the previous years positioned businesses that opened during this era for success. Jewish-owned businesses, few of which had opened during the downturn, opened with greater frequency in these years, placing them in the right place at the right time. Their success was also enhanced by working directly with freedmen. Needing to start from scratch in order to grow crops as tenant farmers or sharecroppers, freedmen, whose emancipation was far from complete, did have the autonomy to work with merchants of their choosing during this era. It made good business sense for merchants to work with freedmen, and a significant proportion of Jewish merchants who opened their doors in this era counted freedmen among their clientele. This confluence of forces and opportunities cemented the Jewish niche economy.[48]

Although 1868 ushered in a period of relative prosperity, the challenges of 1866–1867 were still fresh in the minds of merchants and lenders who had lost much of the capital that had poured into the Gulf South in the years immediately following the war. Operating in an atmosphere of heightened risk, merchants needed prodding to lend money, so legislatures passed crop lien laws that allowed farmers and plantation owners to legally pledge their future crop as collateral. This, believed legislators, would jump-start the economy—Mississippi even called their lien law an "Act for Encouraging Agriculture." Mississippi's lien law went into effect on February 18, 1867, and in Louisiana, an 1867 act changed the Civil Code such that debts owed for furnished plantation supplies or cash advances took priority over other debts.[49]

Despite the security provided by the lien laws, a loan backed by a crop that was months away from harvest—and as the previous two years had demonstrated was subject to destruction by a host of forces unleashed by Mother Nature—was hardly a sound investment for New York and international financiers. This was especially so as the Industrial Revolution provided capitalists with far less risky investment opportunities. In order to mitigate their risk with Southern investments, financiers charged Gulf South merchants high rates of interest. These rates were generally no less than 10 percent and, in some instances, rose to 25 percent—even for merchants with the most impeccable credit. Merchants, who were now paying high rates of interest to their creditors and who had also taken the gamble that the economic situation and Mother Nature would play to their favor, in turn charged very high rates of interest to their customers. On one plantation in Leflore County, Mississippi, croppers paid 25 percent interest on food and 35 percent on clothes to the merchants who supplied them with their goods. As a result, interest charges ate away at farmers' bottom lines, and they were forced to grow more cotton to repay their debts.[50]

While financiers and merchants assumed a significant amount of risk, high interest rates also ensured that they would be rewarded handsomely if crops turned out well and if other contingencies went according to plan. For the most part between 1868 and 1872, they did. For Abraham Levy, mercantile activities in 1868 were intended to cover the debts that he had incurred during the poor crop years of 1866–1867. "I do need the money to make payments in [New Orleans] of over all [indebtedness] from 1867 & 1866 to gett [sic] my Rest Once more," Levy wrote in late 1868. He continued to work with Meyer Brothers in Clinton, as he had done during the war, and the firm apparently collected cotton on his behalf. "How is it going with my bills that I turned over to you all in Clinton," Abraham wrote to Henry Meyer. One particular farmer "wants to pay for his cotton. I hope that you are [trying] to get all the money for me, as much as possible, since I want to pay all my debts, so that I get everything in order." Further, Levy continued, "be so good as to write now to Bayou Sara how it's going with the oats & cotton bills that I gave you all for collection." In another letter, Levy wrote to Emanuel Meyer that "*in regard to Kelly's cotton* I. do. nat. understand you. [Yesterday you said] Mr. Kelly has no [funds] and then [you] Say Mr. Kelly has given You A Draft on A Levi [New Orleans] . . . & [he] paid [when he] has funds on hand."[51]

The passage of lien laws, coupled with Mother Nature's cooperation and strong cotton prices, meant that merchants were in the driver's seat for a short period beginning in 1868. In several towns, this was also a period where more Jews arrived on the scene in greater concentrations. In Bayou Sara, while the challenging years of 1866–1867 saw an influx of short-lived non-Jewish businesses, Jewish merchants opened their doors in greater percentages and numbers between 1868 and 1873. While precision is not possible through extant records, mercantile reports indicate that six new cotton economy businesses opened their doors in 1868, four of which were operated by Jews. The following year saw four new businesses, all of which were Jewish owned. In 1870, around a dozen new businesses appear to have opened, and about half of them were operated by Jews. In 1871 three new businesses opened, one of which was Jewish owned, and in 1872, two more businesses emerged on the scene, one of which was operated by a Jewish merchant. Finally, in 1873, before economic panic swept the nation, eight new businesses emerged on the scene, five of which appear to have been operated by Jews. Thus all told, between 1868 and 1873, over half of the new cotton economy businesses that arrived on the scene were opened by Jews. These businesses were in the right place at the right time, as legal, economic, and environmental conditions aligned in their favor.[52]

How does this compare to other towns in the region? In Greenville we see a similar pattern, in which mercantile reports indicate that Jews operated about half of the approximately fifty new cotton economy businesses that opened their doors over the same 1868–1873 period. In the critical transition year of 1868, all four Jewish businesses that opened lasted more than eight years. In the larger metropolis of Shreveport, while Jewish percentages were lower, numerically more Jews settled than they did in the smaller river towns. Jews operated about one-third of the approximately 100 firms that opened their doors in Shreveport at this time. In the critical 1868 transition year, the six new Jewish businesses that opened lasted an average of eleven years.[53]

While more Jewish businesses opened during this period than had in the 1866–1867 years, what is perhaps most notable about this period is the overwhelming number of new Jewish businesses that emerged that worked with freedmen. While scholarship has tended to focus on whether to ascribe either benevolent or sinister motivations for this economic relationship, what is clear is that good business practices dictated that merchants should work with freedmen, as the abolition of slavery and the emergence of sharecropping created a large group of potential new customers for the region's merchants.

When Abraham Lincoln signed the Emancipation Proclamation on the first day of 1863, declaring that over 3 million of the nation's slaves "are and henceforth shall be free," the debate immediately began as to what the South's new labor system would look like. With demand for cotton as high as ever, contemporaries feared that without the labor system upon which they had long relied, the South would be unable to keep up with demand or resume its critical position in the global cotton empire. Given this reality, it was clear that new labor relationships would hold the key to the resumption of the region's cotton production, and contemporaries robustly debated what that system would look like.[54]

Freedpeople, for their part, eagerly awaited the freedoms that emancipation should have brought, but those freedoms were not forthcoming. Many maintained that only ownership of land would give them true autonomy, yet it soon became clear that ownership was not what planters and government officials had in mind. Despite the wishes of some radical

Republicans, rather than providing freedmen "forty acres and a mule" to farm their own land, freedmen were instead bound to land that was not their own. Such labor systems took many forms, but most common was for the laborer, or "tenant," to produce the crop and pay a percentage at the end of the season as rent to the landowner. Many freedmen would purchase their supplies on credit from landlords or merchants, and their pay would be a share of the crop after their debts were repaid.[55]

These systems spread rapidly, and, by 1900, three-quarters of all black farmers in Arkansas, South Carolina, Mississippi, Louisiana, Alabama, and Georgia were either sharecroppers who earned a share of the crop or renters who paid rent to landlords but who kept the full crop. Yet while these systems ensured that the region would continue to grow cotton and address the worldwide demand, they also ensured that freedmen would remain tied to the land of others, and that they would spiral into a cycle of poverty from which it would be nearly impossible to dig themselves out. This new system would come to define the economic structure of the postbellum South.[56]

When freedmen would not work "willingly," planters resorted to coercion to ensure that their hegemony would be maintained. One British minister noted that "everywhere measures are being taken to force the Negroes to work, and to teach them that freedom means working for wages instead of masters." An editorial in the *Economist* claimed that "it is clear that the dark races must in some way or other be induced to obey white men willingly." When coercion failed, state governments passed black codes and other legislation that in reality bound former slaves to cotton plantations. In some areas, landlords forced yearlong contracts upon their workers in an attempt to bind them to the fields through the harvest. Mississippi passed a law in late 1865 that forced freedpeople to sign contracts that restricted their mobility. For groups such as the Ku Klux Klan, so-called labor discipline became a key plank in their practices. And the political coalition that embraced white supremacy also utilized economic coercion to control black labor. "We have the capital and give employment," noted one Civil War general in an address to black voters. "We own the lands and require labor to make them productive. . . . You desire to be employed. . . . We know we can do without you. We think you will find it very difficult to do without us. . . . We have the wealth." In some instances, merchants cut off credit to blacks who attended Republican meetings, and landlords warned that they would evict "any negro who will not swear never again to vote the Radical ticket."[57]

In addition to economic coercion, some Southerners turned to violence to brutally repress black political participation and representation. Black leaders began to organize events that called for civil and voting rights, and many also took a greater role in statewide conventions, later holding prominent state and federal offices. But as black leaders yearned for political representation, it was met by brutal violence from those who hoped to maintain their own hegemony. Groups such as the Regulators, the Redeemers, the Young Men's Democratic Clubs, the Invisible Empire, and the Ku Klux Klan used violence and intimidation to keep blacks out of politics and to push white Democrats into power. The Klan gained notoriety, and their "reign of terror" included assassinations of elected officials.[58]

Violence against blacks was widespread. Freedman Henry Adams claimed that "over two thousand colored people" were murdered around Shreveport in 1865, and the following year, after "some kind of dispute with some freedmen" near Pine Bluff, a group set ablaze a black settlement. In the aftermath, "24 Negro men woman [sic] and children were hanging to trees all round the Cabbins [sic]." Black political meetings, black churches, and black schools were also the targets of violence. In Texas, 1,000 black people were murdered between 1865 and 1868 for "reasons" such as failing to "remove his hat," for refusing to "give up his whiskey flask," or simply, claimed one white man, "to thin out the niggers a little." In Bayou Sara, W. G. Schaefer wrote in his diary in 1868 that he "saw [a] Negro man hung named Edmond Harrison." Women were not afforded a reprieve from the violence.[59]

The spate of brutal violence didn't escape the attention of Congress, which passed the Ku Klux Klan Act of 1871, moving certain crimes into federal jurisdiction. This calmed much of the violence and temporarily brought a degree of stability to the South. Republicans did well in the election of 1872, and the growth of the Redeemers, those seeking to bring states back to "native" Democrat control, seemed to be halted, and violence was reduced.[60]

Although their economic and political freedoms were severely restricted in the 1868–1872 period and they were the victims of brutal violence, freedmen were generally given the autonomy to choose the merchants from whom to purchase their goods. And this meant that freedmen were a significant new customer base for merchants. There also may have been a stigma associated with working with freedmen. In Bayou Sara, the *New York Times* noted that "it may appear strange to the readers of THE TIMES that these stores should be outside of the town, but the business done is entirely with the country negroes, who bring their cotton and products for barter. It is therefore a better locality than within the precincts of the town." Although it is not clear just how many non-Jewish merchants worked with freedmen, a significant number of Jewish merchants in the Gulf South during the 1868–1873 period did.[61]

Again, Bayou Sara provides an excellent lens through which we can see this phenomenon, which included some of the town's largest businesses, such as the powerhouse firm of Julius Freyhan & Co. Freyhan's firm had its roots in the antebellum years, and in 1872 a Dun recorder claimed that the bulk of Freyhan's business was conducted with freedmen. Moses Mann was also one of West Feliciana Parish's most prominent businessmen, and while we know that he had owned slaves prior to the war, it is unclear if his own postbellum businesses worked with freedmen. Nonetheless, Mann financially supported his brother Abraham, who by 1872 was conducting "considerable [business] with negroes + [small] farmers," and he was also a partner in Mann & Levy, which conducted "a good business principally with the colored laborers."[62]

While Freyhan and Mann's firms had emerged in the antebellum years, those that opened in Bayou Sara during the 1868–1873 period—both large and small—were characterized by their business with freedmen. This was the case for Adolph Teutsch's general store, which became one of the strongest firms in the parish. Teutsch was born in 1850 in Venningen, Bavaria, and by 1871 had a small West Feliciana store that was "dependent upon crops" that were "short in this parish." A Dun recorder noted no fewer than six times between 1871 and 1873 that this "small negro store" conducted business "chiefly" with freedmen and was engaged in the "negro trade." By 1878 Teutsch was "first class, good, reliable."[63]

Picard & Weil was another of the town's largest businesses, and while it is unclear if the firm worked directly with freedmen, two firms with which it was closely affiliated did. S. Weil & Bro., a partnership between Simon Weil (of Picard & Weil) and his two brothers, first appeared in

1868. The small firm was backed by Picard & Weil, and a Dun recorder claimed that they "trade principally with negroes" and worked with "small farmers." By late 1871 the firm transitioned to the leadership of Lazard Weil, and the business remained fairly small, although it continued to be backed by Picard & Weil. Dun recorders indicated that Lazard "sells chiefly to coled. [colored] people" and conducted "principally a negro trade" and that his business was "principally confined to advancing to freedmen." While he didn't "stand as high as his brother," Lazard Weil's business nevertheless appeared to have done fairly well and lasted through 1880.[64]

While the parish's strongest firms and leading businessmen worked either directly or indirectly with freedmen, so, too, did many other smaller, Jewish-owned firms that emerged in the 1868–1873 period. This included that of Jacob Mitchell, who from the start "trades with negroes," claimed a Dun recorder. He was soon conducting "considerable" business, still "chiefly" and "principally with negroes," according to his credit reports. The prejudices of Dun recorders came through Mitchell's credit reports, as one reporter claimed that, because he dealt with freedmen, his business was "a risky one" and thought him good for "limited" credit.[65]

Several other Jewish-owned businesses that worked with freedmen also emerged between 1868 and 1873. B. Landman's St. Francisville general store was open in late 1869, conducting business "chiefly with negroes." Landman, however, was out of business by 1871. Solomon Heidingsfelder arrived in Bayou Sara in 1869, armed with a small amount of capital from his father, and he traded "principally with the negroes." His firm was also short-lived—before the end of 1871 he had left town. One Dun agent opined that he did "not consider that persons doing such [business] are [good] for large orders or long [credit], their success depending too much on the crops and the honesty of negroes." Joseph and Louisa Aronstein's general store opened in 1869 in Louisa's name, and the business advanced a large amount of supplies and received payment in cotton. They fell behind in their collections in 1871 and were "struggling along" financially, and the store "always appears to be 'hard up.'" Nevertheless, the Aronsteins conducted "a considerable [business] with negroes," "advancing considerably" to them. The business closed in 1878.[66]

These short-lived businesses were not alone. The widow of Ernest Newman conducted a so-called "negro [business]" that opened in 1871, and Meyer Brothers, which also opened around 1871, "traded principally with [the] colored population advancing supplies buying cotton etc." By 1876, Meyer Brothers had dissolved. In 1872, D. Rosen opened a "small store for [the] negro trade," which was "more adapted for trade with [the] colored population." Also in 1872, M. Goldman opened a general store where he "deals with negroes in furnishing them." The business quickly fell into "bad repute," and Goldman was deemed "a sham," although the business remained until 1880. Joseph Stern apparently opened his dry goods and grocery store in 1873, and he was soon doing a "principally negro trade," operating through 1880.[67]

Also opening in 1873, Benjamin Lehman's small general store "deal[s] with negroes on time, [is] dependent on crops," and was good for small orders. His business was "depending entirely on his collections from" freedmen, which, according to the Dun reporter, was "a very risky" business, and he was "not regarded reliable" for any amount of credit. He had failed by 1874. His brother, M. Lehman, operated the "same kind of business" as Benjamin, dealing "with negroes on [credit], dependent on crops," owning no real estate, and he was good only for small orders. He was "dependent on [freedmen] for success which," according to the Dun recorder, "is rather dubious caution is recommended."[68]

All told, between 1868 and 1873, Dun recorders observed that about three-quarters of the new Jewish firms were conducting business with freedmen. Other firms may have been doing so as well, although Dun recorders may not have noted this. But new firms working with freedmen during this era were in no way unique to Bayou Sara. Upriver in Greenville, Joseph Radjesky's store opened shortly after the war, and his "trade is almost exclusively with the negroes," observed a Dun reporter. "I think he has credited them imprudently, which will [probably] cost him most of his profits," claimed one report. The "only trouble with him," observed another report, was "that he credits the negroes too much and has trouble collecting." Also in Greenville, Isenberg & Massenger were "Jew peddlers" who opened around 1870, and a recorder noted that "their dealings are all in the country with the Negroes + we know little" about them.[69]

Downriver from Greenville, Jewish-owned businesses opening in the 1868–1872 period in Port Gibson also counted freedmen among their customers. Moses Kaufman, Sr., opened his fancy dry goods and general store in 1872 and was noted to "sell and advance to freedmen." Moses Kaufman, Jr., was the proprietor of a dry goods and grocery store in Port Gibson, and in an odd account, a Dun agent reported that "he encourages negroes to steal jewelry + spoons + he buys in quantities. 'He is a thief.'" Additionally, Jacob Riteman arrived in Port Gibson from Vicksburg in 1872, and a Dun reporter noted that his general store sold principally "to Negroes for cash."[70]

The same can be said for businesses opening elsewhere throughout the Gulf South in this era. In Shreveport, Max Blum was known to be "trading principally with negroes of low [character]." In Benton, Alabama, Benjamin and Samuel Wolff "made money fast out of the freedmen + do very little of any other trade." In Huntsville, Solomon and Daniel Schiffman arrived from Cincinnati and conducted business "on a side street mostly with negroes."[71]

While Jews certainly had extensive economic relationships with freedmen, there are also some examples of Dun recorders highlighting non-Jewish businesses that also worked with freedmen. In Bayou Sara, Peter Fisher and his wife opened a small "store in town," and a Dun recorder claimed that Mrs. Fisher's "trade principally in the country is with negroes." A. B. Briant opened a small country store in 1870 that "deals altogether with negroes," and William Krenly opened a small "country grocery" sixteen miles from town and conducted business "principally for freedmen." Jeff Hamilton was a "planter on a [small] scale, on land belonging to his fathers [sic] estate," and he had "interest in a [small] country store, put up for trade with negroes."[72]

While there are only a handful of non-Jewish businesses in Bayou Sara known to work with freedmen, this does not necessarily mean that Jews conducted business with freedmen at a higher rate than their non-Jewish neighbors. However, Dun agents *recorded* a significant number of Jewish businesses in town that worked with freedmen, but they recorded only a handful of non-Jewish businesses that did so.

The merchant-freedmen relationships were not limited to businesses that emerged between 1868 and 1873. We have already seen how antebellum Jewish merchants Julius Freyhan and Moses Mann worked directly or indirectly with freedmen. But new postbellum Jewish-owned firms that opened in other years follow the same pattern. In Port Gibson, one particular merchant operated a fancy dry goods and general store and in 1873 was noted to "sell + advance to Negroes." In West Feliciana Parish, J. L. Brown took over a small dry goods and grocery store from his mother-in-law in 1877, and his business was supposedly "confined to [the] negro trade." His business had failed and closed by 1879. Henry Jacobs and his brother had opened by 1874 as "energetic" businessmen with a small amount of capital and were conducting a "small negro trade." Some non-Jewish firms that opened outside this period also worked with freedmen. Emile Weber conducted "considerable [business] with negroes + small farmers," and his mother also "trades only with freed men, white people never go into her store."[73]

Weber's willingness to work with freedmen may have been informed by his active involvement in Republican politics, and Emile and his brother Don were considered "the leading Republicans of the Felicianas." Don Weber's life had "been frequently threatened of late," noted the *New York Times*, and another newspaper claimed that he was "shot down without a word of warning, as he was walking along the street about 3 o'clock in the afternoon on his way to dinner." Emile Weber had "every reason to believe that D.A. Weber has been murdered by the bulldozers for political vengeance," the *Times* observed, maintaining that "this is the voice of bloody Feliciana, in debatable Louisiana." Another newspaper correspondent had no doubt that the "dastardly assassination" could "only be ascribed to political reasons."[74]

Nonetheless, the structural factors specific to the 1868–1873 period—including a stronger economy, advantageous laws, and stronger crop yield—were all important factors that fostered mercantile success during these years. Jewish firms, which opened in greater numbers than had been the case during the 1866–1867 downturn, were thus in the right place at the right time. And in addition to the more conducive environment in which they operated, a significant number of Jewish businesses worked directly with freedmen, which made good business sense. All of these forces converged to make 1868–1873 a robust era for Jewish merchants.

While the 1868–1873 period was a strong one for cotton businesses—and Jewish mercantile establishments in particular—several outside forces came together to make 1873–1879 a challenge for all merchants in the region. Ushered in by financial panic, the uncertainty in this era also included political instability, race violence, disease outbreaks, fires, floods, and challenges to lien laws. Once again, merchants who survived relied on saved capital, ingenuity, and credit networks.

During this era, the nation's political instability created an uncertain environment in which to operate. Democrats began to sweep into power in the South, "redeeming" states from Republican control. So-called Redeemer politicians diminished the opportunities available to freedmen and ratcheted up their campaign of violence to squelch their political opponents, including a significant number of lynchings. In Mississippi, the 1874 election provided an excuse for Democrats to violently destroy the Republican apparatus and to prevent blacks from exercising their right to vote. Two years later in Louisiana, fifteen prisoners, who were brought to New Orleans by steamship from Bayou Sara, had been "charged with conspiracy and the intimidation of negroes in July last." All of the prisoners were white, they were required to appear before a U.S. court, and they were held until bail. By the 1890s, racial segregation was the legal norm; blacks were often prevented from serving on juries, and Redeemers used force to maintain control over their labor. All of this led to the rise of Jim Crow laws throughout the region.[75]

Closely tied to race politics, the period 1873–1879 was also characterized by the effort to repeal the lien laws that had encouraged merchants to give credit more freely—including lending to freedmen. Opponents of the lien laws were furious that, in the case of default, a merchant's lien won out above all others and that the merchant stood a better chance of recouping his losses before others. Landowners resented this subservience to the merchants, and one Mississippi legislator claimed that Mississippi had "suffered more from the lien law than Radical rule."[76]

Democrats led the charge to reshape these laws, and attempts at repeal occurred throughout the region and led to uncertainty for merchants. Georgia was the first state to prevent merchants from taking crop liens in 1874, and Alabama debated repeal throughout the late 1870s before finally passing a measure in 1884. Repeal was attempted but failed in Louisiana in 1878, and a partial repeal was enacted in Mississippi that same year. South Carolina repealed its lien laws in 1877 but reversed course a year later, recognizing that farmers could no longer get the supplies they needed under their new system. Without assurances that their loans would be repaid should crops fail, merchants were more reluctant to deal directly with farmers, black or white.[77]

The critical factor in that reluctance was the Panic of 1873—which disrupted the nation's system of credit and was the worst economic crisis to date in the Union. With the failure of Jay Cooke & Co. on September 18, 1873, one of the nation's most prominent financial firms utterly collapsed. At the New York Stock Exchange, one publication declared that "dread seemed to take possession of the multitude." One reporter noted a "mad terror" and described scenes of men who "rushed to and fro trying to get rid of their property, almost begging people to take it from them at any price." The following day, another major firm, Fisk & Hatch closed its doors, and on September 20 the New York Stock Exchange closed for the first time in its history.[78]

While the economy would struggle for the next two decades, the period between 1873 and 1879 was one of particular uncertainty for the financial system. In those years, 414 banks closed their doors, and while bankruptcies numbered 5,100 in 1873, they rose to 10,478 in 1878. Railroad construction slowed considerably, and by 1876 half of the railroads had bankrupted. Railroad speculation had been partially to blame for the financial collapse, and their failures brought down not only the banks that had supplied the capital but also the industries that were counting on the success of railroads. With less demand for rails, for example, the market for iron dropped precipitously, further affecting the financial sector.[79]

New York's economic elite took a beating between 1873 and 1879. "Everything looks dark," claimed August Belmont. "I have met with greater losses . . . than I have ever known in the many years of my mercantile experience." The Chamber of Commerce was "unable to record any thing satisfactory" about the iron trade. "It is probable that never in the history of the trade . . . has a darker cloud rested over its prospects than now." In 1878, New York's mayor was concerned that "vacant shops, stores, and manufactories . . . stare at us in every street." Manufacturers also struggled mightily, and merchants and bankers who had taken the most risks were often the most likely to feel the negative impacts.[80]

The panic spread beyond New York. The Bank of California, for example, failed. But several of the Jewish banks that provided credit to the Southern cotton trade survived, in large part through ethnic networks.

Isaias Hellman's Farmers and Merchants Bank weathered the storm, possibly because it was more cautious in lending and kept larger cash reserves, but also because it leveraged family and ethnic networks to raise the capital necessary for survival. When the panic reached California, Hellman was away in Europe, and he asked his brother-in-law Mayer Lehman for a $20,000 loan to weather the storm. In response to the financial disaster, Hellman's bank closed its doors for thirty days while Hellman and his partners sought the capital necessary to survive. Hellman secured a loan from the Jewish banking house of Lazard Frères, a cousin secured $15,000 from the Jewish firm of Haas Brothers of San Francisco, and other associates found enough funds to keep the bank solvent. Hellman's bank survived.[81]

While the Panic of 1873 certainly affected Northern and Western banks, it also spread to New Orleans. Mere days after the failure of Jay Cooke & Co., New Orleans banks suspended currency payments and made no new loans. In the Crescent City, gas lights were turned off on moonlit nights in order to save money, property values plummeted, suicides increased, and a quarter of all tax revenue due in January 1875 could not be collected. The Freedmen's Savings Bank, with branches in New Orleans and Shreveport, failed in 1874, and $300,000 of freedmen's savings disappeared.[82]

As the reality of the banking environment became clearer, panic set in among farmers and merchants in the Gulf South. Planters were encouraged to bring their cotton to market as soon as possible so merchants could pay their Northern debts. Economic activity slowed, land prices dropped, and crop prices declined throughout the rest of the nineteenth century. This pressured farmers to grow even more cotton to compensate, which prevented those farmers from instead growing the staple crops that could have made them more self-sufficient. Meanwhile, interest rates skyrocketed, credit was particularly hard to secure, and the cycle of debt deepened.[83]

As if politics, lien law repeals, and economic collapse weren't enough, merchants had to deal with flooding again, as the "Great Overflow" of the Lower Mississippi Valley in 1874 affected the region's ability to climb out from under the financial disaster. One newspaper reported in February that 14,000 square miles of Louisiana, Arkansas, and Mississippi were underwater and claimed that that 50,000 people were homeless and in need of aid. The citizens of Catahoula Parish resolved

> that it is a solemn and sad fact that the extreme high water which now covers our entire rich alluvial lands, is bringing with it great distress among the people, who have no money, no credit, and not more than ten days rations. This want of money and provisions in this district, arises from the fact that crops were almost a total failure last year; the people are in debt, and no one will advance them money, credit or provisions.

They urged that Louisiana's governor and the president of the United States "be notified of and made acquainted with the hunger, destitution and want of this section of country, and that they be requested to furnish the poor, destitute people of the district with meat, meal and corn." By May, one Shreveport newspaper claimed that "the crevases are fifty miles in width. Through them flow streams greater and more powerful than the mighty Mississippi itself, and which pour out on this devoted country 2,000,000,000 cubic feet of water every hour."[84]

In addition to flooding, fires also continued to make life more challenging for merchants in this period. For example, a fire swept through Greenville on September 2, 1874, starting in the storehouse of B. Seelig & Co. It quickly spread, and by the time the flames had been fully extinguished, sixty-two businesses and forty-five dwellings had been destroyed. Twenty-five of those businesses were owned by Jews, including the firms of Weiss & Goldstein and Leopold Wilczinski. The following year a second large fire swept through Greenville, and although not as large as the previous fire, it nevertheless destroyed eight mercantile establishments.[85]

Finally, yellow fever outbreaks also provided challenges to mercantile activity and continuity. Shreveport in particular faced a major outbreak of the disease in 1873, which killed between 800 and 1,000 residents. One contemporary recalled that

> graves were filled as fast as they could be dug. All during the night horses could be heard carrying the dead, and the moans and weeping of the bereaved families swept over the town. Girls who were well today were dead from the terrible fever in a week's time. . . . As fast as victims died, they

were buried without much ceremony to ease the pain of those left. When entire families were swept out by the fever, their clothes and everything in the house was burned.

Although there was a major outbreak of the disease in Memphis and New Orleans in 1878, Shreveport was spared this round in part because of a strict quarantine—enforced by shotguns—that was likely inspired in part by a recollection of the disaster five years prior.[86]

The 1878 outbreak also reveals how ethnic mercantile networks doubled as support networks. According to the *Jewish Messenger*, appeals for help, including a telegram from James Gutheim of New Orleans, have "aroused our merchants to liberal action." In response, several firms rallied the mercantile community from around the country to donate to relief efforts. Among the leaders of this effort was Lehman Brothers, which collected money from Meyer, Weis & Co. and Lazard Frères, among a host of other firms. Other Jewish merchants donated to the cause, including the Seligmans, the Hallgartens, S. Loeb, and Jacob Schiff.[87]

While Shreveport escaped the 1878 epidemic, Greenville was not so lucky. Cases multiplied over August and September, until an early frost on October 15 and a heavy frost in late October slowed the spread of the disease. When all was said and done, 291 Greenville residents had died, as well as 37 in surrounding villages. Curiously, the Jewish death toll seemed to be a significantly lower percentage of the population. Only eighteen of the known yellow fever victims were Jews.[88]

Despite the challenges of the 1873–1879 period, many firms survived and thrived. Julius Weis's cotton commission business, for example, which had received 30,000 bales of cotton in 1868–1869, received 130,000 bales of cotton in 1875–1876, which Weis estimated to be perhaps "the largest cotton commission business ever done in the City by any one house." Many of the firms that survived were able to do so because of saved capital, in much the same fashion as they had weathered the 1866–1867 downturn. Others survived because they were able to adapt, and many relied on lifelines and extensions from their creditors, revealing just how important trust-based economic networks actually were.[89]

Such was the case for Mann, Fischer & Co., which was "solvent" in 1869, and the partners conducted a "large + safe" business, "supplying planters." The 1873–1879 downturn does not appear to have affected them to a significant degree. Shortly after the onset of panic, they were the proprietors of "quite a large establishment," and while the partnership dissolved later that year, Moses Mann carried on the business in his own name, and it continued to thrive. By 1875, the business was "said to be quite wealthy," and moving forward, the firm continued to have "a large surplus of capital" and was considered to be "first class. Regarded as entirely reliable" and safe. It remained strong into 1880, when recovery from the downturn began.[90]

Moses Mann had strong networks with New Orleans and New York, which aided him during a period that many others struggled. Mann had interests in at least two businesses in New Orleans—first, he was the proprietor of Meyer & Mann of New Orleans, a commission house that was a partnership between Mann and his cousin, with whom he had partnered for a brief time in postbellum Bayou Sara. Second, and more important, was Mann's interest in Katz & Barnett, which was located on Canal Street. This wholesale dry goods and notions firm was "doing very well" and was operational by 1866 and receiving cotton by 1867. The firm also provided Mann with a direct link to New York. "Wholesale traders in N.Y.C. speak well of them," and it was said that it had credit "in some of the European markets," wrote a Dun reporter, and Katz & Barnett also appears to have had a branch or a close connection in New York.[91]

E & B Jacobs's Shreveport store was valued at $150,000 in 1868, and it appears to have survived the Panic of 1873 almost flawlessly. By 1874 it was already deemed "out of debt," worth an estimated $250,000, much of which was in real estate, mortgaged security, and its stock. That same year it conducted "a large wholesale" business, had "unlimited" credit, and was "the largest in this section of the Country." E & B Jacobs were the "richest men in town," and the firm reached an A/1 credit rating by 1880.[92]

In Selma, M. Schwartz & Co. survived the 1873–1879 downturn because of cash reserves. By 1876 the firm was solely a cotton factorage house, and while other firms were struggling, Schwartz "has cash means" and "employs it with great" advantage. When Schwartz retired, the firm became M. Gusdorf & Co., which received credit from Lehman

Brothers, and in 1879 it was considered a "strong firm" that conducted a "large safe and lucrative business."[93]

In Natchez, Henry Frank also survived. "Frank bears the reputation of a man of integrity," wrote a Dun recorder, noting that he also "stands very high here." The recorder specifically noted that Frank took little risk in business sales, which may have helped him to weather the impending storm. Moreover, noted the agent, his business had flexibility, as "should he find wholesale trade unprofitable he can at any time return to the combination of" wholesale and retail. His caution and aversion to risk may have paid off, although in 1873 he "had a hard time this year" but was "still solvent" and "stands high." The following year he was "no doubt solvent," but a Dun recorder believed he was overstating his means." Frank's business in 1874 "has not been large," the recorder noted, and "he has done but little cash business and has sometimes been 'pushed' to pay rent." Nonetheless, he had recovered by 1876, as he was doing a large business and "pays promptly."[94]

E. Schaefer & Co. of Yazoo City was considered to be the best dry goods store in town in 1870 and in 1873 remained "one of the leading merchants of Yazoo City," who was doing a "large" business. Yet Emile Schaefer apparently had a vice—he was a "reckless card player" and "frequently loses heavily." His penchant for gambling may have also led him to speculate "by attempting to plant with fair prospects of success." A Dun agent noted that he "gambles + loses always," yet he seems to have succeeded in his planting venture—by 1873 he ran a plantation in addition to his store. He struggled during the downturn but nonetheless survived. He was "prompt but like many others [considerably] in debt" in 1874, yet he continued to be regarded as a merchant with a "first rate" business ability. By 1878, his estimated worth was approximately $15,000, and he made a reported $10,000 in 1879 on cotton. In 1883, Schaefer transitioned from the mercantile business to planting, and within several years, he owned 1,500 acres of land and produced about 250 bales of cotton annually. In 1886 he also invested in the Yazoo Oil Works.[95]

Another merchant who had strong credit networks and who survived the downturn was Isaias Meyer, who had diversified with an ownership stake in a New Jersey silk factory, Pelgram & Meyer. The firm was operational by the late 1870s, and by 1879 its capital was estimated between

$300,000 and $400,000. Isaias Meyer himself was worth a reported half million dollars in late 1881, and with this large nest egg upon which to draw, the firm "asked for no credit in this country outside of foreign exchange for raw silk which they imported directly." While it is unclear if the firm worked with Lehman Brothers in the 1870s, extant ledgers show that it did as early as 1881. It paid an interest payment in January 1881 and separate interest payments in 1884. Isaias Meyer himself worked with Lehman Brothers in 1883.[96]

Firms operated by non-Jewish merchants also survived the 1873–1879 downturn, including the small Bayou Sara firm of Mrs. E. Weber. Hatch & Irvine, which J. W. Dorr called one of the "principal merchants of the place" before the war, also made it through. In 1870 Hatch & Irvine was "doing the largest [commission business] in the Parish" and later owned a "large plantation." J. F. Irvine supposedly had an interest in J. H. Harris of New Orleans, which may have connected him to the New York market, [and he was] "perfectly good, doing a large business." His business also appeared to be quite nimble. While he conducted "quite an extensive business," he did not have a large stock on hand, but he could still "replenish his stock on short time." Irvine also diversified and added a saw mill to his portfolio in the late 1870s.

In Union Springs, Alabama, the dry goods and grocery store of Wright, Frazier & Co. emerged after the war and by 1872 was considered the "best + most [prosperous] House in this place." It took "cotton in trade largely, + speculate," and in 1873 it had a reported 181 bales of cotton and $72,000 on hand. It borrowed heavily and had large debts, but it had apparently built quite a nest egg, having paid cash for New York purchases. By 1874 it was deemed the "largest + best grocery house at the Springs." The following year it had "cash on hand + cotton in ware house [sic]," and by 1877, it was the "largest + one of the safest" businesses in town, and also owned three or four plantations.[97]

Not all Jewish businesses survived the tumult, as many of those businesses with strong capital reserves, effective credit networks, and impeccable credit, nonetheless still suffered during this depression. Isaias Meyer's other firm, Bodenheim, Meyer & Co., fell victim to these forces. In 1871, the firm had "abundant means" but was "not believed to have made any money, since they embarked in this" business. "Their trade is all in the South, which has not been satisfactory in point of payment."

While business seems to have picked up in 1873, the following year they "had a good deal of trouble with their collections in the South + West this Spring + this has caused them to be a little behind in their payments." But they were "not known to have made any serious losses." They had recovered somewhat by 1875, and the firm seems to have been on stronger footing, having conducted a business the previous year of about $250,000. But still they "did not make anything beyond expenses," although they were nevertheless "meeting their engagements promptly now" and were making money in the West. But Henry Bodenheim fell into a significant amount of debt in Vicksburg, and his creditors sued him.[98]

Unable to cope with the financial ruin that befell him, Bodenheim took his own life, and in so doing became part of a heartbreaking trend of mercantile suicides during this era. "Henry Bodenheim, a broken down merchant, of New York, committed suicide on Wednesday," reported the *Brooklyn Daily Eagle*. He "died mysteriously," reported *Pomeroy's Democrat*, and "he had failed, and his creditors were to have met with him" a few days hence. Washington's *Evening Star* also reported the suicide on its front page, and the *Canton Mail* claimed that "grief, disappointment and mortification were too much for him." South Carolina's *Daily Phoenix* graphically reported that Bodenheim had died "by cutting his throat with a penknife, because of business reverses." Bodenheim's failure led to the dissolution of Bodenheim, Meyer & Co., and such mercantile failures were not uncommon during these years.[99]

Although the percentage of Jewish firms in the 1873–1879 period increased in some towns, success or failure during this downturn was not preordained by ethnicity. Some Jewish firms failed, as by the end of 1873, Bayou Sara's Jacob Mitchell was seeking compromise with his New Orleans creditors. He proposed paying twenty-five cents on the dollar, but when his offer was rejected, he apparently placed the business in his wife's name—a popular tactic to shield assets. She "succeeds him in everything but his bad character," a Dun recorder noted, and by 1876 the Mitchells had apparently failed and left for Texas, although they appear to have later returned.[100]

By the beginning of 1879, the United States was finally beginning to recover from the Panic of 1873, but the remainder of the nineteenth century would continue to be characterized by financial ups and downs.

Agricultural production increased, enlivening business prospects, and business continued to grow between 1879 and 1882, in large part because of a boom in railroad construction. The number of miles built in 1882 reached 11,569—four years earlier that figure had been only 2,665 miles. According to one study, 15 percent of the nation's capital formation in the 1880s came via the expansion of the railroad. Building construction also increased in these years, the balance of trade increased supplies of gold, unemployment was low, and so, too, were interest rates. Capital was also easier to come by.[101]

But the relative uptick would not last, followed soon after by the Depression of 1882–1885. The fortunes of the railroad again played a significant role. Expected profits declined, poor management upended public confidence, and investors grew weary. Responding to decreased demand for steel rails, the price of steel plummeted, sending aftershocks throughout the steel industry. Steel workers lost their jobs, wages decreased, and the same situation befell other parts of the manufacturing and mining sectors. A financial panic hit New York in 1884 when some banks were forced to close, stock prices declined precipitously, and interest rates rose dramatically. Over 100 banks across the United States failed, and unemployment increased. Some ruminated that the United States would need to leave behind the gold standard, and international investors sold American securities. During the 1882–1885 period, business activity declined by nearly 25 percent.[102]

By 1885 the economy was again looking up, as business improved and crop yields showed encouraging signs, and confidence in railroads had returned by 1886. Yet the cycle of highs and lows continued with the Panic of 1893, which was caused in part by questions over gold, silver, and monetary policy. Interior banks hoped to withdraw deposits from New York, and many banks were forced to restrict cash withdrawals. This situation lasted until the economy began to pick up in 1896, and Congress made the gold standard the sole monetary standard in the United States in 1900.[103]

All of these financial ups and downs, from 1866 to the end of the nineteenth century, created an uncertain situation for those in the cotton industry. The U.S. Census noted an increasing number of debtors, yet crop diversification, improved growing methods, and improvements to shipping all suggested that the farmers' troubles may have been over.

But financial unease, price fluctuations, the rise of futures trading, and the growth of new overseas cotton production all made life challenging for those in the industry. An 1895 U.S. Senate committee report on agriculture and forestry observed that "generally the financial condition of the [cotton] farmers is bad, a very large percentage insolvent, and that very few indeed are substantially increasing in the possession of property." The committee also noted "that with the prices prevailing in the years 1891–92–93 in nearly every part of the cotton-producing region the cost of production equaled, if it did not exceed, the value of the cotton raised."[104]

* * *

Overall, the cotton industry's move to the interior brought Jews from the margins of the cotton industry to the mainstream. But timing mattered, and dividing the years after the war into three subperiods reveals not only how changes in structural factors affected the region but also how they affected Jewish businesses in seemingly different ways than their non-Jewish neighbors. Jewish businesses in the region appear to have been less affected by the lean years of 1866–1867 because fewer Jewish businesses appear to have opened. Conversely, more new Jewish businesses emerged between 1868 and 1873, and a willingness to work with freedmen positioned those business owners to reap the benefits of a stronger economy and the advantageous changes to laws. Finally, while 1873–1879 challenged businesses throughout the region—both Jewish and non-Jewish—capital reserves and ingenuity were two factors that allowed businesses to survive.

But another factor that allowed Jewish businesses in particular to survive the 1873–1879 downturn, as well as other vicissitudes in the postbellum economy, was a reliance on ethnic networks of trust. Merchants often lost big during the downturns, particularly in 1873–1879, and without extensions from their creditors, many failed. But those who had access to credit via ethnic networks were often able to weather these financial storms. How these networks funneled credit to merchants, and then from merchants to farmers, is the subject of the following two chapters.

4

Networks from Above

Surviving the volatility that defined the postbellum economy required credit, and farmers obtained that credit via ethnic networks, which connected global investors to rural cotton farmers scattered throughout the Gulf South. These networks operated on two primary tiers. At the top, global capital moved from Europe or the Northeast down to large retailers or wholesalers in the interior towns of the Gulf South. And at the bottom, those retailers or wholesalers provided credit to smaller businesses or directly to the region's farmers.

This chapter analyzes the top portion of this network and does so through the lens of Lehman Brothers, which linked scores of cotton businesses across the Gulf South to the global investment they needed to survive. This global investment was essential for the cotton industry to rebuild, but working across oceans was risky for bankers. Trust networks, therefore, became the key to successful international commerce, and the social separation of the era fostered trust networks that left Jewish and non-Jewish banks operating largely in separate spheres. As a result, non-Jewish firms such as J. P. Morgan & Co. funneled investments to America through relationships and syndicates via largely fellow Anglo-American banks, and Jewish firms such as Lehman Brothers brought European investment to America through largely Jewish networks. Ethnicity mattered.

With access to global investments through ethnic networks, ethnicity continued to matter as Lehman Brothers extended credit to cotton merchants scattered throughout interior towns in the region's most fertile cotton lands. Many, although certainly not all, of those merchants were fellow Jews, and with credit from Lehman Brothers and other sources, they could not only survive the major downturns that defined the era but also in many cases thrive in the postbellum milieu. As Lehman Brothers developed a large footprint in the Gulf South, it thus played a

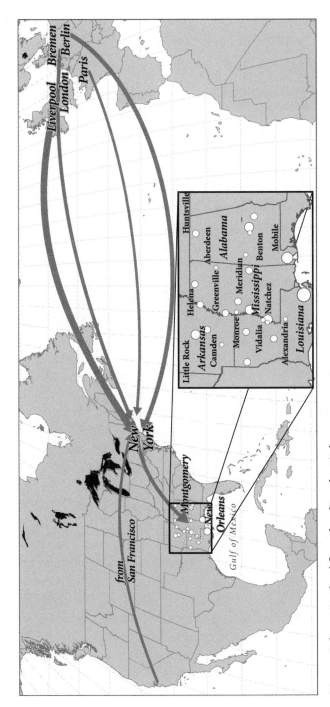

Map 4.1. Lehman Brothers' flow of credit and capital

central role in an ethnic economy that linked the region's merchants to the global investment they needed to succeed.

* * *

As the Civil War came to a close, Lehman Brothers' antebellum and wartime activities meant that it was poised to become one of the most significant and prolific cotton businesses in the world. As we have seen, it had been "a very rich house" in the antebellum years, selling supplies to farmers and accepting cotton as payment. The firm also leveraged family and ethnic networks to access the markets and capital of Europe and New York. When the war broke out, it was dependent upon the North-South trade that had been severed by the blockade, and it "lost heavily." Lehman Brothers also lost a potential fortune when retreating Confederates burned its cotton warehouses. But at the same time, in the later years of the war Lehman Brothers also used cotton trading permits wisely, and it worked with the state of Alabama to trade cotton between Union and Confederate lines. All of this meant that, according to a later estimate, the firm was worth no more than $250,000, and—with cash in hand, with an established customer base in the interior Southern towns that were becoming the center of the cotton economy, and with ethnic networks already in place that connected those towns to global investors—the firm was ripe for success in this new postbellum milieu.[1]

Recognizing New York's place as America's financial center, Lehman Brothers moved its primary operation to New York, opening as grocers and commission merchants on Chambers Street in September 1865. The firm was considered "prudent" and "not speculative," and in 1868, Mayer Lehman moved to New York to join his brother Emanuel, who had operated Lehman Brothers' New York operation before the war. Success was almost immediate, and in 1865 a credit reporter claimed that they had "all the capital they want," buying for cash or on thirty days, and the firm maintained a daily balance of approximately $20,000 in their Importers and Traders Bank account. By the mid-1870s, members of the firm estimated their worth at $1.5 million, and banks confirmed their claim that they had no indebtedness. By the 1880s, Lehman Brothers was classified as receivers and cotton commission merchants, and the firm made "heavy advances to consignors." The brothers were "personally popular" and had the "reputation of being good merchants," and they always appeared to be "easy in money matters." They claimed to have "made more or less money every year since 1865," and in 1883 their credit rating was a stellar AAA1. The firm continued to thrive until its 2008 collapse.[2]

While the New York firm would later diversify, it initially focused "largely in cotton" and in making "cash advances on consignments." R.G. Dun listed the firm as a "cotton commission" house into the late nineteenth century, and its agents noted that they "have been very successful operators in Cotton" and that they continued to "make advances on Cotton as heretofore." Many of Lehman Brothers' other investments were

Figure 4.1. "Mayer Lehman." Image courtesy of the Jacob Rader Marcus Center of the American Jewish Archives, Cincinnati, Ohio (PC-2946).

also in the South, including real estate, railway securities, and Southern municipal bonds.[3]

Because Mayer and Emanuel Lehman moved to New York, John Wesley Durr took control of the Montgomery branch's daily operations. There, Lehman, Durr & Co. continued its general merchandising, although on a smaller scale, and it increasingly focused on cotton. The firm rebuilt its warehouses, some of the largest in Alabama. Coupled with Lehman Brothers' strong capitalization and excellent credit, this allowed the firm to buy cotton directly from growers and to store it until prices rose.[4]

Meanwhile, in New Orleans, Mayer and Emanuel entrusted their branch to family. Mayer's brother-in law, Benjamin Newgass, took over day-to-day operations of the firm, and Lehman, Newgass & Co. quickly grew into a key cog in the Lehman Brothers operation. "A new house. Appear to be doing well," wrote a Dun recorder in the fall of 1865, estimating the firm's capital at $500,000—the majority of which came from the Lehmans themselves. By 1867 the firm had "considerable means + large facilities" and was good "without doubt." Dun agents classified the firm as a cotton commission business, which was deemed "one of our strongest + largest houses" with the "highest grade of credit." They had very little paper out and were "ready to discount any of their own paper offered at 7%."[5]

When Benjamin Newgass left New Orleans for Liverpool, further internationalizing Lehman Brothers' cotton operation, Henry Abraham, one of Newgass's relatives, took over the firm. Now known as Lehman, Abraham, & Co., the firm was presumed to be the third-largest receiver of cotton in New Orleans by 1877, and its credit rating was "unquestionably one of the most solid in the State." The business was "generally considered an A.1. house" and continued to enjoy "unquestioned" credit and standing locally. The firm also owned "considerable" real estate, including an estimated $450,000 in productive city real estate, "a large + elegant [building] to be used as offices for themselves + others," and Lane Cotton Mills. In the mid-1880s, Henry Abraham left the business, and Maurice Stern was promoted to partner of what became known as Lehman, Stern, & Co.[6]

As partners came and went, the New Orleans branch's success was due in large part to its access to credit, which, according to a Dun recorder, "in Banking + commercial circles is as high as ever." Much of that was because of its access to the New York market through the primary Lehman Brothers branch. "They only occasionally use a [moderate credit] on this market, and . . . the bulk of their indebtedness when they have occasion to use their [credit] is negotiated through Lehman Bros of N.Y. City," claimed a recorder. Between 1877 and 1880, the firm also had acceptances from the State National Bank and Citizens Bank, as well as smaller transactions with Canal Bank.[7]

The firm was also reliant upon international networks. Lehman Brothers had a direct connection to Newgass, Rosenheim & Co., its agent in Liverpool, to sell the cotton that Lehman's Southern branches had purchased from growers and in turn had sold to the New York branch. In an era when reliable information was hard to find, these close connections between markets were invaluable. But the importance of these connections to Europe went deeper. The United States was a debtor nation, in need of European capital to fund its investments. But a provision of the 1863 National Banking Act prevented commercial, nationally chartered banks from opening overseas branches. So private banks, including Lehman Brothers, J. P. Morgan & Co., and others, filled the void and played a critical role in bringing European investment to America's industries—including the cotton industry.[8]

The networks that brought European investment to American firms were largely ethnic in nature. There were few means by which contracts could be enforced across vast oceans and national borders, so in an era where, as we have seen, personal trust fostered economic trust, ethnicity engendered separate, although overlapping, economic spheres. For example, J. P. Morgan & Co. had Paris and London branches and acted as an intermediary between European investors and American investments—particularly in the railroad sector. Morgan worked closely with Kidder, Peabody & Co., the American agents for Baring Brothers, and while Jewish banks such as Kuhn, Loeb & Co. did participate in J. P. Morgan & Co.'s syndicates, their participation almost always ranked below Kidder, Peabody & Co. These economic relationships reflected the social milieu in which the firms operated. J. P. Morgan & Co. continued to view itself as a bank for the social elite in the twentieth century, identifying as an Anglo-American and non-Jewish firm. Differentiating his bank from Jewish banks during the era of mass East European Jewish migration, Morgan insisted that his bank and Barings's representatives were the only "white firms in New York," and Morgan avoided one particular opportunity that he found to be "a little too Jewish." Additionally, J. P. Morgan & Co. and its various incarnations had no Jewish directors until the mid-twentieth century, further reflecting the limited opportunities for trust-based relationships between Jewish and non-Jewish firms.[9]

While J. P. Morgan & Co.'s networks were primarily with Anglo-American and non-Jewish firms, Lehman Brothers developed close networks with global banking houses operated by fellow Jews. Just as J. P. Morgan & Co. worked with Kuhn, Loeb & Co., whose partners, including Jacob Schiff, were all Jews, Lehman Brothers also had economic ties with non-Jewish firms, including Latham, Alexander & Co. But in order to access the capital and credit necessary to fuel its growing business, Lehman Brothers had close ties to Hallgarten & Co., a German-Jewish firm that served as a conduit between German capital and American markets—particularly in the railroad sector. It also worked with L. Rosenheim & Sons of Liverpool, Johannes Roth of New Orleans and Bremen, Germany, and F. Goldstein & Co. of Berlin. Lazard Frères, which operated a banking network that included New York, Paris, and London, had a small sundries account with Lehman Brothers in 1878. That grew to a much larger exchange account for just over $35,000 in 1881 and transactions of well over $150,000 in 1882–1883. Lehman Brothers also worked with Kuhn, Loeb & Co., one of the largest Jewish banks in New York, whose European connections—including M. & M. Warburg, a German investment house led by Felix Warburg's brother Max—brought European capital into American markets. Lehman Brothers had "gold" and "special" accounts with Kuhn, Loeb & Co., and the two firms conducted extensive transactions with one another.[10]

Lehman Brothers also worked closely with J. W. Seligman & Co., a Jewish firm that had branches and interests across the globe and cultivated ethnic networks that brought European investment across the Atlantic. J. W. Seligman & Co. got its start in the antebellum cotton town of Selma, Alabama, but unable to break into Southern markets while the factorage system had been in place, it diversified into the risky Californian market during the gold rush. While this left it "less dependent on Southern customers than their rivals were," argues Adam Mendelsohn, its presence in the West "became a lifeline in desperate times when other commerce was disrupted." The firm had extensive dealings in Europe during the Civil War, and its presence in the American and European markets also served as a hedge against down times in any one particular market. The San Francisco branch of the Seligman firm had purchased gold to hedge currency and to sell in the European market and depended on bills of exchange to acquire francs or pounds with which they could make purchases in Europe. The New York branch also served as agents for its offices in London and Frankfurt, securing payment from American importers who utilized European credit to buy their goods, and significant percentages of Jewish merchants were on both the European and American ends of these transactions. The Seligmans also established a relationship with Baron Lionel de Rothschild of the London Jewish banking family, and Joseph Seligman encouraged his New Orleans branch to work with Liverpool Jewish cotton financier J. H. Schroder & Co.[11]

It was through the New Orleans branch of J. W. Seligman & Co. that Lehman Brothers' New Orleans branch transacted a significant amount of business. While the Seligmans left Selma prior to the war and set down roots in New York and California, the firm recognized the potential for significant profits through banking, cotton, and the importation of goods in the postbellum years. So the firm returned to the South immediately after the cessation of hostilities, opening a New Orleans branch under the leadership of Max Hellman, Jesse Seligman's brother-in-law. Seligman, Hellman & Co. planned to specialize in banking and clearing bills and drafts from the cotton industry, and it brought an influx of currency to the Crescent City—selling greenbacks in New Orleans and gold in New York to hedge against fluctuations. Max Hellman's role was to purchase bills and drafts in New Orleans that were drawn on cotton buyers to be resold in New York.[12]

When Max Hellman left the New Orleans branch to become a partner in the Seligman Paris operation, his younger brother Theodore succeeded him—again highlighting the importance of family connections. Theodore Hellman was born around 1844 and emigrated from Munich to America in 1859, around the age of fifteen. He began his career as an errand boy in the Seligman firm and soon became the chief bookkeeper. Theodore married Frances Seligman, a daughter of Joseph Seligman.

Now a member of the family, he was tapped to lead Seligman, Hellman & Co. at the age of twenty-four. Theodore Hellman also served as vice president of the Union Bank and a director of the Louisiana National Bank. He owned a mansion at the corner of St. Charles Avenue and Second Street, which was described as "the palatial mansion" with a "beautiful lawn and ornamental grounds," located at "what is known as the choicest residence square in the Garden District." In that home, Hellman hosted a ball where General Ulysses S. Grant met with Confederate General P. G. T. Beauregard.[13]

Under the leadership of Max and then Theodore Hellman, Seligman, Hellman & Co. prospered almost from the beginning. "We are getting the name of having the choicest Southern bills, which tells to our advantage," Joseph Seligman wrote to Max Hellman in 1867. The firm's networks and capital helped it to survive the lean crop years of 1866–1867, as Joseph Seligman claimed that, with the exception of Hellman and one other banker, "we have reason to know that every other banker has lost money this season in purchasing bills in New Orleans." Praise for the firm did not come only from within. By 1869 the firm was considered by credit reporters to be "A1 in all respects" and soon was deemed "very reliable" and" worth over a million dollars." By the late 1870s, Seligman, Hellman & Co. was considered a "first class banking establishment," but the firm's growth was not without bumps in the road. Following the Panic of 1873, the firm lost $23,500 by advancing funds to a cotton shipper without proper security. "Dear Theodore," wrote Joseph Seligman. "Be spared similar mistakes in the future, as I would rather lose double the amount than to be published as a dupe." In 1877, Seligman, Hellman & Co. accused Mortimer Carr of producing false bills of lading to Theodore Hellman, obtaining nearly $37,000.[14]

Seligman, Hellman & Co. was "indebted by one of the largest firms of the city," and whether or not this notation referred to Lehman, Abraham & Co. the Lehmans and Seligmans nonetheless transacted a significant amount of business with one another. For example, in January 1877 alone, Lehman ledgers show cash drafts of $55,000 over a two-day period. A week later came transactions of $15,000 and $50,000, followed a week later by a $25,000 transaction, and transactions continued between the two companies. Early 1879 saw a similar pattern, with cash drafts of $50,000, $50,000 and $25,000 in mid-January, followed by two $25,000 transactions in late January, two $25,000 transactions in early February, and large transactions continued through April. Their significant business relationship continued. In one month alone the firms conducted over $200,000 worth of business.[15]

In addition to its relationship with Seligman, Hellman & Co., Lehman Brothers also worked closely with the wealthy California banker Isaias Hellman—another Jewish banker with financial interests that linked California to Europe and New York. Hellman's connection to Lehman Brothers went well beyond ethnicity and religion, and again highlights the importance of family. Hellman married Esther Newgass, whose sister Babette was married to Mayer Lehman, and whose brother Benjamin Newgass was Lehman's business partner in New Orleans. Hellman came to America as a poor Jew from Germany in 1859, and he had a small merchandise account with Lehman Brothers in 1877. Hellman ultimately built three of the West's most important banks: Los Angeles' Farmers and Merchants Bank, San Francisco's Nevada Bank, and the Wells Fargo Bank. Hellman was also the president or director of fourteen other banks, and by 1910 he oversaw over $100 million in capital. He was also a major investor in California and a promoter for banking, transportation, education, land development, water, electricity, oil, and wine.[16]

While Isaias Hellman was a key figure in Jewish banking circles, he made a concerted effort that his operations not be confined solely to the Jewish ethnic economy. "I have to be a better man than you are," Hellman wrote to a colleague, "because I am a Jew. You can do things I cannot do. If I did them I would be criticized, while you will not be. I have to keep that steadily in mind, in all my dealings." When he set up a bank in 1890, he noted that he had "selected an excellent Board of Directors, all strong men, privately speaking seven Christians, and including myself four Jews. I have done this to avoid the idea which exists with other banks here of making a Jewish bank or a Catholic or any other institution; I want it to be a popular institution and I think it is so considered, if not I will endeavor my best to make it so."[17]

Despite the ties of family and ethnicity with Lehman Brothers—or perhaps because of them—the relationship was not without its difficulties. In 1891, Hellman was short on cash and withdrew some of his funds from Lehman Brothers—which also happened to be short on cash at the time. Mayer Lehman was furious, and wrote, in Isaias's words, "a contemptible letter [and] a second one followed from the office of Lehman Brothers the day following." Hellman drew Benjamin Newgass into the dispute: "The truth of the matter is the Lehmans have had for years past many favors from me," Hellman claimed. "They have had hundreds of thousands of my money, without even the acknowledgment of a promissory note or an acceptance and without collateral they have allowed me whatever rate of interest they saw fit." Newgass, however, apparently sided with Lehman, informing Hellman that Mayer Lehman "was very angry that you had [acted] so very inconsiderably in taking away so much money without any previous notice." Further, Newgass wrote, "I must tell you frankly you have not acted right + with due consideration toward Lehman Bros. + especially Mayer. You know they have made great sacrifices for me." The family dispute continued until the end of 1892, when social ties appear to have been restored, paving the "way to reconciliation and good feeling between us." Nonetheless, together, Isaias Hellman, Mayer Lehman, and Benjamin Newgass were involved in purchasing and selling stocks and bonds, providing credit, and investing in each other's banks and business ventures.[18]

With ethnic networks connecting the firm to global capital, Lehman Brothers was a critical cog in an economic network that funneled that capital through New York and down to the cotton businesses of the Gulf South. All three branches of Lehman Brothers—New Orleans, Montgomery, and New York—continued to advance that capital to Southern cotton businesses. For example, Lehman Abraham & Co. in New Orleans was "advancing largely to Planters, etc.," buying cotton directly from rural growers and merchants. This provided these growers and merchants with goods for the growing season and a reliable outlet for their cotton. The firm was flush with capital and rarely needed credit, and one Dun recorder claimed that, on the occasions that they did actually need credit, it was negotiated by the New York branch. Lehman, Durr & Co. in Montgomery also purchased cotton from farmers, which it then stored in its extensive warehouses before selling at a time dictated by the market. Finally, Lehman Brothers in New York also "offered to advance money to a large extent to Southern planters to move their crops." Although the firm would diversify, by 1880 Lehman Brothers was still "advancing largely to planters." This economic network was mutually beneficial; it increased Lehman Brothers' footprint in the South as well as the firm's bottom line, while smaller firms grew rapidly with access to Lehman credit.[19]

With a significant amount of capital and a direct network to European investment, Lehman Brothers survived difficult times, such as the downturn that followed the Panic of 1873. For example, the firm was "among the heaviest receivers of Cotton" in 1873, and as the panic set in during the following year, a Dun recorder noted that banks still "readily accept" its paper. In 1876 it had recently completed "a large + elegant building," and in the following year it was "unquestionably one of the most solid in the State." Its ability to survive this major downturn meant that businesses that relied upon it were in far better shape than merchants who had relied upon firms or banks that had collapsed.[20]

Lehman Brothers worked with a plethora of firms, and in so doing assumed a central role in an ethnic network that moved capital and credit to the Gulf South. Its ledgers from the late 1870s through the 1880s read as a veritable "who's who" of Southern cotton businesses, allowing us to reconstruct the network that Lehman Brother's footprint left throughout the Gulf South. Here again, these networks were built upon trust, and ethnicity mattered. Many, but certainly not all, of the Southern firms with which Lehman Brothers worked were owned and operated by Jews.

Lehman Brothers had a large footprint in Vicksburg and the Bends, where it worked with many of the region's Jewish-owned cotton businesses. For example, Lehman, Abraham & Co. worked closely with Benjamin Dreyfus of Waterproof, Louisiana. Dreyfus and his brother Simon were Alsatian Jews who opened their general store around 1870. They operated a second branch in nearby St. Joseph, and they also opened an additional branch house in Vidalia, across the river from Natchez. The business was fairly small at the outset—Dreyfus had about $5,000 in stock and owned real estate at both Waterproof and St. Joseph. The firm was "reliable in means," and the partners "built a fine store."[21]

While Dreyfus and his brother conducted a "splendid [business] at first," trouble lurked beneath the surface. The brothers were "supposed to be very reckless in [business] and not regarded as responsible men to do business with," and their honesty was very "questionable." As a result, Dun recorders could not recommend credit. Without a positive credit report, the firm turned to Lehman, Abraham & Co., and "placed

Map 4.2. Vicksburg and the Bends

Note: Black circles representing cities and towns are sized by their total 1880 population. Shaded gray dots represent 100 bales of cotton produced in 1880, distributed randomly throughout county and parish borders. Railroads depict extent of tracks in 1880.

on record a mortgage" on all of Dreyfus's real estate in Tensas Parish, Louisiana. Dreyfus also had other references, including "plenty of good backers, among N. O. merchants."[22]

The economic downturn following the Panic of 1873 was not kind to Dreyfus. In 1875 he "settled with his creditors at 40%," and it didn't take long for trouble to hit again. According to Dreyfus, he was pushed financially as he purchased "too many goods in St. Louis," but the weather was "bad for crops." With farmers unable to pay, he "became embarrassed," so he returned "some of the goods." Yet while "some sent their claims for collection," Dreyfus was not sued. One Dun recorder had another explanation for Dreyfus's struggles, suggesting that his failure was in part because most of his accounts were with freedmen and because he had done no "advancing so as to give him control of cotton." Dreyfus was granted a one-year extension on debts that he held in St. Louis, but he remained "in trouble," owing "more than he can pay."[23]

While Lehman, Abraham & Co. provided mortgages that helped Dreyfus meet his obligations, he ultimately failed when he lost Lehman's trust. In 1878, his real estate was again mortgaged to his commission merchants, Lehman, Abraham & Co., for more than its $5,000 value. While one estimate claimed that Dreyfus was indebted to Lehman for $8,000, another claimed that he owed the Lehman subsidiary $10,000, which represented only a third of his total debt. Nevertheless, Lehman, Abraham & Co. vouched for Dreyfus when credit reporters asked, telling a Dun recorder that Dreyfus had total assets of $27,800 and liabilities of $11,250, and they spoke "in high terms of his honesty, industry, &c." That trust was misplaced. In late 1878, Lehman, Abraham & Co. "discovered him shipping cotton [that was] pledged to them to another party, evidently with intent to defraud." While Lehman's recommendation and mortgages had allowed Dreyfus to survive, after uncovering the fraud they "immediately closed him out."[24]

Elsewhere in Vicksburg and the Bends, Lehman Brothers provided the Vicksburg Jewish firm of Baer & Bro. with access to global investment and the New York market. Baer & Bro. opened in 1863, and brothers Victor and Abraham Baer started small, buying for cash in New York. They were "regarded with favor by merchants" but not by bankers, who did not regard them as "substantial" and feared that they may "leave at any time." The firm survived the 1866–1867 downturn, and their estimated capital in 1867 was between $15,000 and $20,000. They were conducting business "principally with negroes," doing "mostly a negro trade," and caution was advised in giving them credit. The firm was soon "considered perfectly reliable for a reasonable line" of credit. The fortunes of the firm grew rapidly, as they didn't "seem to have felt the panic" that rippled through the economy—likely a reference to 1873 and its aftermath. By 1876, Baer & Bro. was "one of the most solvent houses in our City," conducting a "large" business. They "buy for cash" and conducted their retail business "principally for cash." A Dun agent soon called the firm "prosperous," and it became a "strong house," worth an estimated $50,000 by 1879. They had "as good credit as any firm in town," and business was still increasing in 1880, when credit reporters considered them "the safest + the best [dry goods] house in the City."[25]

Lehman Brothers and its subsidiaries worked with other Jewish firms in Vicksburg, including Sussman & Metzger, which had financial relationships with both Lehman Brothers and Lehman, Abraham & Co. Sussman & Metzger began as a small country store at Beachland by 1877. The proprietors were "good for their wants" and did an advancing business, and by 1878 the firm had opened its store in Vicksburg. That year, Lehman Brothers' ledgers recorded a $50 cash loan, and the two firms had a more extensive relationship through the end of 1879, conducting nearly $35,000 of business. The ledgers also record notes with other firms, such as Vicksburg Bank, Mississippi Valley Bank, and Hallgarten & Co. Sussman & Metzger was soon worth between $25,000 and $35,000, and the partners' credit was good as they "always paid their paper promptly." Sussman & Metzger remained on the mercantile reference book rolls through 1890 as "cotton factors and [a] commission" house.[26]

South of Vicksburg, Lehman Brothers worked with Samuel Bernheimer's dry goods and grocery store, which grew to become the strongest business in postbellum Port Gibson, Mississippi. Bernheimer arrived in Port Gibson around 1850, and Dun agents initially struggled to figure out Bernheimer's background. There was a rumor that he or a brother had failed two or three times previous to opening in Port Gibson, but that was apparently unsubstantiated. In addition, Dun recorders initially declared that the Bernheimers were Jews but later claimed that they "deny being Jews." Finally, a recorder declared definitively that they were Jewish, which, in his opinion, was important because it increased the chances of what he called a "Jew failure," by which he meant "a total failure to pay anything." Moreover, the agent maintained that he could uncover little information about them, as one could "judge of 'Jew merchants' only [from appearance]." They "stand [very] well for Jews," he claimed, but "being Jews this is [about] all we know, or can tell [about] them."[27]

In 1850, Samuel Bernheimer and his brother were selling a "large" amount of goods, some of which they imported from Switzerland and Italy, and others they ordered from New York, Philadelphia, or New Orleans. The brothers were doing a profitable and very good business, selling "exclusively for Cash or nominal [credit]," and soon had an eight-month draft "on a good [New Orleans] house" and were "growing in the confidence of our people." On the eve of the war, they were "presumed to be rich" and were "doing the largest [dry goods] business in the place." Though they had earlier owned real estate, they had "little property except goods" on the eve of the conflict, and they were estimated to be worth $20,000 to $30,000.[28]

While the war significantly disrupted the Bernheimer's business, they soon rebuilt and were thriving again. After the Crescent City fell to Union troops, Samuel Bernheimer joined a New Orleans firm, but his tenure there was short, and by the end of the conflict, Bernheimer had returned to Port Gibson. Yet he returned with debt, and much like other businesses that tried to shield assets while maintaining good credit, Bernheimer recommenced in another name—that of partner and brother-in-law William Cahn. Credit reporters knew that Cahn's business was the "Sham Successor of that illustrious firm" of Samuel Bernheimer & Co., and had been organized so that Cahn could enjoy good credit, "at least till his 'clerks' [presumably a mocking reference to Bernheimer] get through settling up with their soft headed [creditors] at 20 cents on the $." The recorder claimed that Cahn had "no means of his own," and though the business had a "good stock," he called the members of the new firm, which the agent claimed enabled the Bernheimers to "cheat creditors," "Jew-swindlers."[29]

The next phase of Samuel Bernheimer's reorganization was to provide the capital for his twenty-one-year-old son, Marcus, to commence business in the junior Bernheimer's name. The reorganized firm survived

1866–1867 and by 1868 had an estimated stock of $30,000 to $35,000. But while Samuel provided capital, he had no credit, as "his settlements on the closing up of the old firm having been [very] unsatisfactory to his [creditors]." Marcus's credit, however, was "[very] good," and with Samuel remaining in the store, business was "flourishing." Soon the Bernheimers were again doing "by far the largest [and] best business of anyone here," and by 1870, Samuel was out of debt. With his name cleared, Samuel renamed the business S. Bernheimer & Son, which later changed to S. Bernheimer & Sons when the firm admitted Marcus' brother Louis. The Bernheimers, however, tried to safeguard against future bankruptcies by placing a residence in the name of one of their wives.[30]

S. Bernheimer & Sons survived the Panic of 1873 and the ensuing downturn. By 1871, they were "first rate, rich, [and have] paid all old debts," and were soon the "No. 1 strongest [and doing] the best [business] in the place." They were "building a store," and the partners were "rich and punctual [and] buy largely for cash" and had no liens or judgments against them. On the eve of the panic, the firm conducted a "very large extensive trade," and the firm recovered quickly. By 1876 the Bernheimers were still good "for anything they contract." They soon kept "the largest variety stock in town" and owed nothing. By 1880 the firm's estimated worth had grown to $80,000 clear.[31]

In order to reestablish his business while digging himself out of debt, Samuel Bernheimer needed credit, and initially Dun agents did not indicate where it came from. They knew that he had real estate that was mortgaged for borrowed money, but his creditors were initially unknown to Dun agents. They presumed that they "deal with 2 or more," but admitted that they "don't know" who their commission merchants were. M. Bernheimer soon established a commission house in St. Louis which was conducting a "large" business, and would later be called a "branch house" to the Port Gibson business. In addition to the St. Louis connection, the Bernheimers also worked with Lehman Brothers at some point between 1889 and 1892.[32]

North of Vicksburg, in Helena, Arkansas, Lehman Brothers worked with Simon Seelig, whose small business was operational by 1867. Seelig had a "fine reputation as a prompt business man," declared a Dun recorder. He owned real estate in St. Louis and had several creditors in St. Louis who do not appear to have been Jewish. One of his creditors said that Seelig and his firm "always have money" and that Seelig "does a sort of Banking [business] in connection with his other [business]." He quickly recovered after the panic, and by 1874, he was considered "one of the solvent merchants of this city" who "stands very well as a business man." "Nobody has apparently done better than" Seelig, claimed one credit reporter, and Simon Seelig also had large landholdings—a community called Seelig soon emerged near Helena. Seelig also had a relationship with Lehman Brothers in the early 1880s.[33]

While Vicksburg and the Bends was an important cotton region where Lehman Brothers had a presence, the firm also had an extensive network in the Black Belt region, where it worked with H. Long, who was Jewish. Long arrived in Selma in the 1860s. He preferred cash transactions, and his clientele was largely composed of freedmen. Long was soon "one of the most successful men in the place," and by 1877 he operated a plantation and continued to run a successful general store.[34]

While ethnicity mattered, and many of the Black Belt firms with which Lehman Brothers worked were operated by fellow Jews, Lehman Brothers did not limit its business to Jewish-owned firms. It also worked with Renfro & Andrews, a wholesale grocery and provisioning company in Opelika, Alabama, which had additional branches in Lafayette and Alexandria City. Renfro & Andrews commenced business around 1872, and while it had taken on significant debt by 1874, the firm was also doing "the largest [wholesale] business here." It was doing "a very extensive [business] by advancing to 'Farmers,'" and it had a cotton warehouse to supplement its "large mortgage business" and cotton merchandise sales. Also in Alabama, Lehman Brothers worked with the dry goods and grocery store of Wright, Frazier & Co., which by 1877 was considered the "largest and safest" business in town.[35]

Lehman Brothers also worked with non-Jewish firms outside of the Black Belt. Led by Edmund Richardson and Augustus H. May, the New Orleans firm of Richardson & May also had a close financial relationship with Lehman Brothers. Richardson & May was operational by 1867, and it took only a couple of years for the partners to be considered "wealthy." By 1877, the firm had become the "leading house in their line" and was deemed "probably the largest receivers of cotton here," worth an estimated $500,000 to $750,000. Members of the firm "generally pay cash" and "seldom + never" ask for credit, and they "always have a surplus on hand for safe investments." By 1880, Richardson & May was "considered to do the largest amount of cotton and wealthiest," and the partners also "stand high both commercially + socially."[36]

Richardson & May did not operate only in the New Orleans market; it also controlled a large and "presumably lucrative" business, principally in Mississippi. One Dun recorder speculated that Richardson was "said to be the richest man in the state." He was also deemed the largest owner of real estate in Mississippi, owning several plantations, and he was connected to Wesson Mills in Copiah County. He had stores on "or near most of his plantations, where he usually has a managing" partner, for whom the support of Richardson & May carried a tremendous amount of weight with credit reporters. Augustus May's son also had the advantage of his father's good name, and his "connections are such as to assure them all the capital + assistance they may need." Another entry noted that May's son "starts under favorable auspices, as his father—of the wealthy Factorage house of Richardson + May, controls for him an extensive trade."[37]

But a significant amount of Lehman Brothers' business was transacted with fellow Jews, and while this included firms in Vicksburg and the Bends and the Black Belt, Lehman Brothers also worked with Jewish-owned firms that were located along the Mississippi's tributaries. This included the Shreveport firm of Levy & Bodenheimer. S. Levy opened a "large store" of Western produce in 1867, which was deemed a "good" business. The firm opened at an inopportune time, in the midst of the 1866–1867 downturn, and a Dun recorder noted that it "may be in debt some." Yet the firm survived, and by 1870 Levy had joined forces with Henry Bodenheimer under the name Levy & Bodenheimer. By 1871 they were considered "known merchants, in high repute," who ran a "cautious" business that made money. In June 1872, shortly before the Panic of 1873 hit, one observer believed that they were "succeeding in establishing a permanently prosperous" business, and while their actual worth was difficult to gauge, he believed by mid-1873 that they may be worth "a great deal." Again, the firm survived, and by 1877 Lehman Brothers and Levy & Bodenheimer were conducting a substantial amount of business together.[38]

In Alexandria, Louisiana, also located along the Red River, Lehman Brothers worked with Baer & Mann, a dry goods and general store that was in reality operated by Abraham Heyman, a "stranger here + a Jew." Heyman commenced business in July 1865 with a $50,000 stock of goods, although he owned no property. Heyman was considered good for "any of his debts," and by the fall of 1866, he was operating what was said to be the largest dry goods firm in the parish. He purchased "principally in New York," had a "large [stock] of goods on hand constantly," and "sells for cash principally" at "cheap" prices. He survived the difficulties of 1866–1867, and by 1870 he remained the "leading merchant of the place" with a stock between $60,000 and $80,000. He continued to make money, which he invested in real estate. Heyman built a "fine brick store" that was valued at $30,000, and he soon had "put up another large brick storehouse."[39]

While the 1860s were kind to Abraham Heyman, the 1870s were not. They "have sustained some small losses" in the past year, noted a credit reporter in 1873, and they were "pressed and are poor to pay." Yet Heyman insisted that he was worth at least $80,000 to $90,000, and the only money he owed was $10,000 on a plantation. However, a recorder was "convinced that [his] liabilities are considerable" and maintained that the "past season has been exceedingly dull with them, as well as all merchants here," but he believed that the firm would survive because of its assets in stock and real estate.[40]

Heyman apparently believed that the Panic of 1873 would quickly subside, but he badly misread the market, purchasing a stock of goods in New York valued between $75,000 and $100,000. At least one observer realized that they wouldn't be able to sell one-tenth of the recent stock they had purchased and conjectured that "they wont make enough for the next 12 months outside their current expenses to more than pay interest on what they owe." A Dun recorder believed that "the shortness of our crops, the stringency of money, together with their past & future liabilities will lend greatly to press & complicate their business." The past growing season "was disastrous to all our large merchants + the present no better, with gloomy prospects for the future." When "uncollected claims" arrived from New York, the credit reporter feared that "they are venturing rather much for the safety" of their creditors.[41]

With a bad investment and a poor economic environment, Heyman's business continued to spiral downward. They "have recently lost heavily in the north," and were "in constant consultation with the [attorneys] who have claims vs. them," one reporter declared. By November there were $6,326 in suits pending against them, with "other suits preparing to be filed." They owned a half interest in a plantation, which was mortgaged for $20,000—its full value—and they also sold a brick warehouse. The problem for Heyman remained the large stock of goods he had purchased from New York in 1873. Though the firm was seemingly doing a "big" business, it failed to mask the reality that they had "too much stock." "Accruing interest on their [liabilities] (so far as they are known) will be more than the annual profits of their sales," warned a recorder. To protect their assets, their wives "had property of marriage + will no doubt seek to secure their premarital claims," and they spoke of "all of the benefits of homestead law." By June 1874, Heyman's firm was "broke and in bankruptcy."[42]

Despite the bankruptcy, Heyman managed to retain about $8,000 of his stock, and he opened a dry goods and general store under the name of Baer & Mann. Heyman was "the ostensible [agent], but in reality he owns the stock," observed one Dun recorder, and Heyman kept no property in his name. Dun agents called him "tricky," "thoroughly dishonest and unreliable," noting that creditors should be careful. He was recently bankrupt and "a corrupt man," they claimed. Yet despite the deception, the firm was almost immediately conducting a "fine business" with $20,000 capital and could "readily pay." The new firm continued to grow and was "doing a good business" by 1878, but remained under the name Baer & Mann. "Heyman is ostensibly agent but is the owner," cautioned one Dun recorder. Baer & Mann conducted business with Lehman Brothers—in 1880 the two firms executed a transaction worth $3,819.37, as well as several transactions between March and June of that year, including a payment of $11.50, representing 6 percent interest. Transactions continued into 1881, and Heyman himself appears in the Lehman ledgers in 1878 with a transaction of $656.15.[43]

In Camden, Arkansas, a town along the Ouachita River, Lehman Brothers and its subsidiaries worked with at least two firms, including the successful dry goods and grocery business of Block & Feibelman. Solomon Block was a young Jew but deemed "an [exception] to that race," who before partnering with Feibelman arrived in Camden at some point around 1850, and he was thought to be very industrious. He initially owned nothing but his stock of goods and sold for cash only, but was soon beginning to do a good business and purchased real estate and was "doing well" by 1854. Before joining the business, Block's eventual partner, Edward Feibelman, had conducted fairly small businesses on his own in Arkansas, where he "stands well" and sold "a [good] many goods."[44]

By 1858, Block had taken Feibelman into his firm, and the "money [making] men" were soon conducting a safe business. Yet the partners faced significant hurdles to their success. Shortly after the partners commenced, the firm fell victim to a fire and sustained "heavy" losses, estimated at about $12,000. In addition to the fire, a poor crop also posed challenges. In 1860 a Dun recorder suggested that if they could collect 40 percent of their assets during this period, "they will be able to pay all their liabilities. But this was doubtful" because of the poor crop, and "it will take most all the cotton made." Nonetheless, in 1860, a Dun recorder noted that members of the firm "buy [considerable] quantities of cotton."[45]

Block & Feibelman was not operational at the end of the conflict. Feibelman had bankrupted during the war, and his name was no longer good, but the partners planned to "make arrangements with their creditors" to resume business and get their financial house in order. They apparently rebuilt quickly, surviving the 1866–1867 downturn. Block appeared to be the first of the partners to clear his name. By 1868 the firm was conducting a "small safe business" under the name of Solomon Block. Though Feibelman's name was no longer on the store, he remained with the business, and the expectation was that when his debts were paid he would likely become a partner again. Within a year, the firm was worth an estimated $30,000 plus $14,000 in real estate, and by 1874, Feibelman's name had returned to the masthead. The firm survived the panic, and by 1877, Block & Feibelman was "reliable + among the very best here," with a combined capital of $75,000.[46]

While Block & Feibelman had been rebuilding in Camden in the war's aftermath, the firm was also laying down roots in New Orleans. The Camden branch remained "under the management of S. Block," but Feibelman left for New Orleans, where he went into business. He soon brought in additional partners, likely leveraging his "wealthy connections who are thought to have" an interest in the business. By early 1881 the New Orleans firm's means were estimated at over $100,000, and it was considered "one of our largest firms . . . in their line." It was doing a "lucrative" business and ranked high in credit with banks and merchants.[47]

While Feibelman's work in New Orleans linked the Camden branch to the Crescent City, Block & Feibelman also had a relationship with Lehman Brothers and its affiliates that connected it to the New York market. This relationship had already begun in 1876 as Block & Feibelman carried forward a balance of $35,780.59 into 1877, and it continued into the 1880s.[48]

Lehman Brothers' connection to Jewish businesses in Camden was not limited to Block & Feibelman; the firm also worked with Jewish merchant Meyer Berg, who operated a dry goods and grocery store. Berg had been in business for five years in Macon County, Alabama, prior to arriving in Camden by 1860. Before the war he had a very large stock of goods, observed a Dun reporter, and claimed to have "purchased them principally for cash." Berg and his partner were "steady + appear to understand" their business.[49]

The war, however, created a new economic reality, and like Edward Feibelman had done with his business, Meyer Berg took his name off the masthead, "perhaps to ward off creditors." By 1865, Meyer's wife Gette was running the business in her name while her husband struggled with debt. The business got an infusion of capital when Gette's uncle in New York "deeded in trust for her use" $14,000, and it was "invested in the goods here." The infusion of New York capital helped them to survive the immediate aftermath of the war, and while they operated a business that was "not large," Meyer was nevertheless "energetic + economical."[50]

While Berg survived the immediate aftermath of the war, the business was soon thriving, and it did not appear to be affected by the downturn. By late 1866, agents believed that Meyer had "settled most of his debts," and the following year he had "put his own shingle out," opening the business in his own name, and credit reporters assumed he "will make money." Meyer Berg was soon considered "a first rate Jew [merchant]," and the "money maker" was presumed to be worth $25,000 clear by 1871. Like other cotton businesses in the region, Berg's generally took "mortgage security for goods put out on time," and because he "credits prudently" and "collects well," he made "large profits." Berg was working with Lehman Brothers and Lehman, Abraham & Co. in January 1878 and in March 1881. Berg was also rumored to have an interest in another

Camden business, and his reputation was such that a recorder commented that if the rumor was true, Berg's "connection with the concern makes it sound without considering its own intrinsic strength."[51]

Lehman Brothers also worked with businesses along the Arkansas River, including that of Simon Gans, who arrived in Little Rock in 1860. After serving the Confederacy during the war, he opened a clothing store that later sold dry goods, and he soon partnered with Moses Katzenstein. The first credit record of the firm was from 1868, when it was "not doing much business." It survived the Panic of 1873, and by 1874 the firm was said to "pay promptly" and had enough credit for their wants. A credit reporter was concerned, however, that they "sell a little too much" on credit but were "close collectors" and were of good character. In 1876, they conducted business "so closely that Banks [sic] here know but little" about them except that their credit was "as good as any firm here." They dealt in cotton, worked the country trade, and had a large assortment of dry goods. The firm worked with Lehman Brothers between 1877 and 1879.[52]

Lehman Brothers also worked with Simon Gans's relative, Jacob Gans, who arrived in Little Rock around 1872. According to a Dun reporter, Jacob had had a business in Memphis that had closed, and Dun agents claimed that he had "swindled" his creditors. The recorder claimed that he was a "trickster" who was "wholly" unreliable and should only be sold to for cash. As a result, assumed the reporter, Jacob Gans conducted business in the name of his wife, Bluma DeYoung Gans, likely to protect his assets, although the store was "attended to by her husband." Regardless of the arrangement, the business was soon thriving, and by 1875 she was doing the best business in her line, and this sentiment was echoed in 1878. The firm conducted a largely cash business and paid its debts promptly, and it was also in business with Lehman Brothers in 1882.[53]

Bluma Gans, however, seems to have had more of a hand in the business than Dun recorders either realized or let on, suggesting that women may have played a more important role in the ethnic economy than credit reports revealed. She was born in Philadelphia in 1835, and by the 1880s she operated a millinery, fancy dry goods, and dressmaking business. The Mrs. B. Gans Company soon had eighty-six employees, spread throughout the various sections of the firm, and the firm expanded in 1884. She purchased from Eastern markets, selecting goods herself, and

Figure 4.2. "Receipt for Bonnet from Mrs. B. Gans." Image courtesy of Temple B'nai Israel, Little Rock, Arkansas.

she also purchased in Paris, in addition bringing back seamstresses who were skilled enough to "do justice" to the fabrics she was purchasing. The store was considered to be a "delightful" place to visit, and mothers and their young daughters could be found shopping together.[54]

Following the death of her husband in 1900, Mrs. Gans moved to New York to be with her daughter, but her family members carried on the business. In 1912 the Little Rock Board of Trade wrote that no dry goods store or millinery could beat the "well stocked and enterprising establishment of Mrs. B. Gans." The company's slogan was "Outfitters for All Womankind," and in 1912 the firm had thirty-three assistants and remained one of the leading stores in Little Rock. Gans died in 1915, and she was buried in the Oakland Jewish Cemetery in Little Rock.[55]

Downriver from Little Rock, Lehman Brothers also worked with Gabe Meyer in Pine Bluff, Arkansas. Meyer was born in Bavaria in 1834 and arrived in New Orleans via Antwerp at the age of fifteen. He began as a peddler, and from 1852 to 1856, he owned a shop in Marion, Louisiana. According to an oft-cited story, Meyer decided to visit his cousins in Grand Lake, Arkansas, but he was forced to detour through Pine Bluff because of extensive flooding. He ended up settling in Pine Bluff around 1856, and once there, he purchased a stock of goods from New York, quite possibly with the aid of his uncle Isaias Meyer, the mercantile scion who, as we have already seen, had a strong presence in New York, Natchez, and Bayou Sara. In Pine Bluff, Gabe Meyer opened a shop on what became the main thoroughfare of the city.[56]

Gabe Meyer apparently lost money during the war, so he needed to start essentially from scratch in the postbellum years. When Gabe and his brother Bennett opened G. Meyer & Bro., they planned to "promptly settle the indebtedness of the firm," and they "were in a bold fix after the war but came out all right," noted a Dun recorder. By 1867 they were considered a "good house" in excellent credit and standing, and they were slow in their payments in 1868 because of the "smallness" of the previous years' crop. But they weathered the downturn, and by 1870 the firm had become "one of our best houses." They were "reputable Jews," "have the confidence of the community," and they operated a "flourishing" business. The firm sold "principally" on credit and "dealt in Cotton considerably," although at times they claimed to "have lost money on it."[57]

The firm conducted an estimated $80,000 in business in 1873 and had an estimated capital of $75,000. While it, like most others, appear to have been in a bit of financial trouble in 1874, it seemed to be on more solid footing by 1875, when it was "generally considered" to be worth $100,000. Meyer sold out in 1876, although the firm remained in the family, but one credit reporter nevertheless supposed that it continued to be backed by Gabe Meyer because nobody else had any visible capital. Meyer also "cultivates about 3500 acres of cotton" and "raises about 15 bales from his own plantations," and according to one source, Meyer owned twenty-one plantations.[58]

Gabe Meyer's excellent reviews, as well as his ability to weather periods where he was "somewhat behind" with some creditors, were primarily because of his contacts in New York, where his firm purchased their dry goods and had strong credit. Its sound financial backing came in large part because it was "assisted by" Bodenheim, Meyer & Co., which, as we saw in the previous chapter, was financed in part by Isaias Meyer and operated by Isaias's nephew Abraham Meyer. Although a credit reporter claimed that Gabe Meyer had "no connection" with Bodenheim, Meyer & Co. beyond the familial relationship, Dun reporters in New York claimed that Bodenheim, Meyer & Co. had a branch in St. Louis and in Pine Bluff, Arkansas. As if this connection weren't enough, Gabe

Meyer also had credit with Meyer, Weis & Co., as well as with Lehman, Abraham & Co. and Phillips & Co., cotton factors of New Orleans. In 1875, Meyer owed Lehman, Abraham & Co. between $5,000 and $6,000 and also owed Meyer, Weis & Co. a few thousand dollars. The firm had a $10,000 credit line with both Lehman Brothers and Meyer, Weis & Co. He also had small transactions with Lehman Brothers between 1878 and 1880, as well as about $1,000 in 1881. Based on the strength of the firm and the importance of its connections, Dun agents believed that the company was good for its contracts.[59]

While Lehman Brothers worked with firms in the richest cotton lands and along river tributaries, it also worked with businesses in interior railroad towns, including Meridian, Mississippi. This included Marks & Lichtenstein, which emerged in 1873, grew rapidly, and advertised "Choice Family Groceries, dry goods, boots, shoes, and plantation supplies." One credit reporter feared that it did not have enough capital

Figure 4.3. "Architect's Sketch, Marks & Lichtenstein, Meridian, Mississippi." Image courtesy of the Jacob Rader Marcus Center of the American Jewish Archives, Cincinnati, Ohio (MSS 601, box 5, folder 2).

to survive, but much of its growth was likely due to its "very fair credit with certain houses in NY." This included Lehman Brothers, as the two firms transacted several thousand dollars' worth of business in 1882.[60]

In 1877, Marks & Lichtenstein was estimated to sell $75,000 to $125,000 annually, and a credit reporter deemed it the "largest establishment here." He emphatically declared that they "sell more goods than any two houses" and that it had the "largest + best stock in the town." In 1879, it was estimated to have purchased 400 bales of cotton and conducted sales of approximately $100,000, although it was assumed that "they have probably lost on cotton," "considerably."[61]

Lehman Brothers and Lehman, Abraham & Co. also worked closely with businesses operated by the Goldsmith, Haber, and Forcheimer families. These firms excelled in the antebellum years, as we saw in chapter 1, and they survived the war years by reestablishing the New York–New Orleans network that they had solidified before the war. During the war, Isaac Haber operated out of New York, where he was affiliated with the firms of Isaac Haber & Co. and Hoyt, Sprague & Co. Meanwhile, Simon Haber and Isaac Forcheimer led the New Orleans operation. Isaac Haber provided goods for the New Orleans trade, in what appears to have been part of a government contract.[62]

After the war, the firms continued to operate in both New York and New Orleans and were estimated to be worth "safely" $100,000. The New York branch was a "money making" business that was "paying cash" and sustained good credit, and it was "able to buy on 6 [months.]" Forcheimer Brothers in New Orleans sold wholesale groceries and had connections in the West, and the firm also had affiliated firms elsewhere in the Gulf South, including Pensacola, Florida, and a branch in Alabama. Financial connections to Lehman Brothers and its affiliates were in place by 1876, as Isaac Haber & Co. carried forward a balance of $12,900.95 into 1877 and Forcheimer Bros. conducted a significant amount of business between 1877 and 1879.[63]

Although Lehman Brothers worked with non-Jewish businesses such as Richardson & May, it was through its financial connections to a multitude of Jewish-owned businesses that it assumed an essential role in an ethnic economy that connected these businesses with the credit and capital they needed to thrive. But while this top tier of the network brought global investment to many of the region's larger businesses, these networks needed a bottom tier to distribute that investment to the farmers and smaller stores of the Gulf South. That bottom tier of this economic network, and the ways in which credit continued to flow along ethnic lines throughout the region's economy, is the subject of the next chapter.

5

Networks from Below

In an economic milieu in which trust was essential and ethnicity fostered
trust, two tiers of a Jewish economic network operated in tandem to
provide credit to rural cotton farmers as they navigated the vicissitudes
of the postbellum economy. In the top tier, firms such as Lehman Brothers secured global investment, frequently with the aid of fellow Jewish
firms, and they distributed that investment to other Jewish-owned firms
throughout the Gulf South. Once that global investment reached the
Gulf South, the bottom tier of this network distributed that credit and
capital throughout local economies.

This chapter explores how the bottom tier of this network operated.
In some instances, Lehman Brothers' customers provided supplies, staples, and luxury items directly to farmers and plantation owners. But
in other instances, Lehman Brothers' customers acted as wholesalers,
who in turn worked with scores of smaller general stores throughout the
region. These wholesalers extended credit to smaller shopkeepers, who
could then stock their own shelves at the start of the season, sell goods
to their customers on credit, and, if all went well, be repaid by their
customers after the harvest. For these small store owners, leniency from
creditors during economic downturns often separated success from failure. Such leniency, however, was risky business for wholesalers. But just
as shared ethnicity fostered trust at the top tier of the network, so, too,
did it engender trust at the bottom level. As a result, Jewish wholesalers
worked closely, though not exclusively, with scores of Jewish merchants
scattered throughout the Gulf South. This completed an extensive ethnic
network that brought global investment to the South and distributed it
throughout local economies.

* * *

"It is a far cry from the little country store opened here in 1867 by Julius
Freyhan," a Lehman Brothers customer, "to the big department store,

with its various subsidiary branches . . ." declared the silver anniversary edition of Bayou Sara's *True Democrat*. Freyhan's success was predicated largely upon the hundreds of thousands of dollars' worth of business that he conducted with Lehman Brothers, a relationship that catapulted him to the forefront of West Feliciana Parish's economy. Freyhan sold an extensive stock of goods, and it was quite a scene when those goods arrived, either by river or rail. "In steamboat days," the *True Democrat* described, "it was a common occurrence for the big St. Louis and Cincinnati packets to spend from a day to a day and a half in unloading supplies for this concern." Goods also arrived over land, as "before the railroads had reached their present state of development long wagon trains came from the interior, bringing cotton and returning with supplies." The stock of supplies that arrived was diverse, noted the same newspaper, emphasizing that "it would take several books to list completely that company's item of trade." While "Freyhan and Company dealt in plantation supplies," it was far more than just a general store. The *True Democrat* noted that "what they really were were crop suppliers,

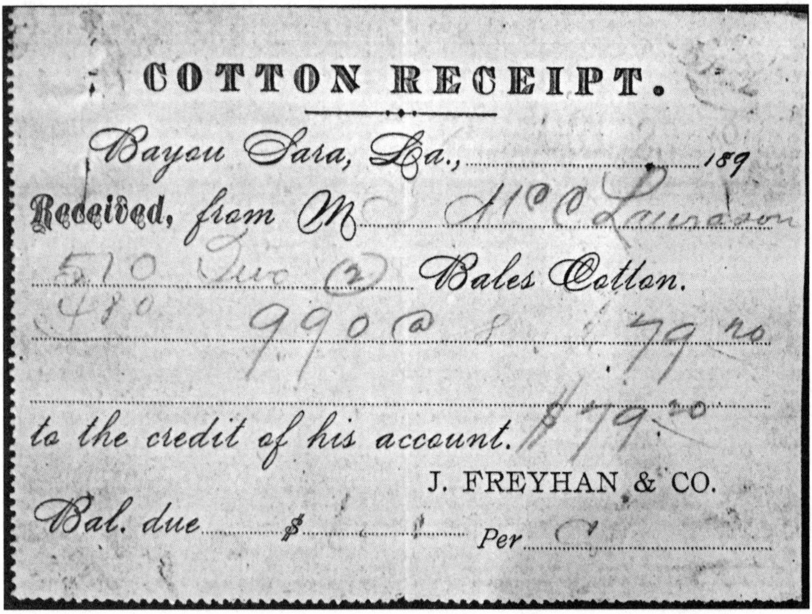
COTTON RECEIPT.

Bayou Sara, La., ... 189

Received, from M ....

.... Bales Cotton.

to the credit of his account.

J. FREYHAN & CO.

Bal. due .... $ .... Per ....

Figure 5.1. "Cotton Receipt from Julius Freyhan & Co." Image courtesy of the West Feliciana Historical Society.

necessary adjuncts to hard times, who sold, on credit and at understand-
ably enormous interest rates, all the seed, tools, etc. necessary to grow
a cotton or corn crop. Incident to actual crop needs were the needs of
house and family." Julius Freyhan & Co. became the parish's largest retail
merchant, and he played a central role in the entire region's economy.[1]

Listed as five feet, four and a half inches tall, Freyhan arrived in
Bayou Sara shortly before the Civil War, passing first through the towns
of Jackson and Clinton, Louisiana. In Clinton, Freyhan met the family of
his future bride, Sarah Wolf, whose brothers Morris and Emanuel would
later become his business partners. After a few years in Clinton, Freyhan
left for West Feliciana Parish, where he was recorded in the 1860 U.S.
Census. He was listed as a non-combat musician during the war and
was captured by the Union after deserting. After the conflict, Freyhan
apparently started anew as a clerk, either in Jackson or in Bayou Sara.[2]

By 1867, Freyhan had opened that "little country store," starting "in a
very humble way, in the dark days of reconstruction," and he was soon
"doing a considerable business with small farmers and planters," working on the retail side of the cotton business. One recorder believed that,
"if crops are good [he] will make money," and by 1871 he had purchased
a sawmill and leased land for a steam gin and grist mill. Business continued to be good, and his investments appeared to have paid off; a Dun
reporter noted that "from all we can learn he last year did a large and
successful" business, in large part because he "was successful last year in
making collections."[3]

Freyhan's store was prominently situated at St. Francisville's central
intersection. It grew rapidly, as it "sprawled across the upper center of
town, a two-story main store, warehouse, general merchandise, another
warehouse, another general merchandise, lunch counter, furniture company, grocery and saloon." The "main store" was "an aggregate of three
buildings at the bus station corner," and the other, the "upper store,"
"incorporated into its melange [sic] the ubiquitous barroom of the day's
general store, and knew its share of shooting fracases." A Dun agent
claimed that Freyhan was doing a "large" business, "principally with the
negroes," but while he continued to do a considerable business of advancing, Dun recorders later stopped mentioning connections to freedmen. One person recalled that "Saturdays," the Jewish Sabbath, "saw the
country folk by the droves piling into town in mule-drawn wagons to

purchase their goods and supplies for the coming week or even month at J. Freyhan & Co."[4]

In addition to its retail business, the firm was involved in wholesaling, and to broaden its St. Francisville presence, the firm also had warehouses by the river in Bayou Sara. "This venture prospered," claimed the *True Democrat*, "and the firm built up an enormous business in the parishes of East and West Baton Rouge, East and West Feliciana, Point Coupee, Avoyelles and Concordia Parishes, in Louisiana, and Adams, Amite and Wilkinson Counties, in Mississippi."[5]

Despite the rise and fall in cotton prices, one observer noted, Julius Freyhan & Co. "has been uniformly successful through high and low prices of cotton," and the business survived the Panic of 1873. Before the panic he shipped 1,500 bales of cotton annually, but in 1874 that had risen to 2,000 bales. His business was in good shape, and his prospects were favorable. Freyhan, noted a local newspaper, "lived to the time when his firm had become the principal source of supply for nearly a dozen Louisiana parishes and Mississippi counties, selling as much as a million dollars' worth of goods and handling from twelve to fourteen thousand bales of cotton in a single year." By 1875, Freyhan was doing "as much [business] as all the other merchants of this place together," shipping between 3,000 and 4,000 bales of cotton, and he also had cash on hand—a reported $32,000 deposit in New Orleans—and his estimated net worth was between $75,000 and $100,000.[6]

Freyhan's footprint continued to expand at St. Francisville's prime intersection. In 1885, his complex consisted of a large general merchandise store, two warehouses, a lunch counter, and a roadside dwelling on the north side of the street. Toward the back of this lot was a cotton ginnery with four Pratt gins, bailing presses and condensers, as well as several wells. Across the street stood Freyhan's furniture store, grocery store, and kitchen, as well as an abandoned frame building that was once used as a cotton gin. Freyhan also owned the lot on the other side of the intersection. Within several years, Freyhan had added several billiard halls and saloons around his mercantile and dry goods establishments, as well as a coffin warehouse and a shop selling confection and cigars. He expanded his ironclad cotton ginnery with platforms, and he also had a warehouse for cotton and seed that was connected to the ginnery with conveyors.[7]

Despite the downturns of the economy, Freyhan's business had a rapid upward trajectory, but it also survived several fires. In 1886, a fire "of incendiary origin" hit Bayou Sara, and the biggest loser in that conflagration was Freyhan. Total damage for the town was estimated at about $118,000—and of that, $100,000 was the loss of Freyhan's stock and building. It appears that three-quarters of Freyhan's losses were covered by insurance. Two years later "a large steam ginnery belonging to J. Freyhart & Co. [sic], together with 1,000 sacks of seed and 500 boxes of coal, was burned Tuesday night at Bayou Sara. Loss, $8,000; insurance, $5,000." Cognizant of the threat of fire, Freyhan's property soon included a large pond and cistern with a suction pipe to deliver water to the ginning complex, if necessary.[8]

Julius Freyhan & Co.'s continued growth through the ups and downs of the economy was only possible because of access to credit. In 1870 Freyhan was backed by his wife's relative Leon Adler, but a significant line of credit came from Lehman Brothers—a relationship that began as early as 1877, although lost records may obscure an earlier connection. In September 1877, Freyhan received from Lehman four "cash draft from sundries" totaling over $16,000, and by 1884, transactions with Lehman Brothers had increased dramatically. In a six-month span Freyhan's account grew from $100,000 to $250,000, and in the ensuing months he paid approximately $118,000 to Lehman Brothers. Freyhan's connection with Lehman Brothers extended beyond these loans, as he served for a period as president of Lane Cotton Mills, which was owned by Lehman, Abraham & Co.[9]

While Freyhan, a Jewish merchant, shared an ethnic tie to Lehman Brothers, ethnicity also mattered within his business; several of his most important and longest-tenured employees were Jewish. Freyhan also hired family members. His business partners and later successors, Morris and Emanuel Wolf, were his brothers-in-law. He also employed his nephew Morris Burgas, who "kept the books, bought cotton and worked in Bayou Sara and St. Francisville." He had an office in Freyhan's general merchandise store, and when Freyhan later moved to New Orleans, Burgas remained behind, in charge of buying cotton upstate and shipping it downriver. He also kept the books for Freyhan's Lane Cotton Mills, which was directly connected to Lehman Brothers. Morris Burgas eventually struck out on his own, purchasing property from Freyhan and opening a general merchandise store, and he continued to buy cotton and send it to New Orleans.[10]

With the credit extended by Lehman Brothers, Julius Freyhan could stock his shelves with goods, selling those items for cash or on credit to his customers. This included Sarah T. Bowman of nearby Rosedown Plantation, whose ledger with Freyhan helps to demonstrate the central role that Julius Freyhan & Co. played in the yearly cycle of his customers. In 1896, for example, Bowman started with an accounts-receivable balance of $89.35 in February. To this she added a gallon of whiskey, sugar, olive oil, mustard, and hinges, which raised her accounts receivable to $228.40. By the end of March, her account had increased to $346.45, after purchases such as grits, olive oil, peaches, tea, whiskey, syrup, lunch tongue, socks, pants, a shirt, and lace linen. April saw more purchases on the account, including shoes, bacon, powdered sugar, ladies' tan hose, corset laces, crackers, sardines, beef tongues, and ribbon, raising her balance to approximately $434. In May, Bowman purchased pepper, coffee, pins, quinine, paper, soda, a hatchet, jars, toothbrushes, soap, Vaseline, and starch, and the balance on her account rose to $630.68.[11]

Bowman's balance at the end of June, after buying envelopes, cornstarch, peaches, crackers, mustard, and bacon, was $669, and her tab reached $784.05 by the end of July, after purchases including a spoon, matches, cups, saucers, rice, whiskey, flour, lard, tea, salmon, lobsters, and sardines. By the end of August, Bowman's accounts receivable had risen to almost $900, and after procuring from Freyhan grits, lard, oatmeal, vinegar, sausage, calico, spools, silk, soap, and macaroni during the month of September, her balance reached over $1,200 on November 2. After the cotton harvest, Bowman could then repay her debts to Freyhan. While her 1896 repayment is unclear, a statement from October 14, 1895, shows 35 bales of cotton credited to her account, netting her $1,419.69.[12]

Freyhan also supplied Solitude Plantation. "Cotton was the main source of income," Beulah Smith Watts, who lived on the plantation, later recalled. The cotton "was ginned and baled on Solitude and sold to Julius Freyhan in St. Francisville where the baled cotton was then shipped from the Bayou Sara river port to various sections of the states," she maintained. Freyhan, she noted, "sold the cotton seed to local farmers."[13]

While Julius Freyhan & Co. offered credit to clients to purchase their goods, the firm also played an informal banking role in West Feliciana

Parish. "During much of the time of the firm's existence there was no bank in the parish," noted the *True Democrat*. "Its operations had become so extensive and its business relations with the public so intimate that it naturally was entrusted with the care of the entire business of many of its patrons, a deposit there being considered as safe as a deposit with any bank."[14]

Freyhan was in the business of banking and selling on credit, and with the travails of the economy and varying crop yields, it should come as no surprise that some of his customers defaulted on their loans. When default occurred, land foreclosure was often the result. "The day of reckoning came when the harvest was gathered," noted the *True Democrat*, "and while the records indicate oftentimes an exceeding leniency, J. Freyhan and Company became the owners of a great deal of land." Some people viewed Freyhan's business "as an octopus, reaching out tentacles to everything in sight," the newspaper claimed. While Freyhan "no doubt controlled many lives—some harshly," this, claimed the *True Democrat*, "was not only inevitable, but probably necessary. Somebody had to have the hard cash, and they did."[15]

As a result of foreclosures and other factors, Freyhan began to add a great deal of land to his portfolio. He purchased property in St. Francisville and one hundred acres of a plantation from a sheriff's sale. While he may have initially rented his own store, he soon owned property in town, as well as other property outside of town. Over the course of the 1870s he purchased a parcel of land from Henry Williams, along with 2 unpicked bales of cotton, a horse and buggy, and fifty bushels of corn—all for $480. In 1887 Freyhan purchased a plantation from a sheriff's sale for $2,954.55, and in 1895, Freyhan provided $2,344.30 to Kemp Mattingly, who had the right to redeem the 450 acres in property for five years by repaying the debt along with 8 percent interest, keeping up the properties, and paying taxes. By the time Freyhan sold out to his brothers-in-law, his assets included the Rogillio swampland in West Feliciana Parish, the Alfred Doyle place below Bayou Sara, and the S. Miller gin house in East Baton Rouge, as well at least a dozen other properties in East and West Feliciana Parishes.[16]

Julius Freyhan & Co. thus provides an excellent example of how a business, with access to Lehman Brothers credit, extended that credit to farmers and plantation owners throughout West Feliciana Parish and beyond. However, there was another way for Lehman Brothers' customers in West Feliciana Parish and elsewhere to infuse that global investment through local economies, and that was by selling at wholesale to smaller stores. These connections between wholesale and retail firms were based on trust, and they were often between family members or those with shared ethnicity.

While Julius Freyhan & Co. also had a wholesale operation, so, too, did the general store of Picard & Weil, which was by many measures the second largest business in West Feliciana—second only to Freyhan. Picard & Weil was a Jewish-owned firm that distributed Lehman Brothers' credit to other Jewish-owned firms in town. This firm was a partnership between Simon Weil and his father-in-law Henry Picard, and it had begun its relationship with Lehman Brothers by 1881. Within two years, Picard & Weil appears to have had just over $44,000 credited from Lehman Brothers. That number dipped to just over $35,000 in 1884, but the relationship between the two firms lasted until least 1892. This credit facilitated the growth of their business.[17]

Simon Weil immigrated to New Orleans in 1854, and his first years in America are unclear—an S. Weil was listed in the 1860 U.S. Census as living in both Yazoo City and Brownsville, Mississippi. He may have paid taxes in New Orleans in 1864 and in Vicksburg in 1865, and an 1866 credit reporter believed that he had come from Mobile. Nevertheless, during his time in New Orleans he married Henry Picard's stepdaughter Jane, and in 1866, Picard & Weil opened as a dry goods store in Bayou Sara. The early years of the firm were marked by ups and downs. In early 1867, a Dun recorder noted that Picard & Weil "appear to be clever" businessmen, who were "doing good business" and had a "[large] stock of goods." Yet the following year they "lost heavily by the decline in goods" and the "bad collections" that were endemic to the economy following the crop failures. As a result, the firm was "in a failing condition." But business soon picked up as they "advanced somewhat in crops" and sold plantation supplies and dry goods, and they were considered "good" businessmen. They owned real estate and soon had a "large store" and considerable stock, and they survived the Panic of 1873 as well. By 1875 they were "supposed to be in easy circumstances," but in 1880 a fire started in their stable, destroying a block of buildings including their store. Picard & Weil rebuilt, and the firm owned a large complex nestled in the block between the Mississippi River and the Bayou Sara Creek. Facing a cotton yard and cotton freight shed that abutted the levee along the river, Picard & Weil's general merchandise store occupied a prominent place, and the complex included buildings behind the store.[18]

Picard & Weil used Lehman Brothers' credit not only to grow its own business but also to offer credit to a network of local Jewish-owned businesses—particularly those of family members. For example, backed by his brother Simon Weil, Lazard Weil opened a small business in 1872, conducting "principally a negro trade" and selling "chiefly" to freedmen— much like other Jewish-owned businesses in the early 1870s. His business continued to be "principally confined to advancing to freedmen," and he remained in business through 1880. Also "backed by Picard & Weil" was S. Weil & Bro., carried on independently of Picard & Weil by Simon Weil and a brother. This firm conducted a business "principally with negroes and small farmers." Henry Picard also had his own business independent of Picard & Weil, possibly in Deer Creek, Mississippi, just outside of Greenville.[19]

While Picard & Weil worked closely with firms operated by family members, ethnic ties also connected its wholesale operation to smaller, Jewish-owned firms. For example, Joseph Meyers opened for business in 1870, conducting a "small" business in the name of Simon Weil that "sells to Negroes + makes money." Early on, the firm was doing "consid[erable] bus[iness]," still "principally with Negroes." By 1873, the firm conducted business "entirely" with freedmen, which, according to the Dun recorder, was "a very unsafe one in this part of the world." His business failed following the Panic of 1873 but apparently later recommenced in the name of S. Weil, and it continued until at least 1880.[20]

In addition to its work in West Feliciana Parish with Julius Freyhan & Co. and Picard & Weil, Lehman Brothers' footprint was heavy throughout the entire Gulf South. In Natchez, for example, its New Orleans branch, Lehman, Abraham & Co., worked with Simon Jacobs, whose business opened in the postbellum years and became one of the strongest firms in this vitally important inland port. Unlike many other Jewish immigrants to the region, Jacobs came from Eastern Europe, first immigrating to Canada in the 1850s. By 1860 he was a shoemaker in St. Louis, and he arrived in Natchez in 1867 and entered the dry goods business.[21]

By 1869 Simon had opened a dry goods business that his younger brother Adolph would later join, and the pair was soon "building up a [good] reputation." They struggled in the wake of the panic, but one of the ways in which it survived was by charging high enough interest rates to cancel out the bad debts that were not repaid to them. For example, a Dun recorder noted that they had "advanced rather heavily," but because their credit prices were "high, there is probably enough margin to enable them to come out even." Even with these high rates their condition was still "uncertain," but the firm soon began to recover. With the credit provided to them by Lehman Brothers, the Jacobs lent a considerable amount of money to sharecroppers and landowners—between 1867 and 1910 they held 3,082 crop liens and trust deeds, valued at over $668,000. The Jacobses provided credit to black farmers and counted Nathan Wright and John R. Lynch among their customers.[22]

Lehman Brothers' credit also flowed through the local economy in Greenville, Mississippi. One of the town's top businesses was Leopold Wilczinski & Co., which was connected to Lehman Brothers indirectly via the non-Jewish firm of Richardson & May, which served as its New Orleans correspondents. Leopold Wilczinski came to America from Posen, followed shortly thereafter by his brothers Herman and Nathan, and mercantile records indicate that by the summer of 1870 the Wilczinskis' general store was on the scene in Greenville. While Wilczinski did not initially conduct a large business, he was considered "prompt and reliable." Soon after, credit reporters noted that his business "stands well" and seemed to make money. Over the course of the 1870s, Wilczinski's business mirrored the growth of Greenville itself, which developed into one of the most important river ports between Memphis and New Orleans.[23]

During the 1873–1879 economic downturn, L. Wilczinski & Co. thrived, appearing "as prosperous as usual," and apparently had a second branch at nearby Argyle. By 1875 they were considered about "the largest and most successful merchants" in Greenville, according to a credit reporter, who also noted that they were considered "honest," stood "high in credit," and were "firstrate" [sic] businessmen. They were soon deemed the "largest cotton shippers from this place" and were "perhaps entitled to the largest [credit] of any store keepers in this town." They shipped large quantities of cotton, purchased $40,000 worth of stock in New York, and "always have $," observed a reporter. But like other businesses of their type, the Wilczinskis remained "dependent on the cotton crop."[24]

On sound financial footing, Leopold Wilczinski could extend credit to his customers, but with credit always came risk. For example, the Wilczinskis lent money to Dock Early, a white farmer, who purchased a sixty-six-acre farm in 1879. Early soon defaulted on a deed of trust held by the Wilczinskis, who purchased the property in 1880 via auction. The Wilczinskis then resold the property back to Early, who promptly defaulted again. The Wilczinskis then decided to sell the parcel to two black farmers, but despite a court order, Early refused to leave the property. Left with little recourse, the Wilczinskis again sold the property back to Early—who defaulted for a third time, but this time he finally left the property. During this ordeal, which lasted eight years, the Wilczinskis loaned Early nearly $1,000, and do not appear to have collected any repayment from him.[25]

While some white farmers such as Dock Early found themselves unable to repay their debts to the Wilczinskis, so, too, did black farmers such as Lewis Spearman, Sr. In 1873, Spearman leased the Ridgeland Plantation in present-day Humphreys County, Mississippi, and because his cotton crop was very good, he saved enough money to purchase his own land in 1874. In addition to his cultivated land, much of his property was wooded, and with convenient access to the Yazoo River, he could easily float timber off his property. For fourteen years, Spearman increased the acreage under cultivation, purchased additional land, and avoided debt.[26]

As the price of cotton declined over the 1880s, however, Spearman was not immune to the repercussions. By early 1888 he had fallen $325 into debt to the Wilczinskis, who refused to grant him further credit without a deed of trust. Spearman granted that deed of trust to the Wilczinskis in exchange for a $500 credit for purchases and cash advances, and he was supposed to repay the debt plus 10 percent interest. If he failed to repay his debt, the Wilczinskis were authorized to sell his land, crops, mules, horse, and cattle at public auction and to repay the debt with the proceeds of the sale. Cotton prices, however, continued to decline, and unable to repay the Wilczinskis, Spearman took out a separate loan for $1,000 from a Memphis company and used part of that to repay his debt to the Wilczinskis.[27]

While this may have been the end of the story as far as the Wilczinskis' bottom line was concerned, things continued to spiral downward for Spearman. Cotton prices continued to tumble, and just as Spearman had patched together a new loan to cover his debts to the Wilczinskis, he took out an additional loan from merchant G. W. Meek to repay his debts in Memphis, and he was also given another $250 credit for supplies. Spearman's debts continued to mount; in 1894 he sold one parcel of land at auction, and in 1895 he sold the rest of his land at auction. He died shortly thereafter. His experience reflects how many black landowners couldn't hold back the tide of debt in their later years, and Spearman's son never attained landownership.[28]

The risks and rewards associated with credit transactions meant that, while L. Wilczinski & Co. continued to grow, its success was not linear. The firm built a two-story brick building in 1885, and in 1889 it "erected the finest block in Greenville, at a cost of $50,000." It owned its own cotton yard, cultivated 400 acres of land of its own, and it also owned a fireproof warehouse that could hold 10,000 bales of cotton. Yet when economic decline hit the Mississippi Delta, its fortunes suffered along with those of farmers such as Spearman. The Wilczinskis were forced to take out a $2,500 loan from the Merchants and Planters Bank of Greenville, and they also negotiated a second lien on a parcel of land. Yet the firm survived, managing to stave off bankruptcy throughout the 1890s.[29]

There were other Jewish firms in Greenville that provided credit to the local economy. Weiss & Goldstein, a partnership between Nathan Goldstein and his father-in-law Morris Weiss, does not appear to have had a relationship with Lehman Brothers, but the firm was nonetheless operational by 1868 and was soon deemed the "largest and most prominent merchants in this city." Yet much like L. Wilczinksi & Co., the firm was dependent upon its ability to collect from those who owed money, as "much depends on Cotton crop + collections." Particularly during difficult years, some farmers could not repay their debts.[30]

For example, William Toler, a black farmer, purchased 160 acres of land, and in the process of improving that land, amassed an $800 debt to Weiss & Goldstein. His debt with the firm continued to increase, and in 1883 he signed a deed of trust on his property for $1,654.06. By 1890, his debt to Weiss & Goldstein had increased to nearly $2,000, and the terms of his loan agreement tightened. Toler was required to sell his entire cotton crop through Weiss & Goldstein, and the firm held liens on Toler's land, mules, and crops. Moreover, he was given a quota of 75 bales of cotton to produce, or he would be charged $1.25 for each bale under 75. Over the next three years, Toler's obligations to Weiss & Goldstein floated between $1,500 and $2,000, and in 1893, he was charged an additional 2.5 percent interest on purchases he made through them. But Toler continued to struggle with repayment, and in 1894, Weiss & Goldstein foreclosed, and Toler's land and six mules were auctioned for $2,000. Toler, however, convinced the bank to sell the land back to him, and much like Louis Spearman did for a time, he continued to find new merchants to loan him money so that he could keep his land.[31]

All of these firms, particularly Julius Freyhan & Co., demonstrate how in many instances credit flowed from Lehman Brothers to Jewish-owned firms and then directly to farmers and plantation owners. But in other instances, Lehman Brothers' credit flowed first to Jewish-owned commission houses or wholesalers, such as Picard & Weil, before continuing along ethnic networks to smaller Jewish retailers. Only then was this global investment loaned to the cotton farmers and plantation owners of the Gulf South. The firm of Meyer, Weis & Co. offers a particularly rich and compelling example of how this wholesale trade unfolded, frequently along ethnic lines.

Meyer, Weis & Co. worked extensively with Lehman, Abraham & Co., the New Orleans branch of Lehman Brothers, which provided the firm with credit. In 1877, Meyer, Weis & Co. had a cash draft transaction of $25,000 with Lehman, Abraham & Co., although missing records may have obscured an earlier relationship, and transactions continued into 1879. One partner in the firm, Isaac Meyer, had his own transactions with Lehman Brothers in 1878 and 1880, including an interest payment on a loan. And Lehman Brothers was not the only Jewish firm that provided Meyer, Weis & Co. access to global capital—the firm also had a financial relationship with Lazard Frères in 1846 and in the ensuing years.[32]

As we have seen in earlier chapters, Meyer, Weis & Co. was thriving prior to the war, with a strong presence in Natchez, Bayou Sara, New Orleans, and New York. During the war, the firm's partners adapted to wartime conditions in order to survive, and successful cotton speculation after the resumption of Mississippi River commerce meant that, at the conflict's end, Meyer, Weis & Co. was in a far better financial position than many of its competitors. It was back on its feet quickly. Already by June 1865, its New York branch was doing a good wholesale business after having "made money by speculating in cotton," and by 1868 the firm was estimated to have capital worth $250,000. The Natchez branch of the business was similarly quick to bounce back, "doing the largest [business] here" in January 1866.[33]

Because the partners wanted to focus on cotton, they sold their stock of dry goods in Natchez to Adolph Meyer, Isaac Meyer's nephew, and to Meyer Eiseman, Adolph Meyer's brother-in-law—extending a Jewish network through familial ties. "Their wealth has been amassed through successful speculation," noted a Dun recorder about the new firm. Adolph Meyer, who had served in the Confederate Army, was "engaged in cotton speculation + must have made a handsome fortune," ventured one Dun recorder, and Eiseman had also "speculated largely in cotton + no doubt made a large fortune." The new firm had "on hand a stock of staple + fancy dry goods" as well as plantation supplies. Meyer and Eiseman, according to a Dun agent, were "keen + shrewd in trading + perhaps would not scruple to take advantage whenever opportunity offers," leading a Dun agent to consider them "trickish."[34]

But with the lean crop years lurking, the new partners made at least two mistakes that would doom their enterprise and return it to the hands of the original partners. First, a Dun recorder noted that they "have money loaned out" in 1866. With farmers unable to repay their debts because of poor crops, the firm braced itself to lose a fortune. But their diversification ultimately doomed the new partners. In addition to the mercantile business, the partners had an interest in planting and were expected to "make a large cotton crop," but they "lost heavily" during the 1866 crop failure. While a recorder still called them "eminently solvent," Adolph Meyer and Meyer Eiseman relinquished control, and the Natchez operation returned to its previous partners. Although the "failure of the crop [no] doubt seriously affected them," noted a Dun recorder, it was nevertheless believed to have "caused the change in the house" from Meyer & Eiseman back to Meyer, Weis & Co. Despite the difficulties, a recorder noted that there was no fear that the firm would fail.[35]

Much as Meyer, Weis & Co. had tried to divest from the dry goods business in Natchez, they sought to do the same in New Orleans. During the war, as we have seen, Julius Weis moved to New Orleans and entered the cotton commission business under the Meyer, Weis & Co. umbrella, also selling dry goods. While the firm was successful during the conflict and immediately afterward, it was not immune to the economic impact of the crop failures that rippled throughout the economy. Julius Weis recalled that, "when cotton goods declined very rapidly with cotton, and as we had a large stock of such goods on hand, we sustained a very severe loss, having purchased them at high figures." Yet because they had "made a large amount during + after the war," Dun agents surmised that they were able to sustain their "heavy" losses.[36]

Julius Weis soon decided to abandon the dry goods business to focus more on the cotton commission part of the operation. As he remembered it, his partner Isaac Meyer "came down from New York, to see how the business was presenting," and when he arrived, Weis "informed him that I was getting tired of the drygoods business, and that I thought it a good idea to close out and go into the cotton commission business entirely." Meyer "declined to do so, thinking it too risky." However, after Weis threatened to dissolve the partnership and enter business on his own, Meyer relented, and in 1868 "we sold out the entire stock of goods on hand at auction" and began exclusively in the commission business. During the 1868–1869 season, Meyer, Weis & Co. received 30,000 bales of cotton, and receipts continued to increase each year. Weis later estimated that at least a million bales of cotton passed through their New Orleans cotton room.[37]

Now focusing on the cotton commission business, Meyer, Weis & Co. grew into one of the largest and strongest businesses in the entire region. By 1871, it was already "one of our largest cotton houses" and worth an estimated half million dollars. During the 1875–1876 season, Meyer, Weis & Co. handled 130,000 bales of cotton, which Weis thought was "the largest cotton commission business ever done in this City by any one house." They continued as "one of the largest Cotton houses here," "rank A1 as merchants," and owned large amounts of real estate. In 1879 they were "said to have made largely on futures," and by 1881, they were "said to be the largest receivers of Cotton firm in this city." The following season, Meyer, Weis & Co. claimed to be worth over $1 million.[38]

Meyer, Weis & Co. was "usually faring better than others when failures occur," and its access to credit and saved capital was crucial in this regard. But its ability to survive failures was also because it had the financial flexibility to be lenient with its customers during downturns, although it was still "known locally as holding their country patrons with a tight rein." It was through those "country patrons" that international credit flowed into local economies. Some of that was through the retail side of the operation, and at least initially, the firm's business was tied to some of the same farmers with whom Julius Weis had worked before the war. Weis retold a story of how a Natchez merchant came to him in 1868 asking for a $500 loan "with which to make his crop. He had lost all of his Negroes during the war, and was then in very reduced circumstances." Weis recognized the man as one who had denied him lodging one night in 1847, when heavy rains prevented Weis from crossing Cole's Creek into Natchez. "I reminded him of the time in 1847," Weis recalled, "and as I had been informed also that he was not very prompt in meeting his obligations, I told him that under the circumstances I could not consistently be of any assistance to him in money matters."[39]

But Meyer, Weis & Co. also provided credit to a broad swath of merchants throughout the region, many of whom were Jewish. In Natchez, for example, where it may have been more closely connected to the Jewish mercantile firms of Natchez than any other business, Meyer, Weis & Co. worked closely with Isaac Lowenburg, Julius Weis's brother-in-law, who served as Weis's local Natchez agent. The brothers-in-law operated plantations in the area, and Lowenburg also owned his own mercantile business. Lowenburg's daughter Clara recalled joining her father "on his annual business trip to New Orleans where he went to make arrangements for handling the cotton plantation products with his commission merchants, Meyer, Weis and Company."[40]

Lowenburg was a Union sutler who remained in Natchez following the war, and in 1868 he had been "engaged since [the war] in planting." He also had a mercantile establishment in which he was "not doing a large [business]," and his success was "doubtful." While his business continued to be slow, he made money in planting in 1868, and his prospects soon trended upward, in large part because "Meyer, Weis & Co. are their backers." By the end of 1869, Lowenburg had "done well for the

Figure 5.2. "Isaac Lowenburg." Image courtesy of the
Jacob Rader Marcus Center of the American Jewish
Archives, Cincinnati, Ohio (MSS 601, box 2).

past 2 years," and by 1870 the firm was "well off," "making money," and
"prompt" in its payments. Lowenburg struggled as a result of the Panic
of 1873, as he was "much in debt," but a credit reporter surmised that "he
will get through" as his "principal [creditors] are Meyer, Weis & Co. of
N.O." After Dun agents spoke with Meyer, they learned that "Lowenburg
has ample means" for his business. He owed them $20,000 at one time,
but he paid them back. This was not the first time that Lowenburg utilized credit to get on his feet. He started with a $2,500 mortgage from
his father-in-law, with no down payment, and he was also the recipient
of at least two loans by Natchez's B'nai B'rith Lodge.[41]

Lowenburg's work brought him a tremendous amount of success,
and he was soon deemed the "best business in his line in Natchez." He

purchased a home that daughter Clara described as taking up "half a city block with an old fashioned plantation style house, a wide sixty foot long front gallery, [and a] wide hall with two rooms on each side." The "parlor was very grand and had stiff Brussels lace curtains hanging from gilt cornices at the four windows . . . the front hall had beautiful varnished marble paneled paper and lovely square shaped chairs and was like a room, with [a] big book case and hat rack and a wall game table." Lowenburg's children Clara and Sim attended boarding schools in Europe, and in addition, Lowenburg was twice elected Natchez's mayor.[42]

Nonetheless, because Isaac Lowenburg was the beneficiary of credit from Meyer, Weis & Co., allowing him to sell goods on credit to local farmers, he was exposed to risk as farmers sometimes could not repay their debts to him. One of the ways he protected his investment was through liens—between 1867 and 1910, Lowenburg held at least 528 crop liens. One such lien was with black croppers Henry and Lucinda Lincoln, and a contract between the two parties read as follows:

> I have received this day from *I. Lowenburg & Co.* in money, and for the purchase of Supplies, Farming Utensils, Working Stock, and other things necessary for the cultivation of a Plantation, the sum of *One Hundred* dollars, for the use and cultivation of a Plantation . . . to be cultivated by me during the present year, and the said *I. Lowenburg & Co.* has agreed to advance me during the present year in money, and for the purchase of Supplies, Farming Utensils, Working Stock, and other things necessary for the purpose of carrying on said Plantation.

Henry and Lucinda Lincoln were also expected to pay Lowenburg "*Ten* per cent commissions for advancing said money, and for interest on such advances, at the rate of *One* per cent per *Month* till paid."[43]

The Lincolns' ability to repay the loan was dependent upon the success of the future cotton crop, which was often a customer's only asset. Therefore, the two parties agreed that the Lincolns would "hereby bargain, sell, mortgage, and pledge to said *I. Lowenburg & Co.* the crop of cotton to be raised by me during the present year." The Lincolns' contract with Lowenburg stipulated that they pledged "to ship to *I. Lowenburg & Co.* in *Natchez* as soon as gathered, and in condition to be sent to market, the whole of the crop of Cotton that I may raise during the present year, to be sold by them and the proceeds to be applied by them in payment and satisfaction of the sums due and to become due to the foresaid." Lowenburg would then return any surplus profit to the Lincolns, but if the crop failed, Lowenburg would not be repaid during that growing season. He could roll the debt over to the next season, or if customers like the Lincolns had other assets, he could seize whatever land or property may have been posted as collateral.[44]

The Lincolns were not the only customers to have crop lien agreements with Isaac Lowenburg. Aaron and Elizabeth Brandon Stanton mortgaged their full cotton crop and agreed to ship it all to Lowenburg for a commission of 2.5 percent. The Stantons used twenty-eight mules as security for an initial advance of just over $2,700, at 8 percent interest, and a credit line of $3,000. The Stantons were able to repay their debt to Lowenburg after their cotton was harvested and sold. Lowenburg also advanced $5,000 of merchandise at 8 percent, plus 2 percent for cash advances, to James Coleman and Michael Mack to open their own stores in Vidalia, Louisiana, across the river from Natchez. The loan was backed by mortgages on their land.[45]

In addition to crop liens, Lowenburg and his fellow merchants could also use trust deeds to secure loans with their customers—between 1867 and 1910, Lowenburg held at least seventy-two trust deeds. Trust deeds differed from other land-backed mortgages because of their scale and because a trustee would hold the title until the debt was paid. For example, merchants might work with plantation owners who held valuable land but had little cash on hand. The merchant would appoint a trustee who would hold the deed in trust, which served as collateral for the merchant in the case of non-payment. After the crop was harvested, and if the planter repaid his debt, the trust deed would be returned to the landowner. However, if a poor crop did not provide enough revenue for repayment, the trustee could seize the land and auction it off with the assistance of the local sheriff and use the proceeds to repay the debt to the merchant. Because the attached land came with debt that often scared off potential investors, frequently the merchant who loaned the money was the winning bidder, acquiring the land at a low price. Lowenburg acted as Julius Weis's agent and held for him several mortgages and trust deeds from Orange and Ann Miles, and he received title to the Clifton Plantation from Meyer, Weis & Co. in 1869. Between 1871 and 1873, Orange and Ann Miles transacted over $10,000 in trust deeds to operate their plantations.[46]

Because many of his loans were backed by liens or trust deeds, when farmers could not pay, Lowenburg could take over the land that had been pledged as collateral. At various times, Lowenburg held title to 27,000 acres. For example, in 1874, James and Richard McCoy, owners of the Galilee cotton plantation, refinanced their debt with Lowenburg as a trust deed for nearly $4,000. The loan was to be paid over three years at 10 percent interest, and a deed to a 975-acre parcel of land was to be held as security. The McCoys also mortgaged another parcel of land with Lowenburg, and they defaulted on both loans. Lowenburg acquired both parcels between 1875 and 1876.[47]

In addition to acquiring land when his customers defaulted, Lowenburg also had a knack for acquiring property that had been seized when their owners defaulted on their tax bills. For example, he bought the 2,570-acre Tekoa Plantation for $1,250, and he operated that plantation for four years before selling it to Julius Weis. In operating a plantation, Lowenburg and Weis were not alone, as sojourner Charles Wessolowsky observed that "here in this part of Mississippi, and in the 'sugar bowl' of Louisiana . . . our Israelites are drifting strongly toward being agriculturists, and a great many of them have a plantation of their own, and are rentors [landlords], and thus reproducing the occupation of our ancestors, and which seems to be to them a very prosperous business." Lowenburg also purchased at a sheriff's sale a one-acre Vidalia parcel that included a steam gin, which was used to process the cotton he purchased in Concordia Parish.[48]

Merchants could come to control land in other ways, including leasing directly from landowners. They could then work with croppers to cultivate the land, and the merchant could reap the proceeds. Merchants could also buy land in a direct sale. Together with Thomas Reber, Lowenburg purchased the Woodlawn parcel of land to develop it into a working-class subdivision, and he also purchased Clifton Plantation, dividing it into a more upscale subdivision called Clifton Heights.[49]

Isaac Lowenburg was not the only Natchez-area Jewish merchant who benefited from the financial backing of Meyer, Weis & Co. So, too, did Isaac Friedler, whose firm was located across the river from Natchez in Vidalia, Louisiana, and who made thousands of loans throughout the area. Friedler served essentially as a Concordia Parish agent for Julius Weis, acquiring goods on credit from him, managing properties, and sending cotton to Weis in New Orleans. Meyer, Weis, & Co. backed Friedler from the early days of his business.[50]

Isaac Friedler was born in Bohemia and came to the Natchez area after first arriving in New York in 1854. He commenced business across the river in Vidalia by early 1870, where his was one of the first businesses in that town, and he grew from modest means in the early 1870s to one of the strongest businesses in the Natchez area by the end of the decade. In 1873 his estimated worth was only $3,000 to $5,000, but that had increased to $10,000 the following year, suggesting that Friedler was not decimated in the immediate aftermath of the Panic of 1873. He owned his own store building and dwelling, "sells for cotton," was "close + saving money," and was good for his wants. He was "advancing to the Freedmen" heavily, and his estimated worth soon increased to $20,000. He was deemed "A1," continued "advancing heavily," and was making large collections. In 1877 he was called "one of our leading merchants," who was "good for all he wants." By the following year he held just under 400 merchant liens on plantations in Concordia Parish, totaling just under $40,000 in credit extended. When businesses to whom he loaned money could not repay their debts, he, like other merchants, periodically turned to the courts.[51]

Friedler made a profit in his mercantile business, and with those profits developed interests in cotton planting, both by himself and also in conjunction with Julius Weis's interests. Some of those opportunities were to be found in leasing plantations, where Friedler profited from the sale of supplies, and he also charged his tenants an average of 3 bales of cotton per lease, which he could then sell in New Orleans. In addition to leasing, Isaac Friedler also made money by purchasing land, including one parcel from Julius Weis in 1884 that was to be paid for partly in cash and the remainder in installments with interest. Friedler planned to operate a plantation supply store, and Weis provided Friedler with credit to purchase the goods he planned to sell. In return, Friedler promised to ship all cotton from the plantation to Weis's firm in New Orleans, and Weis would collect a 2.5 percent commission for selling the cotton, over and above the profits he made furnishing supplies to Friedler on credit.[52]

Meyer, Weis & Co. also worked with other businesses in the Natchez area, but not all of those relationships were as successful as those with Friedler and Lowenburg. For example, Abraham Isaacs, who opened a dry goods and grocery store in 1863 after the flow of commerce recommenced in the region, told Dun recorders in 1870 that he had a relationship with Meyer, Weis & Co. He started slowly, with a "business capacity" that was "not good," but he did have strong references that may have assisted him in getting the credit he needed. He had "parties in NY who know him by introduction from their friends in the south" who claimed that he was "well-spoken of as reliable + of [moderate] means."[53]

By 1870, Isaacs was focusing exclusively on dry goods, and his stock of goods had increased to $8,000. A Dun recorder couldn't account for the sudden increase of his stock "except on the grounds he has a silent partner" because "he certainly is not a [good business] man + does not bear a first rate reputation." He had a "large stock, but sells very little," and despite Isaacs's strong references, the suspicions proved correct. In 1871 Isaacs was "under indictment in Warren County charged with obtaining goods under false pretenses," and he was sued on three counts in Warren County Circuit Court.[54]

The postbellum Natchez dry goods house of Lehman & Smiley also had a long-standing business connection to Meyer, Weis & Co., which gave the firm credit when nobody else would. Just prior to the Panic of 1873, Lehman & Smiley had a small stock, and the partners both had "good reputations," but those reputations were less important than financial realities. After the panic the firm was "very shaky," and in June 1874 they "turned over everything to Meyer, Weis & Co. under deed of trust." At that point they apparently left for Union Church, Mississippi, where they had "no competition" and conducted a good business. Their success in Union Church apparently led to an extension from Meyer, Weis & Co., but a Dun agent doubted if any other creditors gave similar extensions. Some creditors extended them moderate lines, noted a Dun agent, and because business was good in Union Church, he believed that they may be able to pay if granted time. However this was apparently not the case, and by June 1875, Lehman & Smiley had "closed up."[55]

Before Lehman & Smiley closed, a recorder noted that the business worked with C. J. Meyer, a trustee and agent of Meyer, Weis & Co. Cassius (C. J.) Meyer "is a brother of the Meyers of the firm of Meyer, Weiss [*sic*] & Co. + is endorsed by them," noted a Dun recorder. He was also the nephew of Isaac Meyer, and he started small at Bowries Point, near Natchez, worth an estimated $5,000 in 1874. Despite the weight of his family's name, his "habits [were] bad," and he was considered "not trustworthy." He was also a store owner and planter in Concordia Parish, similarly "backed by Meyer, Weis & Co.," although he reportedly closed his store and continued planting. He continued his business in Vidalia, where he was worth an estimated $25,000 clear, and Meyer, Weis & Co. continued to back him. Despite his connections, C. J. Meyer's business ventures were not at the same level of success as those of his brothers Victor and Adolph.[56]

While Meyer, Weis & Co. may have worked with Natchez-area cotton businesses more closely than any other firm, it was also deeply enmeshed in the mercantile life of the Vicksburg and the Bends region more broadly. For example, Meyer, Weis & Co. worked with several businesses in Greenville, Mississippi, although seemingly with less success than some of its relationships in Natchez. That included Moses Seelig's general store, which gave a deed in trust to Meyer, Weis & Co. when it was struggling. Seelig's store was a branch of his main operation in Memphis, and at first an associate ran the Greenville branch, which was initially "doing well" and was considered "generally reliable." Seelig and his associate were keeping a good stock and seemed to be making money and doing well. However, in 1867 they were selling goods at such low prices that "they have created the impression they were preparing to break." They were "regarded with great suspicion," claimed a Dun agent, and "their honesty is doubted." Their problem, noted a credit reporter, was that they did not credit "prudently" the previous year, and as a result, they were "crippled" because of the money due to them. This was similar to scores of other businesses following the poor crop years of 1866–1867.[57]

The firm reorganized, and Moses Seelig took charge of the Greenville branch. Success followed immediately, and the business was soon considered "the best firm in town." One credit reporter proclaimed that "I don't know any Jews who stand so well. They are worthy + can get credit for any [amount] they may require." Yet while they had a good stock of goods, and a considerable amount of real estate, the firm "like all of our prudent merchants are contracting in place of expanding their business." Seelig's commission merchants had been carrying him over with advances, and after the Panic of 1873, things soured. Meyer, Weis & Co. held a mortgage or deed in trust upon his real estate, which it advertised for sale, and they "say that they cannot pay their debts at present." A Dun agent thought that, if creditors would "make a favorable extension, it [would] be well, if not they might as well sue now." Things did not end well for Seelig in Greenville, and by 1874 the firm was in bankruptcy and was also burned out by fire.[58]

Another Greenville firm with which Meyer, Weis & Co. worked was the general store of Joseph Radjesky, which had opened its doors by 1868. One agent claimed that he was doing about "as well as the majority of merchants" after the lean crop years, in that he was "much behind but is pressing his debtors, + appears to be paying up as fast as he can." In Radjesky's case, one credit reporter attributed his lack of success to working with freedmen. "His trade is almost exclusively with the negroes," claimed a Dun agent, who believed that "he has credited them imprudently, which will [probably] cost him most of his profits." Several months later he reiterated his belief that the "only trouble with him is that he [credits] the negroes too much + has great difficulty in collecting." Radjesky could never quite dig out from his debt, and in 1871 he was attached by Meyer, Weis & Co. He claimed that his assets were double his liabilities, and he was soon back on his feet, "making money." Yet he "failed altogether" in 1873, "leaving nothing" to his creditors.[59]

While some firms thrived or survived because of loans and mortgages from Meyer, Weis & Co., the failure of Marx Gensburger's Greenville general store was tied to the unwillingness of Meyer, Weis & Co. to provide credit. Gensburger was a "sober and [industrious man]" who started with a small trade, "principally for cash," and credit reporters "regard him good" for a limited amount of credit. He opened in the late 1860s, and although he seems to have survived the ups and downs of the economy, he only had $2,000 to $5,000 capital in his business in 1876, although he had real estate in his wife's name and was good for credit.[60]

Gensburger soon ran into trouble, stemming from a "misunderstanding" over a bill from Memphis for $168.25. To pay this bill, he made arrangements for an advance from Meyer, Weis & Co., and "out of this he expected to meet the other paper," but the loan apparently fell through.

Instead, to pay his debts, he could only rely on his collections, which he claimed would be "ample" enough to meet his obligations, but this was not the case. By May 1878 there were "suits now pending." Without a lifeline, Gensburger was in bankruptcy by November, and he was "insolvent" by 1879.[61]

Meyer, Weis & Co. worked with businesses elsewhere in Vicksburg and the Bends, backing, for example, Moses Kaufman, Jr.'s dry goods and grocery store in Port Gibson. By 1869 Kaufman was doing a "small business" with a stock of $2,000 to $3,000. He had "temperate" habits, but his character was "not yet established." Initially a relative had "furnished the means" for the business, but soon "his backers" were also Meyer, Weis & Co. Credit reporters understood the weight of his backers and noted that, with their support, "he will no doubt succeed." Yet without those endorsements, they believed, he would be "not [worth] a cent" and "not reliable" to credit. Nonetheless, despite his strong backing, Kaufman's business failed under mysterious circumstances. One recorder claimed in 1874 that Kaufman was "a thief." He was sued, and an attachment was issued against him, and by 1875 he was apparently out of business.[62]

In Waterproof, Louisiana, between Vicksburg and Natchez, the firm of Wise, Moss & Co. relied on credit from Meyer, Weis & Co. over the course of the 1870s. The journalist Edward King traveled through Waterproof, including it among a list of several "primitive settlements" and also noting ironically that Waterproof was "by no means proof against the water." There, David Wise opened for business in 1845, and he owned the property on which he conducted business. He owned a dwelling and "some slaves." Before long, he was the proprietor of a large, "lucrative" business," which was "on the increase," and he was held in the "fullest confidence." Wise had been "doing a good business up until the war," and while he was reported to have been in Natchez at the close of the conflict, he had reestablished his business by 1868. Like other business owners who survived the war but found themselves in debt, Wise put the business in somebody else's name until he could clear his own. While Charles Moss, a "smart, active German Jew," was on the masthead, Wise was "in the house at all times, ostensibly as a clerk, but owning the concern."[63]

The firm survived both the crop failures of 1866–1867 and the Panic of 1873. While the firm was "doing a very fair business," it "sustained heavy losses" in 1867, much like many merchants who were similarly "advancing to planters." Nevertheless, it survived, and by 1870 it was thought "that all claims have been settled." The firm was renamed Moss, Wise & Co., and Moss apparently gained an official ownership stake in the business. By 1870 the firm had an estimated capital of $40,000 to $50,000, sold at both retail and wholesale, and the partners were "safe for all they want." Moss, however, had real estate that was "heavily mortgaged." They also appear to have survived the economic shockwaves associated with the panic, and in 1874 a Dun agent estimated that they "do half the merchandise of this place." The firm was worth a clear $75,000 by 1874, and they were soon deemed the "largest firm in the place."[64]

In addition to the "principal business" in Waterproof, Moss, Wise & Co. owned a cotton plantation that Moss managed, and mortgages from Meyer, Weis Co. allowed them to purchase the land from which they derived income. In 1872 the firm owed $20,000 to Meyer, Weis & Co., a debt it appears to have repaid shortly after the Panic of 1873. Moss and Wise produced an estimated 725 bales in 1875, and in 1879, their only debt was the $18,000 they owed Meyer, Weis & Co. for a plantation that was valued between $28,000 and $30,000.[65]

While Meyer, Weis & Co. had a relationship in antebellum Bayou Sara with Charles Hoffman & Co., the firm had a less direct postbellum presence in West Feliciana Parish, providing credit to businesses, including Jacob Mitchell's general store. Prior to the war, Mitchell was clerking for and living with his uncle, Moses Mann, a prominent Bayou Sara merchant. In 1868, Mitchell opened a St. Francisville general store with "means furnished by Mann," and by 1870 he was the proprietor of a large store and was by then "backed" by Meyer, Weis & Co. of New Orleans.[66]

Jacob Mitchell was soon doing considerable business "in plantation supplies" and was "good at collections." At the start, the Dun recorder noted that he "trades with negroes," and within a couple of years, he was conducting a "very good" business, "chiefly with negroes." But Mitchell's business soon soured, and he developed a poor reputation—he was "not considered honest." Moreover, a recorder claimed that because he dealt with freedmen, his business was "a risky one," so he was recommended only for "limited" credit. Mitchell was in debt in 1873, and while his offer to settle in New Orleans at 25 cents on the dollar was accepted by his creditors, his wife took over the business and "succeeds him in everything except his bad character." She held the store in her own name, while her husband, who was "not in [good] repute," apparently operated the business.[67]

Thus Meyer, Weis & Co. had an extensive footprint in towns along the Mississippi River, supplying credit to firms in all of the prominent towns—Greenville, Vicksburg, Natchez, Port Gibson, and Bayou Sara. But the firm also worked with businesses elsewhere in the Gulf South—including those along the Red River. In Shreveport, for example, Simon and Herman Herold's dry goods, grocery, and general store had only one creditor for a time—Meyer, Weis & Co. The Herold brothers had opened for business by 1866 and were soon "doing well"; they were estimated to be worth $50,000. They soon began to carry on business at separate stores in their own names, and sales between July 1865 and April 1866 totaled over $27,000 and $20,000, respectively.[68]

Simon Herold's part of the business was "thriving," tied largely to the support he received from Meyer, Weis & Co. Just prior to the Panic of 1873 he was doing a "brisk" business with a "large stock of goods on hand," and he had an estimated worth of $65,000 clear. Simon Herald's focus was on the retail cash business, which may have helped him through the crop failures. He was assumed to be good for his debts if he purchased on credit, explained a Dun agent. Yet he did experience some bumps in the road, and he soon found himself in trouble. Following the Panic of 1873, a Dun recorder expected that he "will lose a good deal this year." That is exactly what happened. Meyer, Weis & Co. of New Orleans reported that they were Herold's only creditor, and that he would have the opportunity to work out of his debt. Shortly thereafter, Simon claimed to have "already reduced indebtedness to Meyer, Weis & Co." from the $55,000 that he owed them. He claimed that his assets included real estate "worth all that it is mortgaged for," his stock, and "accounts receivable for supplies furnished to farmers," which he anticipated would pay the rest of his debts. Despite these assets, Simon Herold couldn't quite get ahead. He continued to struggle into 1878, but a credit reporter noted that he "has friends who appear to keep him up." This support helped Herold to remain in business through 1900.[69]

Downriver in Alexandria, Meyer, Weis & Co. loaned money to B. Weil & Bro. and held liens on its property. Benjamin Weil and his brothers John and Edward were initially "pedlars [sic], birds of passage," comparable, he believed, to most of the Jews in the parish. "One day here + another in another place." The first extant record of the brothers as peddlers was in 1851, and they continued to peddle "with a wagon + 2 horses" throughout the parish. The Weil brothers survived the war, reopening their store in November 1865, and they were considered "shrewd active and remarkably attentive to" their business. They soon managed to have a "good stock" worth $15,000 to $20,000 and conducted a "good [business] for this place." At the beginning of 1868, while farmers were still struggling with poor crop years, the Weil brothers "sell for cash principally."[70]

But John Weil was "said to be in debt quite heavily," with "debts contracted before the war," and the firm was never quite able to get out from under the debts with which it was saddled. By 1867 it had compromised on most of its obligations at 25 to 50 cents on the dollar, yet it continued to "owe heavily" and had been sued by New Orleans and New York houses. But it had "obtained an extension" from its creditors. It was able to settle with New Orleans creditors because Meyer, Weis & Co. of New Orleans "furnish the money" to pay twenty cents cash and fifteen cents on its own paper, with Meyer, Weis & Co. "having mortgages on all" of its property. Despite the financial support from Meyer, Weis & Co., the firm was "in bad repute here" in 1870, and the business changed hands shortly thereafter.[71]

Thus Meyer, Weis & Co. underscores the importance of how ethnic ties helped to distribute global investment throughout the postbellum economy. Just as the top tier of the economic network required trust, which was largely predicated on ethnicity, in order to effectively funnel credit from international banks to the cotton businesses of the Gulf South, so, too, did the bottom tier of the network. The Jewish wholesalers and commission houses that worked with firms such as Lehman Brothers then extended credit to scores of smaller general stores throughout the region, many of which were operated by Jews. Of course, as we have seen, Jewish firms also worked with non-Jewish firms, but ethnic networks acted as a competitive advantage for Jewish merchants in the postbellum Gulf South. However, as we will see in the following chapter, that advantage would not last long.

6

The End of the Niche Economy

By the late nineteenth century, changes to the cotton industry meant that the Jewish economic niche was no longer as important as it once was. Structural changes to global capitalism, including vertical integration and the rise of investment banking, changed the nature of credit and lending. Networks of trust, which had been a competitive advantage for ethnic minorities in the industry, began to lose their importance, overtaken by more impersonal cotton exchanges and state bureaucracy. Those who could adapt to these changes might be able to thrive, but those who could not found themselves increasingly marginalized from their once commanding positions.

As the nature of global capitalism was changing, other global and local forces also hastened the demise of this niche economy. The Gulf South had once held a near stranglehold on the cotton that fueled the European economy, but the world's thirst for white gold pushed the European powers toward colonial expansion to find cheaper places across the globe to produce it. Moreover, floods and invasive species ravaged cotton crops in the Gulf South, and a spate of anti-Jewish violence took direct aim at the Jewish niche economy. All of this meant that in much the same manner that structural factors created the niche economy, they also brought it to an end.

* * *

By the late nineteenth century, the economic system in which the global cotton economy functioned was changing, signaling the decline of the merchant who had once been so central to it. In the merchants' place, the rise of investment banking changed the contours of international finance, as a small number of firms became key providers of credit. Investment banks, which had fantastic amounts of capital at their disposal, financed the economy's diversification beyond agriculture and trade and into industry and manufacturing. Cotton and other crude materials dropped from 27 percent of New York's exports in 1860 to 11 percent in 1900, while manufactured goods increased from 24 percent to 38 percent over the same time. Insurance and railroad financing came into the orbit of investment banks, which facilitated the flow of capital into many different sectors. Investment banks became the prime liaisons between industrialists and investors, who now had new options for their capital.[1]

This shift from agriculture to manufacturing and industry, together with the rise of investment banking, portended trouble for Southern Jewish merchants. The manufacturing sector now charted the nation's economic course. As new opportunities shifted money out of the cotton industry, merchants began to deal more in industrial goods than in agricultural commodities, bringing them in closer alignment with the nation's manufacturing sector. Merchants were also no longer the prime sources of credit. The New York Stock Exchange became an important means of raising capital, bypassing merchants in the process.[2]

Further minimizing the role of the merchant was the rise of cotton exchanges, which fostered a system of financing that neutralized the competitive advantage of ethnic networks. Whereas transactions had once rested on the familiarity and level of trust between the parties, cotton exchanges now made those transactions impersonal. The exchanges upended the reliance on personal connections forged through an ethnic economy, and the role of merchants—including Jewish merchants—declined.[3]

The New York Cotton Exchange opened in 1870, joined by exchanges around the world in places such as New Orleans, Vicksburg, Le Havre, Bremen, Osaka, Shanghai, São Paolo, Bombay, and Alexandria. Exchanges created a single "world price" for cotton, which was accessible around the globe, and they also made futures trading the standard for cotton transactions. Futures allowed buyers and sellers to trade cotton in advance of when it was harvested or needed in factories. Under this system, factory owners would agree to buy cotton in the future at a particular price, helping them to plan their budgets and calendars—all while providing farmers with the money necessary to grow and harvest their crops. Traders and speculators would also utilize the cotton exchange, but their interest was to gamble on which direction the market would go, trading in the right to buy cotton without actually trading in the cotton

itself. For example, if the cotton crop was proceeding apace but a speculator heard a rumor of a drought or pest that would limit the amount of
cotton produced and thus raise the price of cotton later in the season, he
could speculatively lock in at the current price for future delivery. If his
read of the market was correct, he could then sell the futures contract
for a profit.[4]

Some Jewish merchants were involved in cotton exchanges, serving
on the boards of directors and in other capacities. Mayer Lehman, for
example, was a founder of the New York Cotton Exchange, and Lehman
Brothers successfully transitioned into this new global economic milieu
in part through pioneering cotton futures. The Lehmans conducted a
large business "advancing on consignment and buying on order," noted
a Dun recorder, and became "large operators in future contracts," making "advances on a large amount of cotton to be held out of this market."
They were also involved in a Georgia lawsuit that tested the validity of
futures, and the suit was decided in their favor. While the New York
branch conducted a good deal of business on futures, the New Orleans
house also did to a moderate extent.[5]

Ethnic networks also became less important as the expansion of cotton took on a more national character, and key elements moved from
the domain of merchants to that of the state. Whereas merchants once
forged the international trade networks that fueled the cotton economy,
these networks became less important as industrial capital became more
important to states, and manufacturers and statesmen viewed these
networks as a threat to their hegemony. The state also took over other
functions that had once been the domain of the merchant—Liverpool
merchants, for example, had previously created standards that defined
quality and benchmark standards. The state also moved into statistics
gathering; from 1863 onward, the U.S. Department of Agriculture reported monthly on cotton production. In 1894 it began to publish the
Agricultural Yearbook, and by 1900, reports were collected by 41 full-
time agents, their 7,500 assistants, 2,400 volunteer county correspondents, their 6,800 assistants, and finally 40,000 volunteer township or
district correspondents. The Census Bureau, too, began to gather cotton-
related data.[6]

The state's role, however, went beyond statistics gathering, as it was
deeply invested in the flow of cotton for social stability and its own

survival. The state's role pushed into new contract laws and property rights, but of particular importance was the ways in which the changing cotton economy shaped colonial and imperial decisions and strategies and how those decisions marginalized the United States in global cotton production. Cotton prices rose 121 percent between 1898 and 1913, and one observer was afraid "to contemplate the consequences which would ensue if anything should again prevent Lancashire from obtaining her share of the cotton crop of America." Fearing these rising prices, European states believed that cotton production on land dominated by imperial states and colonial expansion could satisfy the need for raw material independence and could also help to keep prices down. Colonial expansion and cotton production became inextricably linked, as traditional cotton powers France, Britain, and the United States were joined by Russia, Japan, Italy, Germany, Portugal, and Belgium.[7]

This push for new frontiers marginalized areas such as the Gulf South that were once central to the industry. While the United States in 1860 had a stranglehold on cotton production, the rise of cotton production elsewhere around the globe left the United States with only about 14 percent of the world's cotton production in 2014. Even spindles and looms moved away from Europe and the United States and spread throughout these new regions. The United Kingdom's share of cotton manufacturing declined from 61 percent in 1860 to 43 percent in 1900 and declined again to 34 percent by 1930. Cotton factories in New England collapsed by the 1920s. With the decline of Europe and the United States in the cotton economy came a concurrent rise in growing and manufacturing elsewhere. Brazil saw a rapid rise after the 1890s, and Japan became a particularly important cotton manufacturing center over the course of several decades. India was also on the rise, particularly Bombay and Ahmedabad. Egypt, however, was slow to become a manufacturing center despite its growth of cotton.[8]

While these forces are clear with the benefit of hindsight, the ways in which the "invisible hand" of global capitalism shaped the fate of the cotton industry were not always clear to contemporaries on the rural front lines. This was true worldwide, not just in the Gulf South. For example, the cotton commissioner for the British Indian province of Berar noted in 1868 that "the great rise and then the sudden fall in the price of cotton, and the constant fluctuations in the market, by which the culti-vator, in even the most remote of the cotton-growing villages is affected, has led some of the less intelligent to regard cotton not only with dis-trust, but with a certain degree of awe." He noted that, in more distant areas, people couldn't understand why prices fluctuated so much and that they "find some difficulty in realizing the present state of the trade, and the fact that, by means of the Electric Telegraph, the throbbings of the pulse of the Home markets communicate themselves instantly to Hingunghat and other trade centres throughout the country." Instead, the commissioner noted that these farmers believed that price fluctua-tions were a result of "luck," "war," "kindness of a paternal Government," or that "the Queen had given every one in England new clothes" because of the Prince's wedding.[9]

Nonetheless, with cheaper production around the world came in-creased pressure to produce cotton more cheaply in the Gulf South. Many realized that commissions paid to cotton brokers and importers drove up prices for their cotton, making it less competitive in world markets. Margins for merchants were slashed, as merchants and im-porters realized that they would need to drive down transaction costs through improved efficiencies. As the railroad and other forces made it easier to connect growers to markets, transaction costs dropped—one estimate suggested that they dropped by 2.5 percent between 1870 and 1886. In order to make up for lower profits, merchants had to secure a larger share of the trade, which led to consolidation that pressed smaller businesses.[10]

Other broader forces helped to marginalize cotton merchants, includ-ing changes to banking and purchasing. Merchants had been in many cases the sole source of capital to fuel the cotton industry as it recovered from the war, but new banking facilities challenged that role. St. Fran-cisville, for example, was by 1908 home to The People's Bank, with an advertised capital of $50,000 and with Jews, including M. Wolf and Ben Mann, among its directors. In 1915, the Bank of Commerce was orga-nized in St. Francisville, and the *True Democrat* noted that on the day the bank opened it had 30 depositors, and after its first month it had 128, and its capital stock was soon worth $15,000. New modes of purchas-ing goods also bypassed merchants. The postal service's introduction of rural free delivery in 1896 and of parcel post in 1913 helped mail-order companies such as Sears-Roebuck and Montgomery Ward to supply the goods that were once available only through local merchants.[11]

These broader changes, which stepped on the traditional role of Southern Jewish merchants, pushed merchants to diversify. Julius Weis and Isaac Meyer sold their interests in Meyer, Weis & Co. to Meyer's nephews Victor and Adolph, and to Meyer's son Sol, after the New Orleans branch handled what Weis estimated to be 1 million bales of cotton. With the loss of the original partners, the new firm became known as V. & A. Meyer, and for a time it maintained the strength of its predecessor, receiving an AAA1 rating from Dun in 1890. V. & A. Meyer also bought and sold foreign exchange for the Lazard Frères account in New Orleans, a role that they held until the dissolution of their firm in the early 1890s. Meanwhile, when Julius Weis returned from Europe and reentered the cotton commission business in New Orleans, he took over the role of buying and selling foreign exchange for Lazard Frères. When Lazard asked him to take over the role after the dissolution of V. & A. Meyer, Weis recalled, "I told them I had never had any experience in that line of business," but after due consideration, he "decided to undertake the business." The diversification of his business was lucrative, as at one point he estimated that he grossed $50 million in business with Lazard. Weis's former partner, Isaias Meyer, also diversified beyond his mercantile interests by investing in a silk factory.[12]

While global forces were challenging the niche economy, so, too, were more localized forces. Environmental factors such as flooding played a key role in the decline of cotton in the Gulf South, and perhaps nowhere was this more evident than in Bayou Sara, which was wiped completely off the map. Virtually no trace of the town remains today. Bayou Sara had been a bustling cotton town, and it was home to Julius Freyhan & Co., the largest merchant in West Feliciana Parish. Freyhan had amassed a significant amount of wealth during his tenure in business, and he moved to New Orleans in the 1880s, where he purchased a home that was described as "an immense rambling house, painted white, with a red roof and a three-story tower, bays, covered porches, with clipped topiaries in urns and towering palm trees." Freyhan belonged to the New Orleans Cotton Exchange, and much like Julius Weis and others, he diversified, moving into ventures other than his general merchandise store in West Feliciana Parish. This, in particular, included his central role at

Lehman Brothers' Lane Cotton Mills in New Orleans. Julius Freyhan died in 1904 at the age of seventy-two, while on "his usual summer trip" to New York.[13]

When Freyhan left West Feliciana Parish for New Orleans in the late 1880s, he left his business in the hands of his brothers-in-law, Morris and Emanuel Wolf, and upon Freyhan's death, the firm was renamed M. & E. Wolf. Initially M. & E. Wolf played the same role in Bayou Sara as it had during Freyhan's lifetime. As late as 1917 it continued to engage "in buying the products of the plantation," particularly cotton, and it also supplied farmers with "a large stock of goods so broad in its scope as to cover the needs of the home and the plantation." This included furniture, men's and women's clothing, as well departments for glassware and china. There was a grocery store "where one could buy champagne, other fine wines and all the delicacies of the time, including smoked mackerel, kippered herring and anything the appetite desired." In addition to luxury foods, they also stocked goods such as flour, and "during the Christmas season there were toys for the children and gifts for the grown ups." The firm did not stray far from its roots, as it also "stocked supplies for the farmer." M. & E. Wolf also had a "modern cotton gin," and "it frequently happens that a country man will bring his cotton here, have it ginned, sell it and the seed to M. & E. Wolf, buy his necessary supplies and return home without having dealings with another firm."[14]

While the firm remained one of the strongest in town, its rating from R.G. Dun steadily declined in the early twentieth century, alongside the fortunes of Bayou Sara itself. Major fires tore through Bayou Sara in 1886 and 1888, and the growth of the railroads meant that the river was no longer the prime cotton thoroughfare that it once was. Disease was also a problem; during one particular outbreak, A. Mann was accused of violating the town's quarantine. According to one report, "a lot of dry goods, concealed in sack and moss, was crossed over the river surreptitiously from Red store, Point Coupee, by the business house of M. Mann, Bayou Sara." Further, it was "alleged that these goods were landed in Point Coupee from New Orleans to avoid our quarantine restrictions." In response to this violation, "Mr. A. Mann, business manager and representative of his brother Moses Mann, was promptly arrested and fined $25 for a willful violation of the quarantine regulations of Bayou Sara." The stakes were high during the disease outbreaks in the region. One newspaper editor opined that "there is no standard by which to measure the sordidness which would prompt a man in times like these, with a dread disease staring us in the face, for the sake of a few paltry dollars, thus to endanger the introduction of the pestilence in our midst. Such acts should be promptly condemned and amply punished."[15]

While these factors challenged Bayou Sara, the most critical problem that the town faced was flooding, as the Mississippi River frequently swelled to unsustainable levels and residents were left to hope that their levee system held. Sometimes it did, and sometimes high water was too much. "All through its existence," claimed one newspaper, Bayou Sara "had many bouts with the river, and always came off the loser. Residents moved up the hill [to St. Francisville] and left their homes to the mercy of the river. When it receded, they returned. Merchants carried on their business by placing their goods on the top shelves, with platforms to stand on except when the water was too deep."[16]

As we have seen, the Mississippi overtopped its banks shortly after the Civil War, leaving W. G. Schafer and fellow residents to clean up the mess. Mississippi River floods continued to be a danger, and a *New York Times* correspondent reported in 1890 that "the levee in front of Bayou Sara broke early this morning and the whole town is under water two to seven feet deep. Several buildings were washed off their foundations, but no lives were lost." Another account noted that, in Bayou Sara, "the water rose to the first floors of all the stores and houses, put a stop to all business, and compelled an abandonment of the town by the majority of the population." As soon as Bayou Sara recovered, the town again faced the onslaught of the Mississippi River. In 1892 the *Times* reported on its front page that the town was under four to eleven feet of water after another levee break. The *True Democrat* noted that flood relief was necessary, and "J. Freyhan and Company shipped 10,000 lbs. of meat, filling an order for that amount."[17]

As flood after flood slowly washed away the once flourishing river port, townspeople were forced to confront Bayou Sara's mortality. In 1909, President William Howard Taft was traveling down the Mississippi River toward Bayou Sara. A crowd gathered at the ferry landing as he approached, and as he pulled near, the *True Democrat* reported that "Taft came from within and stood near the railing." After drifting past the landing, the boat backed up, and "President Taft all the while was in full view." As the boat docked at 8:35 P.M., the onlookers quieted as the governor introduced Taft to the crowd, which was followed by a "loud and enthusiastic welcome." The president made a "gracious bow" to the crowd, which was accompanied by a twenty-one-gun salute. Had it been three decades earlier, Taft may have gotten off the boat at what was once a critically important mercantile hub. Some in the crowd believed that he would do just that, but their hopes may have been colored by what the town had been, rather than what it then was. Rather than stopping, Taft's "parade continued down the great river." Just as President Taft passed by Bayou Sara, so, too, did the global cotton economy.[18]

The levee broke again in 1912, and as a result of the rushing water through what became a one-hundred-foot breach, Bayou Sara was again left in shambles. "The Bayou Sara post-office building was in the original path of the waters and it was torn from its foundation and carried across to Principal St.," reported the *True Democrat*. "The kitchen of the Burton Hotel was washed off, and Szabo's saloon was carried up the street near the Irvine residence. Smaller houses were twisted and turned, while light buildings and outhouses of every description immediately entered the swim."[19]

Figure 6.1. "A Flooded Bayou Sara." Image courtesy of the Louisiana State University Special Collections, Elizabeth Dart Collection (121:9, box 3).

Figure 6.2. "Man Surveying a Flooded Bayou Sara." Image courtesy of the Louisiana State University Special Collections, Elizabeth Dart Collection (121:9, box 3).

The town finally succumbed to the river in 1925, much as Grand Gulf, Mississippi, and the antebellum location of Greenville, Mississippi, had done previously. Most of Bayou Sara's remaining residents moved up the hill to St. Francisville, abandoning the river port that had been so important for a good portion of the nineteenth century. In 1926, Louisiana removed Bayou Sara's charter, and, according to one observer, "The little ghost town became a wilderness of willows." The post office was removed around 1928, and when there was no longer a town to maintain the bayou levee, "succeeding floods swept away the houses that were left to show where Bayou Sara had been." One observer succinctly declared that "the Mississippi built the town and the Mississippi destroyed it."[20]

While floods doomed Bayou Sara, the boll weevil also made it a far less attractive investment for merchants and financiers. The boll weevil was a small beetle, approximately a quarter of an inch long, with a noticeable snout. The pest was native to Central America and Mexico, and it entered the United States in 1892, advancing between 40 and 160 miles each year. It soon reached Louisiana, spread to Mississippi by 1907, and by 1909 it had infested the southwestern third of the state. The pest fed primarily on cotton plants, and early in the season it would eat leaves. Later in the season, female weevils would lay eggs in cotton bolls, and they could produce 100–300 eggs in a season. Once the larvae grew to adulthood, the cotton boll would fall to the ground, and although damage could be mitigated by dry, hot summers, the boll weevil ultimately devastated the region's cotton supply. Cotton production declined precipitously, and in Adams County it took six acres of land to produce a single bale of cotton.[21]

The coming of the boll weevil undermined the profitability of merchants, so residents were left without the traditional sources of credit upon which they had come to rely. The *True Democrat* lamented that, "since the ravages of the boll weevil . . . agriculture has been at more or less of a standstill." The article continued to note that "with the boll weevil came hard times. The merchant refused credit and the farmer found that he had to depend upon his soil to raise the actual necessities of life which he had before bought from the country store on credit." M. & E. Wolf, the successor to Julius Freyhan & Co., was extremely cautious in lending after the arrival of the pest. "With the advent of the boll weevil," noted the *True Democrat*, "the business of this firm was restricted to the confines dictated by a conservative policy, for at no time has wild-catting been participated in or encouraged by its proprietors." The newspaper also claimed that, rather than merchants, by 1917 the Bank of Commerce was the institution doing the most for the "financial rehabilitation of West Feliciana, following the disasters that resulted from the invasion of the boll weevil."[22]

Meanwhile, upriver in Natchez, which was built high upon a bluff, the environmental factor that decimated the cotton industry was not flooding as much as it was the boll weevil, which devastated Natchez upon its arrival. A rash of suicides followed the boll weevil's invasion, as prominent planters and merchants took their own lives, unable to cope with the new reality. The building of grand homes ceased after 1908, the city stopped its annual Mardi Gras celebrations in 1909, and already by 1914 the city's merchant class had been reduced by one-third.[23]

The boll weevil did not by itself destroy Natchez's cotton economy. Alongside the global changes that left the town's merchants struggling, agricultural productivity was already declining by the 1890s. Some tried to diversify beyond cotton. Merchant suicides and breakdowns occurred in the 1890s as well, before the boll weevil infestation, and when many of the Reconstruction-era opportunities for freedpeople were rolled back and racism became even more firmly entrenched, many freedmen began to leave the area, in search of new opportunities. Thus the boll weevil was only the final straw in a process that had been under way for two decades.[24]

While environmental factors cut into the South's competitive advantage, and changes to global capitalism minimized the importance of trust and marginalized merchants—particularly the Jewish merchants who relied on ethnic networks—a spate of anti-Jewish violence challenged the idea that the Gulf South was a safe place of opportunity for Jewish merchants. Much of the violence that overtook the region was rooted in economics, but not all of it targeted Jews. Whitecaps, for example, were often motivated by economics, and they used such terror tactics as night riding to intimidate their victims. While they targeted mostly blacks, some of their victims were Jews, and as we shall see, they targeted them specifically because of their ethnic networks and niche economy.[25]

"In some rural portions of the South a prejudice still exists against Jewish merchants among a certain shiftless class of the community," opined the *American Israelite* in 1887. "In several parishes of this State this feeling has latterly manifested itself somewhat violently." In one instance in West Carroll Parish, "the popular feeling" against merchant Simon Witkowski "broke out into actual violence, resulting in the killing of one man and in driving Witkowski from the parish." The *American Hebrew* claimed that the alleged cause of the violence was that Witkowski "had ground down those who were indebted to him, and had pursued a very hard policy in dealing with them."[26]

This was followed shortly thereafter by a similar incident in Evergreen, Louisiana, where perpetrators rode up to one Jewish store "and riddled it and the surrounding fence with bullets." The following day, that store owner and another Jewish store owner in nearby Cottonport were "served with notices calling attention to what the mob had done, and warning them to leave the parish at once if they wished to save their lives." One of those victims was Felix Bauer, whose major supplier was V. & A. Meyer, the successor firm to Meyer, Weis & Co. Those notices consisted of public proclamations that declared that the

Map 6.1. Incidents of anti-Jewish violence

Note: Circles represent direct incidents of violence against Jewish merchants. Triangles represent indirect incidents of violence against Jewish merchants.

perpetrators "wanted no more Jews among them, and therefore advised all Jews to leave the parish by April, under penalty of death." Correspondents from the *American Israelite* understood that backlash against the Jewish niche economy was a key motivator of these crimes, surmising that "business jealousy, coupled, probably, with some of that anti-Semitic feeling which so often shows itself in rural sections," fueled the incidents.[27]

The violence continued unabated. In 1889, Delhi, Louisiana, was the site of more violence against Jewish merchants, when "the stores of several Jewish merchants were attacked by an armed mob and fired into." The mob, according to one source, "numbered from thirty to one hundred men and fired fully one thousand shots that night, not at persons, but into the stores of Jewish merchants." About fifty shots were fired at one store, "smashing the glass front to atoms," and another store's "windows were battered and broken with bricks." Another account claimed that in one store, lamps and windows were broken, "and brickbats were used as well as bullets." Residents awoke the next morning fearing "that a quarrel or feud was being settled by loss of life," but instead, "they were astonished to hear that the Jewish houses of business except one had been fired upon and their doors shattered by bullets." In an era where Russian pogroms against East European Jews were frequent, the *Jewish Messenger* incredulously noted that "the incident did not occur in Russia, but in hospitable Louisiana."[28]

Local and national newspapers made it clear that this was not a random crime against merchants but specifically targeted Jews. The *Morning Star*, a Catholic weekly, called the Delhi attack a "war on the Jew," and the *Baton Rouge Advocate* called it a "Crusade against the Jews." The New Orleans *Times Picayune* claimed that "the trouble has been brewing for some time, although the Jews have been established in Delhi during many years and this is the first outbreak of prejudice." But while Jews were clearly the target, their mercantile activity was in the crosshairs of the perpetrators. The *Daily Picayune* argued that "business jealousy was at the bottom of the whole affair," and the *American Israelite* also attributed "the cause of the disturbance to business rivalry, as the Jews were monopolizing the trade of the town," some claimed.[29]

While Jewish merchants were the target, residents were apparently frustrated that Jewish mercantile establishments employed Jewish clerks rather than non-Jews from Delhi. "The storm which burst upon the Jews has long been brewing," claimed one local woman, who noted that

> there has been a feeling, even among their best friends, that they made no adequate recompense for the immense patronage bestowed upon them. The young men growing up in the town and vicinity, if worthy, would naturally expect to find employment here, but until the Monday following the riot, not one of these within the last ten years has ever obtained a situation in a Jewish store."

Instead, she argued, "they have consequently labored in the fields and shops, or sought employment elsewhere."[30]

The claim that Jewish clerks were the root of the violence was echoed by other sources, including one Delhi Jewish clerk who claimed that "the clerks left because their employers were told they must employ people born and bred there to get along." The Catholic *Morning Star* noted how "anonymous parties" around Delhi "have again, in a most threatening manner, notified the Jewish merchants of that place to discharge their Hebrew clerks and employ Gentiles, or immediately remove their effects and themselves from the parish. The only reason assigned is that it is not proper that business should be done among their people, 'and the Jew take all the money.'" Soon Jewish clerks began to leave, and shortly thereafter, claimed an observer, "the Jewish merchants commissioned a citizen to obtain American clerks for them." The power of this statement—that Jews were not American—speaks volumes.[31]

The violence continued to spread. "More Anti-Jewish Outbreaks," proclaimed the *Daily Advocate*, as "Lake Providence has followed the example of Delhi, and made war upon the Jews." In Lake Providence, located along the Mississippi River between Greenville and Vicksburg, "outlaws shot into stores and posted placards warning the Jews to leave before Jan. 1st." Residents claimed that the stores of two Jews, including the president of their police jury, "were fired into . . . by a few lawless men." One store owner claimed that "about twenty shots were fired into his dwelling near midnight, one of them passing nearly over the bed where his family lay. There were thirty-five empty rifle shells found on the levee this morning in front of their store." The other store owner who was victimized had his store shot into about fifty times. The attackers then apparently referenced the Delhi shootings, as a placard was placed on site reading "No Jews after the 1ˢᵗ of January. A Delhi warning of fire and lead will make you leave."[32]

These instances of violence continued, although in some instances the motivation for violence was not clearly linked to mercantile activity. In 1895, the *Jewish Spectator* reported "dynamite being used in Bayou Sara, La., against Jewish residences, and of threats to various Jews in that city to remove from buildings owned by other Jews." In Tigerville, Louisiana, William Vorhees murdered Solomon Ellenstein after demanding to see his business license. In Greenville, Mississippi, prominent Jewish merchant Lee Hexter was shot by Caleb Stone, although it was not considered serious. Also in Greenville, a prominent citizen, Lewis Taylor Rucks, was killed when he intervened on behalf of Herman Gottschalk, a Jewish night clerk of a hotel. In Port Gibson, Jewish sojourner Charles Wessolowsky noted that "in one case the murderer and in another the murdered party were Israelites." According to one account, robbers stormed Jacob Simon's store in Breaux Bridge, Louisiana, murdering him and then "made away with the booty."[33]

With violent outbursts and no concrete action to prevent it or to bring perpetrators to justice, Jews begrudgingly began to accept that the hospitable environment that had cradled their ethnic economy was waning. "For a long time we were incredulous concerning the rumors we heard of lawlessness against the Jewish merchants of several towns of Louisiana," noted the *American Hebrew*, whose editors "hesitated in believing" it and hoped that it "would at least be only temporary." However, the editors soon admitted that "the trouble is more serious than we supposed." The editors linked this violence to a broader American turn toward anti-Semitism, including social exclusion, yet they still argued that there were more hospitable places for Jews than the Gulf South. "The merchants have lost heart at the failure to secure protection for their property, safety for their lives, and security for their rights, and have resolved to move from the neighborhood, close up their business, and seek elsewhere the opportunity to earn a livelihood. They will, undoubtedly, have no difficulty in finding at once a place where they can make a living in peace."[34]

All of these factors—violence, environmental challenges, and changes to global capitalism that neutralized the competitive advantage of networks—spelled doom for the Jewish niche economy. It did not, however, mean the end of Jews or the Jewish general store in Southern towns—the "Jew Store" remained relevant and was an iconic image well into the twentieth century. Moreover, Jews continued in roles of social and economic prominence, serving as mayors and acting as philanthropists to larger causes within the communities in which they lived. But as the importance of ethnic networks waned along with the industry that had once shaped global capitalism, some Jews began to leave the area. The size of the Jewish community of Natchez peaked with the arrival of the boll weevil, and its population never recovered from the emigration that followed. In West Feliciana Parish, one observer highlighted in 1894 "the exodus of Jewish people that has taken place within the last few years," prophesizing that "in a very few years hence Bayou Sara will be nearly depopulated of her Jewish inhabitants." That onlooker noted that "many have gone to large cities, drawn thither by the educational advantages for their children, while others have removed, to be near relatives and friends. I do not intend this as a prophesy, but 'Coming events cast their shadows before.'"[35]

Other Jewish merchants successfully transitioned into new sectors of the economy, led by firms such as Lehman Brothers, J. W. Seligman & Co., and Lazard Frères, which all diversified into new forms of banking, manufacturing, and industry. Lehman Brothers, for example, transitioned away from a sole focus on cotton and moved more toward investment banking. The firm increasingly turned its attention to a range of commodities, buying and selling petroleum, coffee, and sugar. "Now inclining more to Banking," Lehman Brothers moved its New York offices to Exchange Place.[36]

These larger firms ushered some of the most successful cotton merchants into the new global economy along with them, highlighting how ethnic ties continued into new economic sectors. Julius Freyhan moved to New Orleans and transitioned into another side of the cotton industry by operating Lehman Brothers' Lane Cotton Mills in New Orleans. Isaias Meyer remained in New York, where he invested in Pelgram & Meyer, a successful New Jersey silk factory, and through that business he continued his financial relationship with Lehman Brothers. And Julius

Weis began to buy and sell foreign exchange for Lazard Frères in New Orleans.[37] But even as these former cotton merchants transitioned into a new global economy, their stories are emblematic of what once was—a Jewish niche economy in the cotton industry that was nurtured by structural factors and fueled by ethnic networks.

Conclusion

Jewish merchants cultivated an economic niche in the Reconstruction-era cotton economy that catapulted them into the forefront of the American economy and global capitalism. With conditions ripe for success, they drew upon ethnic networks of trust that enabled their businesses to survive during market downturns by ensuring access to credit. Jews clustered in the cotton industry, and as a staggering number of Jews operated dry goods and general stores, Jews became deeply enmeshed in the nation's—and perhaps the world's—most important industry.

That immersion proved significant. Jewish success in the cotton trade fostered a golden era for Southern Jews during the roughly two decades following the Civil War. It redrew the American Jewish map, as scores of Jewish merchants settled in market towns located in regions of high cotton production and marketing. Jews also concentrated in towns that sat along river or rail lines offering easy transportation access for cotton shipments. The internal dynamics of Jewish communities also changed significantly, as Jews transitioned from a wandering, peddling-based lifestyle to one that featured more stable Jewish communities with burial grounds, synagogues, and social organizations. Success in the cotton trade redefined the terms of Jewish integration in the cities and towns in which Jews lived, and Jews reshaped the growth and development of the towns themselves.

The Jewish niche economy in the cotton industry also provides an excellent lens through which to see more broadly how niche economies emerge and function and how ethnicity has long mattered in the development of global capitalism. It demonstrates the importance of structural and environmental forces within capitalism, particularly within micro economies. In the case of Jewish merchants, those structural factors began in the antebellum years, when a core group graduated from peddlers to shopkeepers in interior towns, accumulating the capital necessary for upward mobility. At the same time that merchants were reaching prominence, their stores were becoming more important to the cotton industry, foreshadowing on a smaller scale the credit system that would become widespread in the postbellum years. The same Jewish store owners were also cultivating network connections with the Northeast. All of these factors meant that on the eve of the Civil War, Jews stood fortuitously positioned in an economic sector poised to shape global capitalism.

Structural factors continued to play an essential role in the emergence of the niche economy after the outbreak of Civil War. Although the Union's economic blockade threatened to upend Jews' toehold in the cotton industry, global demand for cotton ensured that they would still have the opportunity to maintain their livelihoods. Smuggling and blockade-running became particularly lucrative, and a dearth of goods in the South made clandestine trade all the more attractive; profit margins proved immense at both ends of the transaction. The demand for goods also made legal trade within the South extraordinarily lucrative. External circumstances continued to create opportunities for merchants after Grant's victory at Vicksburg, as the legal cotton trade resumed amidst tremendous global demand. The world's thirst for cotton allowed many merchants not only to survive the war but also to thrive.

After the war, structural forces continued to create a milieu conducive to Jewish success in the cotton industry. Cotton factors, who had been central to financing the antebellum cotton industry, now found themselves marginalized as technological advances, including the telegraph, cotton compresses, and railroads, made it easier to market cotton in the interior. As the factorage system collapsed, interior general and dry goods stores, which Jews had begun to operate in the antebellum years, filled the void and became the economy's lifeblood. Additionally, emancipation provided a new potential customer base. It made good business sense for Jews to welcome freedmen as customers, and that is what they did. But despite these changes, success proved neither easy nor linear. Crop failures in 1866–1867 meant that saved capital or lenient creditors were necessary for a store to survive. When business opportunities brightened between 1868 and 1872, as new legislation encouraged lending and crop yields improved, merchants' success also rose. But the period of good fortune ended spectacularly with the Panic of 1873, which ushered in a period of uncertainty lasting until 1879. Again, accumulated capital or lenient creditors proved necessary to survive.

Just as structural factors led to the rise of the niche economy, they also brought it to an end. Changes in global capitalism, including the rise of investment banking, made lending more impersonal, neutralizing a clear competitive advantage for Jewish merchants who relied on ethnic networks. The Gulf South also found itself marginalized in the global cotton industry, as a fear of higher prices convinced European powers to open new lands for cheaper cotton production, harnessing the power of colonialism to the detriment of American cotton. Concurrently, environmental forces such as floods and the boll weevil ravaged the industry in the Gulf South, decimating cotton crops. As the situation deteriorated, these forces, combined with anti-Jewish violence, converged to marginalize merchants. Although many Jewish merchants remained in the South, the Jewish niche economy collapsed.

If structural factors created the necessary conditions for Jewish merchants to function within Southern capitalism, Jewish merchants still could not have actually succeeded in the absence of ethnic economic networks. Networks supplied the trust upon which economic transactions relied. Credit reporters did not trust Jews, and they cautioned against loaning them money. Since Jews and Gentiles were confined largely to separate social spheres, little opportunity existed for conventional social ties to overcome this distrust. Instead, Jews, much like other ethnic minorities, trusted one another more than they trusted strangers with whom they had no connections. This trust was cultivated largely through ties of family, kinship, or ethnicity that operated within businesses and between businesses. Shared ethnicity fostered the networks of trust that provided Jews with credit, and this provided them with a clear competitive advantage.

Ethnicity mattered for Jewish merchants in the Gulf South prior to the war. They developed ethnic networks that connected family members within firms, that connected Jewish merchants with credit sources in New York and abroad, and that ultimately provided outlets for their cotton. These networks crystallized in the postbellum years, as businesses such as Lehman Brothers secured global investment largely through trust networks with other Jewish firms. Overseas transactions were particularly risky, and networks of trust could mitigate that risk.

Once Lehman Brothers acquired this global investment, they would send that investment to the South—again through relationships of trust that were often predicated on ethnicity.

Once that investment reached the South, ethnic networks played an important role in distributing it throughout the economy. In some cases, Jewish businesses that received credit would work directly with farmers—some of whom were freedmen. But in other cases, the networks would have an added layer, with stores acting as wholesalers or commission houses and working with smaller dry goods and general stores in the region—many of which were owned by Jews. Here again, ethnicity mattered. With these networks in place, smaller Jewish businesses could access credit—the lifeblood of the economy, which allowed them to survive the vicissitudes of the postbellum economy and encouraged Jews to cluster in this niche. But as the importance of trust-based networks declined, and as lending became more impersonal with the rise of investment banking, Jewish merchants in the industry lost their competitive advantage. Although many remained in the region, their niche economy collapsed.

The experience of Jewish merchants in the cotton industry accounts for American Jewry's golden age during the Reconstruction era. It also demonstrates the importance of economics in dictating the ways in which Jews shaped, and were shaped by, the milieu in which they lived. But it is a far more universal case study that speaks to niche economies and minority entrepreneurship more broadly. It shows that the economic environment in which a niche economy emerged was critical. And it demonstrates that within that environment, ethnic networks fostered the trust upon which capitalism relied. Taken together, the experience of Jewish merchants in the cotton industry reveals the ways in which ethnicity mattered in the development of global capitalism.

NOTES

INTRODUCTION

1 Julius Weis Autobiography (JWA), n.d., Ida Weis Friend Collection, MSS 287, box 7, Louisiana Research Collection, Tulane University Special Collections (TUSC), 5–6, 8, 10–11, 13; Susie J. Pak, *Gentlemen Bankers: The World of J. P. Morgan* (Cambridge, MA: Harvard University Press, 2013), 2, 12; and *Money Trust Investigation: Investigation of Financial and Monetary Conditions in the United States under House Resolutions 429 and 504 before a Subcommittee of the Committee on Banking and Currency*, Parts 1–29 (Washington, DC: U.S. Government Printing Office, 1913), 1083–1084; see also 1049–1054, 1080–1085. J. P. Morgan was asked questions by Samuel Untermayer.

2 Early modern economic niches appear in Francesca Trivellato, *The Familiarity of Strangers: The Sephardic Diaspora, Livorno, and Cross-Cultural Trade in the Early Modern Period* (New Haven, CT: Yale University Press, 2012); as well as that Adam Teller, *Money, Power and Influence in Eighteenth Century Lithuania: The Jews on the Radziwill Estates* (Stanford, CA: Stanford University Press, 2016). Modern European economic niches emerge in Derek J. Penslar, *Shylock's Children: Economics and Jewish Identity in Modern Europe* (Berkeley: University of California Press, 2001); and Michael K. Silber, ed., *Jews in the Hungarian Economy* (Jerusalem: Magnes Press, 1992). Transnational economic networks appear in Sarah Abrevaya Stein, *Plumes: Ostrich Feathers, Jews, and a Lost World of Global Commerce* (New Haven, CT: Yale University Press, 2008); and Adam D. Mendelsohn, *The Rag Race: How Jews Sewed Their Way to Success in America and the British Empire* (New York: New York University Press, 2015). See also Marni Davis, *Jews and Booze: Becoming American in the Age of Prohibition* (New York: New York University Press, 2012); Hasia R. Diner, *Roads Taken: The Great Jewish Migrations to the New World and the Peddlers Who Forged the Way* (New Haven, CT: Yale University Press, 2015); Eli Lederhendler, *Jewish Immigrants and American Capitalism, 1880–1920* (Cambridge: Cambridge University Press, 2009); and Rebecca Kobrin and Adam Teller, eds., *Purchasing Power: The Economics of Modern Jewish History* (Philadelphia: University of Pennsylvania Press, 2015).

3 William R. Kerr and Martin Mandorff, "Social Networks, Ethnicity, and Entrepreneurship," Working Paper no. 16–042 (Cambridge, MA: Harvard Business School, June 14, 2016), 2. Ethnic niches can be accompanied by an accusation that an ethnic group holds monopolies on trade in particular sectors at the expense of "natives." Although it has not been specifically Jewish traits or characteristics that

have fostered these niches, Jews in particular have been singled out, as the alleged phenomenon can fit neatly into the Shylock stereotype. But if we utilize a global lens, it becomes perfectly clear that Jews were the reviled intermediaries between global forces and Gulf South cotton farmers, just as Greek, Armenian, and other merchants were reviled by cotton farmers in Egypt, India, Anatolia, and throughout the world. In each of these places, virtually the same charges levied against Jews in the Gulf South were also levied against these non-Jewish merchants, clearly demonstrating that this is in no way a singular Jewish phenomenon. For more on this global context, see Sven Beckert, *Empire of Cotton: A Global History* (New York: Knopf, 2014).

4 Chinese launderers clustered in early twentieth-century California, and contemporary examples of ethnic niches in the United States include motels owned by Gujarati Indians, Vietnamese nail salons, Yemini groceries, Punjabi Indian convenience stores, and Korean dry cleaners. Quantitative analysis reveals that immigrant minority groups were more concentrated in self-employed entrepreneurship than the general population. See Kerr and Mandorff, "Social Networks, Ethnicity, and Entrepreneurship," 1–2, 5. Kerr and Mandorff argue that, while studying "the relationship between ethnicity, occupational choice, and entrepreneurship," they have discovered that "immigrant groups in the United States cluster in specific business sectors." Korean entrepreneurship in dry cleaners is thirty-four times that of other immigrant groups, and Gujarati-speaking Indians are over one hundred times more concentrated in motel management. Kerr and Mandorff "develop a model of social interactions where non-work relationships facilitate the acquisition of sector-specific skills. The resulting scale economies generate occupational stratification along ethnic lines, consistent with the reoccurring phenomenon of small, socially-isolated groups achieving considerable economic success via concentrated entrepreneurship. Empirical evidence from the United States supports our model's underlying mechanisms," they maintain.

5 I will frame this question within the classic debate of Jewish economic history—do Jews, as a minority in the Diaspora, have a learned or acquired propensity to sense and fill economic needs because of their characteristics and backgrounds? Or is there something about each particular place, time, and situation that pushed or encouraged Jews to enter each particular field? Several of those who emphasize propensity point to the uniformity in the Jewish economic experience across time and place. This approach is in large part grounded in the work of Werner Sombart, *The Jews and Modern Capitalism* (New York: E. P. Dutton, 1913). According to Ira Katznelson, Sombart suggests that "the rootless mentality, urban-oriented culture, acquisitive nature, and rationalistically inclined religion of the Jews had placed them at the head of western capitalist development." See Ira Katznelson, "Two Exceptionalisms: Points of Departure for Studies of Capitalism and Jews in the United States," in *Chosen Capital: The Jewish Encounter with American Capitalism*, ed. Rebecca Kobrin (New Brunswick, NJ: Rutgers University Press, 2012), 21. Sombart's work spawned the "middleman-minority theory," but others, including Werner Mosse, have turned to a different approach, termed

the "new institutional economic theory." See Werner Mosse, "Judaism, Jews and Capitalism: Weber, Sombart and Beyond," *Leo Baeck Institute Yearbook* 24, no. 1 (1979): 3–15. This approach largely argues that individual economic actions cannot be studied in a vacuum; rather, the Jewish economic experience must be viewed within the context of the broader economy. Certainly the story of Jews in the American cotton trade requires us to understand the particular economy and capitalism in which Jews were operating, which is detailed throughout this book. But it also draws similarities to other minorities' niche economies across time and space, including those of Jews, Greeks, and others. Thus our story pushes us toward a new paradigm for understanding such niche economies.

6   Many recent scholars have challenged Sombart's thesis, favoring instead Mosse's focus on analyzing particular situations. "Understanding specifically Jewish institutions and attitudes, including those that promote cohesion and solidarity, is inherently insufficient," argues Ira Katznelson. Instead, Katznelson maintains that scholars "should depict with quantitative and qualitative exactness how Jews were embedded within particular capitalisms." Further, he maintains that, "when over-representation and a niche economy was uncovered, a systematic and compara-tive analysis of institutions, networks, opportunity patterns, and other structural arrangements must be mounted to discover persuasive causal explanations." See Katznelson, "Two Exceptionalisms," 23. Following Katznelson's call, Rebecca Ko-brin's *Chosen Capital* explores several niche economies. For a particularly strong historiographical overview of this theory, see Mendelsohn, *The Rag Race*. See also Avner Greif, *Institutions and the Path to the Modern Economy: Lessons from Medieval Trade* (New York: Cambridge University Press, 2006).

7   Many who have followed in the footsteps of Sombart argue that there is a Jew-ish cultural propensity to take on certain professions—a propensity motivated by particular Jewish characteristics or backgrounds. They often point to Jewish communities scattered across time and place and note the striking similarities in economic life, including Jewish participation in occupations that were deemed "unproductive" by their larger societies, involvement in banking, connections to Jewish firms elsewhere, and a flourishing in times of economic backwardness that slowed as the economies grew. This approach has been co-opted in some cases by those who wish to tie distinct racial characteristics to Jews vis-à-vis capitalism. Others have pushed this approach to include distinctive elements of Jewish culture that clustered Jews into particular capitalisms. However, the idea that Jews had a propensity to gravitate toward capitalism and business in many ways spawned the "middleman-minority theory," which posits that minority societies more broadly tend to concentrate their economic activities in high-risk professions that are considered undesirable by the larger society. These profes-sions, which generally have low start-up costs and low barriers to entry, often position the minority as middlemen, situated between elites and the masses. However, so the argument goes, by utilizing characteristics specific to minority middlemen—such as group solidarity, thrift, and an entrepreneurial spirit—they

achieve economic success, often angering others in the population. Others have suggested, correctly I argue, that minorities benefit from the networks of trust and kinship that minorities possess. For more, see Kobrin, ed., *Chosen Capital*, esp. Katznelson, "Two Exceptionalisms," 21; Michael K. Silber, "A Jewish Minority in a Backwards Economy: An Introduction," in Silber, ed., *Jews in the Hungarian Economy*, esp. 5; Mendelsohn, *The Rag Race*, 233; Howard E. Aldrich and Roger Waldinger, "Ethnicity and Entrepreneurship," *Annual Review of Sociology* 16 (1990): 111–135; and Jonathan Karp, *The Politics of Jewish Commerce: Economic Thought and Emancipation in Europe, 1638–1848* (New York: Cambridge University Press, 2008), among others.

8 Beckert, *Empire of Cotton*, xvi–xvii, xi, xii, 441. "The empire of cotton was," argues Beckert, "from the beginning, a site of constant global struggle between slaves and planters, merchants and statesmen, farmers and merchants, workers and factory owners." See Beckert, xii.

9 Ibid., 105–109; Gene Dattel, *Cotton and Race in the Making of America: The Human Costs of Economic Power* (Chicago: Ivan R. Dee, 2009), 51, 78–81; Scott Marler, "Merchants and the Political Economy of Nineteenth-Century Louisiana: New Orleans and Its Hinterlands" (PhD diss., Rice University, 2007), 18. See also Dattel, *Cotton and Race*, 81, for a list of pursuits that ultimately failed to utilize slave labor. Cotton and slavery were so intertwined that historian Gavin Wright notes that the "slave economy ultimately came to resemble the geography of natural cotton-growing areas." See Gavin Wright, *Slavery and American Economic Development* (Baton Rouge: Louisiana State University Press, 2013), 86.

10 Wm. F. Switzler, U.S. Department of the Treasury, *Report on the Internal Commerce of the United States: 1882, 1885, 1887, 1889* (Washington, DC: U.S. Government Printing Office, 1888), year 1887, 146.

11 Harold D. Woodman, *King Cotton and His Retainers: Financing and Marketing the Cotton Crop of the South, 1800–1925* (Washington, DC: Beard Books, 2000), esp. 12–14. "The factor," argues Woodman, "became the cotton planter's commercial alter ego, his personal representative in the marketplace." Planters relied on cotton factors for the marketing and selling of their crop, as the factor would be responsible for shipping the cotton to market and for warehousing the cotton until prices reached a favorable level. He would charge a commission plus expenses for his services. "Although his primary concern was with the sale of the crop and the needs of the plantation," Woodman maintains, the factor "also performed many other personal services for the planter," including purchasing goods and supplies—generally on credit until the season's cotton could be sold. Cotton factors were inclined to work with large-scale planters, as proceeds from small-scale planters and farmers frequently did not justify the work required to market their crops. This created an opportunity for merchants. In some instances, merchants would come directly to the plantation, offering to trade goods for cotton, or they might offer cash for cotton that they would later seek to sell at a profit. In other instances, planters would bring cotton to a general store, where they could either

sell their cotton or trade it for goods. Merchants often served hundreds of farmers and planters in crossroads villages and merchant towns, and this scale made their work profitable. See ibid., 75, 78. Scott Marler argues that, because "planters were clearly the dominant class in the Old South," historians have generally overlooked the antebellum success of these smaller stores, and they have suggested that these stores were "either primitive trading posts or mere 'appendages' of the city-based factorage system." However, Marler correctly argues that these stores were critically important because they "paved a path" for postbellum success for merchants. He maintains that, in the antebellum years, "hundreds of rural storekeepers succeeded, thereby establishing a foundation for their enhanced role in the transformed plantation system after the Civil War," and it was "largely because of lessons they learned before the war [that] rural merchants suddenly found themselves well situated to reap the benefits of those changes." "This foundation," he maintains, "has been insufficiently acknowledged by historians of the nineteenth-century South, who have grown increasingly accustomed to emphasizing the radical break (or, to use older terminology, 'discontinuity') with the past represented by slave emancipation after the North's victory in the war." See Scott P. Marler, *The Merchant's Capital: New Orleans and the Political Economy of the Nineteenth-Century South* (Cambridge: Cambridge University Press, 2013), 89–90, 102, 115–116.

12 Improved communication technology after the war meant that interior merchants could sell cotton at the best time and highest prices without the aid of cotton factors in ports such as New Orleans. Additionally, merchants in the interior could ship directly to cotton markets—including New York—via emerging and growing overland rail routes, bypassing the factors of New Orleans altogether. Moreover, compression equipment that had previously only been available in larger cities emerged in small towns; compressed bales significantly reduced transportation costs. See Woodman, *King Cotton*, 96, 273.

13 Southern currency and Confederate bonds were rendered worthless, so many of those who had invested unwisely or who had relied on banks found themselves destitute. Yet plantation owners remained tied to the yearly cycle whereby they would buy goods and supplies on credit at the beginning of the season and repay their debts after harvest. Additionally, when former slaves were freed and became tenant farmers or sharecroppers, they were forced to start from scratch. They generally had no supplies or equipment of their own to plant their first crop, and they also needed basic necessities such as food, clothing, and household goods. With payday coming *after* the crop was harvested, credit was absolutely necessary for postbellum white and black farmers to produce cotton. See ibid., 282.

14 Following the Civil War, and with the end of slavery, business as usual could not continue, so new labor arrangements were necessary to continue production. Without a labor force, production would grind to a standstill, so states passed black codes and other legislation that essentially bound former slaves to cotton farms. Even the commissioner of the Freedmen's Bureau wanted former slaves to

"return to plantation labor, but under conditions that allowed them the opportunity" to graduate from the wage-earning class. See Eric Foner, *Reconstruction:
America's Unfinished Revolution* (New York: Harper & Row, 1988). In fact, argues
Gene Dattel, the Freedmen's Bureau, "for the most part, became an employment
agency for cotton farms." Rather than giving freedmen "forty acres and a mule"
to farm their own land, freedmen were tied to the land of others through a labor
system that revolved around tenant farming and sharecropping. Although these
labor systems took many forms, the most common was for the laborer, or "tenant," to produce the crop and, at the end of the season, pay a percentage of the
proceeds to the landowner as rent. See Dattel, *Cotton and Race*, 246, 251, 293, 321.

15 As Hasia Diner reminds us, Jewish peddlers "sold to everyone and anyone. White,
black, or tawny, it made no difference; customers were customers, business was
business. The color of the customer's skin mattered not at all to the peddler who
exchanged goods for cash." While there were social stigmas and threats of violence against those who worked with freedmen, Diner argues that Jews had been
faced with color divides before. "Nearly every place the immigrant Jewish peddlers went," Diner argues, "with the exception of the British Isles and Scandinavia,
they stumbled into societies in which color mattered." In some of these places, she
argues, "the color divide followed a native-versus-European colonist divide." The
United States, the Caribbean, and large parts of Latin America "fissured along a
tripartite color spectrum," whereby "those of European lineage held all or nearly
all political and economic power, while African slaves and their descendants, as
well as the native peoples and other nonwhites, contended with powerlessness,
economic deprivation, and lack of meaningful (or any) citizenship. Immigrant
Jewish peddlers," she argues, "came to places where their whiteness, as defined by
custom and law, facilitated their migrations and made their peddling fundamentally successful." See Diner, *Roads Taken*, 43.

16 Although there has been a significant amount of scholarship on this relationship
between Jews and freedmen, very little has focused on their actual economic
relationship and has instead become part of a politicized conversation surrounding black-Jewish relations and moral responsibility. Titles such as "Friend or Foe,"
for example, characterize much of the scholarship. While this subject is certainly
important, my aim is to deconstruct the specific economic relationship between
Jews and freedmen in Reconstruction America. For more on this historiography,
see these works by Hasia Diner: *Roads Taken*; "Between Words and Deeds: Jews
and Blacks in America, 1880–1935, in *Struggles in the Promised Land: Toward a
History of Black-Jewish Relations in the United States*, ed. Jack Salzman and Cornel
West (New York: Oxford University Press, 1997); "Drawn Together by Self-
Interest: Jewish Representation of Race and Race Relations in the Early Twentieth
Century," in *African Americans and Jews in the Twentieth Century: Studies in
Convergence and Conflict*, ed. V. P. Franklin, Nancy L. Grant, Harold M. Kletnick,
and Genna Rae McNeil (Columbia: University of Missouri Press, 1998); and *A
Time for Gathering: The Second Migration, 1820–1880* (Baltimore: Johns Hopkins

University Press, 1992). Also see Melissa Walker, "Consumption and Consumers," and Edgar D. Thompson, "Country Stores," both in *Agriculture and Industry*, vol. 2 of *The New Encyclopedia of Southern Culture*, ed. Melissa Walker and James Cobb (Chapel Hill: University of North Carolina Press, 2008); Eric Goldstein, *The Price of Whiteness: Jews, Race, and American Identity* (Princeton, NJ: Princeton University Press, 2008); Daniel R. Weinfeld, "Samuel Fleischman: Tragedy in Reconstruction-Era Florida," *Southern Jewish History* 8 (2005): 31–76; Clive Webb, *Fight against Fear: Southern Jews and Black Civil Rights* (Athens: University of Georgia Press, 2001); Louis Schmier, "'For Him the "Schwartzers" Couldn't Do Enough': A Jewish Peddler and His Black Customers Look at Each Other," in *Strangers and Neighbors: Relations between Blacks and Jews in the United States*, ed. Maurianne Adams and John Bracy (Amherst: University of Massachusetts Press, 1999), 223–236; John Dollard, *Caste and Class in A Southern Town* (New Haven, CT: Yale University Press, 1937); Arnold M. Shankman, *Ambivalent Friends: Afro-American View the Immigrant* (Westport, CT: Greenwood Press, 1982); Jerrell H. Shofner, *Nor Is It Over Yet: Florida in the Era of Reconstruction, 1863–1877* (Gainesville: University Presses of Florida, 1974); Beth Kreydatus, "'You Are a Part of All of Us': Black Department Store Employees in Jim Crow Richmond," *Journal of Historical Research in Marketing* 2, no. 1 (2010): 108–129; Gerald David Jaynes, *Branches without Roots: Genesis of the Black Working Class in the American South, 1862–1882* (New York: Oxford University Press, 1989); J. Ida Jiggetts, *Religion, Diet, and Health of Jews* (New York: Bloch, 1949); Abraham Peck, "That Other 'Peculiar Institution': Jews and Judaism in the Nineteenth Century South," *Modern Judaism* 7, no. 1 (1987): 99–114; Mrs. Kate E. R. Pickard, *The Kidnapped and the Ransomed: Being the Personal Recollections of Peter Still and His Wife "Vina," after Forty Years of Slavery* (Syracuse, NY: William T. Hamilton, 1856); Clive Webb, "Jewish Merchants and Black Customers in the Age of Jim Crow," *Southern Jewish History* 2 (1999): 55–80; and Jack Salzman, *Bridges and Boundaries: African Americans and American Jews* (New York: George Braziller, 1992). See also the work of Jonathan Karp, whose research in this area is particularly important.

17 When the factorage system broke down in the postbellum years, these rural shopkeepers, Scott Marler argues, who "had cut their credit-provisioning teeth by dealing with the white yeomanry before the war . . . were thus better positioned to furnish the needs of small farms afterward." See Marler, *The Merchants' Capital*, 115–116. As Hasia Diner has shown in *Roads Taken* and elsewhere, many Jews began as peddlers, and the more successful were able to earn enough money to open storefronts.

18 See Pak, *Gentlemen Bankers*, 2, 12; and *Money Trust Investigation*, 1083–1084; see also 1049–1054, 1080–1085. Morgan was asked questions by Samuel Untermyer.

19 Pak, *Gentlemen Bankers*, esp. 9–10, 83–88, 96–97. Pak argues that "history often diverges from theory. In reality, competition did not self-regulate. Financial efficacy was not the goal of all economic decisions." See also "Editorial," *Christian*

Advocate, April 20, 1893, as cited in Pak, *Gentleman Bankers*, 88; and Kerr and Mandorff, "Social Networks, Ethnicity, and Entrepreneurship," 2. Kerr and Mandorff argue that "self-employed entrepreneurs can benefit from social interactions outside of work (e.g., family gatherings, religious and cultural functions, meetings with friends). At these social events, self-employed entrepreneurs have the opportunity to discuss recent customer trends, share best practices, coordinate activities, and so on. The model describes how a small ethnic minority group that has restricted social interactions can have a comparative advantage for self employment."

20 Pak, *Gentleman Bankers*, 81–82. Other historians have observed the critical importance of these Jewish networks for economic success more broadly. For example, the first Jews to arrive in America in the seventeenth century were welcomed in large part because of their access to a worldwide family and ethnic trading network, positioning them at the forefront of the New World's economy. With regard to the nineteenth- and twentieth-century South, see Elliott Ashkenazi, *The Business of Jews in Louisiana, 1840–1875* (Tuscaloosa: University of Alabama Press, 1988); Stephen J. Whitfield, "Commerce and Community: A Business History of Jacksonville Jewry," *Southern Jewish History* 12 (2009): 115–226; and Henry Givens Baker, *Rich's of Atlanta: The Story of a Store since 1867* (Atlanta: Division of Research, School of Business Administration, Atlanta Division, University of Georgia, 1953). Contemporary journalists have also highlighted this phenomenon in a non-Jewish context; for example, the importance of Chinese ethnic networks in spurring growth in China. See "The Magic of Diasporas," *Economist*, November 19, 2011, 13. These high-profile entrepreneurs have been termed members of "Our Crowd" by Steven Birmingham, and they constituted the upper crust of American Jewry. While they left lasting legacies with such names as Goldman, Sachs, Lehman, and Seligman, this same networking dynamic was also at play for scores of lesser-known firms. See Steven Birmingham, *Our Crowd: The Great Jewish Families of New York* (New York: Harper & Row, 1962).

21 Pak, *Gentleman Bankers*, 14; and William D. Cohan, *Money and Power: How Goldman Sachs Came to Rule the World* (New York: Doubleday, 2011), 26–27. This interaction is according to Birmingham, *Our Crowd*.

22 Historians, according to Scott Marler, "have been slow to acknowledge kinship as a category for understanding how social structures were created and maintained among the widely dispersed population of the nineteenth-century South." See Marler, "Merchants and the Political Economy of Nineteenth-Century Louisiana," 107.

23 Farmers and merchants were often in a great deal of leftover debt from the war years. On the eve of the conflict, notes Woodman, "as usual, most planters were in debt to their factors, having anticipated the proceeds of their crops through advances." Though much of the 1860 cotton crop was sold and debts repaid before a Union blockade, the same could not be said for the 1861 crop. With supply lines disrupted and no clear outlet for the cotton crop, it became increasingly difficult

for planters to sell their cotton and repay their debts to factors and merchants. Solely in New Orleans, reported one Mississippi legislature committee, "it is not an exaggerated estimate to say that over one hundred millions of dollars will fall due . . . within the next eight months . . . for which the growing and future crops are pledged." Planters couldn't pay merchants or factors, who in turn couldn't pay their financial backers in the North, so the credit system began to break down. See Woodman, *King Cotton*, 201, 206.

24 Beckert, *Empire of Cotton*, esp. 150, 233, 239, 316.

25 Ibid., xvi, 232–233, 515. For more, see Alexander Kitroeff, *The Greeks in Egypt, 1919–1937: Ethnicity and Class* (Oxford: Ithaca Press for the Middle East Center, St. Antony's College, Oxford University, 1989), 1, 76, 82, 88; and Christos Hadziiosif, "La Colonie grecque en Égypte, 1833–1856" (thesis, Université de Paris–Sorbonne, 1980), 118, 119.

26 Beckert, *Empire of Cotton*, 233; Mark Twain, *Concerning the Jews* (1899; reprint, New York: Harper & Bros., 1934), 11; and Frederick Law Olmsted, *Cotton Kingdom: A Traveller's Observations on Cotton and Slavery in the American Slave States* (New York: Mason Brothers, 1861), 1:252.

27 Edward King, *The Great South*, ed. W. Magruder Drake and Robert R. Jones (Baton Rouge: Louisiana State University Press, 1972), 274. The pieces in this book were originally published between 1873 and 1874 as part of *Scribner's* "Great South" series. The book also contains articles written by King but not published in *Scribner's*.

28 Robert Somers, *The Southern States since the War* (London: MacMillian & Co., 1871), 150–151, 198.

29 Roger L. Ransom and Richard Sutch, *One Kind of Freedom: The Economic Consequences of Emancipation* (Cambridge: Cambridge University Press, 2001), esp. 387n34.

30 Ashkenazi, *The Business of Jews in Louisiana*, 1, 4.

31 Thomas Clark, "The Post–Civil War Economy in the South," *American Jewish Historical Quarterly*, 55, no. 4 (June 1966): 425, 428, 430, 433. Based largely on contemporary observations, limited data sets, and vague hunches, historians have been divided on whether Jews dominated mercantile life in cotton regions. Some historians, including Clark, seem to agree with this sentiment. Clark, for instance, notes that "economically the Jew seldom if ever competed directly with the Southerner in his main economic activities," suggesting that Jews were concentrated in their own particular sector of the economy. Yet Harold Woodman cautions us that this may not be the case. Although he does not offer statistics to support this assertion, he nevertheless claims that Jews did not "dominate the furnishing merchant business." See Woodman, *King Cotton*, 304.

32 Several historiographic examples offer guidance in quantifying R.G. Dun materials (R.G. Dun & Co. records, Baker Library, Harvard Business School) in the Gulf South's cotton economy. Ransom and Sutch utilize the Dun reports, among other sources, to produce a list of towns that "seemed to play a prominent enough

role in the commercial activity of their regions to warrant designation as at least
'minor' cotton centers" in 1880. See Ransom and Sutch, *One Kind of Freedom*,
300. Since I am looking for Jews in the Gulf South who were involved in the cotton industry, Ransom and Sutch's work offers a geographic starting point. They
looked at four factors to determine the relative importance of a town to the cotton
industry: its 1880 population; the presence of banking facilities; the presence of
commercial facilities such as warehouses, cotton gins, or factorage houses; and
the proximity of transportation facilities. They then identified 158 cities and towns
important to the cotton south—60 of which were in the Gulf South region that
I am analyzing. By utilizing the Dun records, Ransom and Sutch then determined
for those 60 towns the number of general stores, which, as we will see, provided
both goods and credit that fueled the cotton industry. Although their study is not
without its flaws, their statistical analysis nevertheless points us to most (though
not all) cotton towns—precisely the places where we would expect to encounter
Jews. A more recent study by Scott P. Marler, "Two Kinds of Freedom: Mercantile Development and Labor Systems in Louisiana Cotton and Sugar Parishes
after the Civil War," *Agricultural History* 85, no. 2 (2011): 225–251, looks closely
at two Louisiana parishes—Ascension Parish, which is known for sugar production, and West Feliciana Parish, which was central to the cotton industry. Marler
uses empirical data mined largely from the Dun reports to show the pecuniary
strength of businesses in each region, and he also demonstrates how mercantile
life changed from the antebellum to the postbellum periods by highlighting
the continuity of businesses in each parish from the antebellum to postbellum
periods. While Marler's work compares antebellum to postbellum mercantile life,
Louis M. Kyriakoudes, "Lower-Order Urbanization and Territorial Monopoly
in the Southern Furnishing Trade: Alabama, 1871–1890," *Social Science History*
26, no. 1 (2002): 179–198, offers us another framework by demonstrating how
postbellum mercantile life changed over time. For example, while Alabama saw
a 52 percent population increase between 1871 and 1890, Kyriakoudes uses the
Dun ledgers to demonstrate that over the same period it saw a 93 percent increase
in the total number of business listings and a 249 percent gain in the number of
general stores. By looking closely at the data, he further discovers particular spots
where we are likely to see high concentrations of newcomers who were driving
that growth (see esp. 186, 195).

33   These figures are as close an approximation as possible, given the limitations
of the data. Records have been compiled from the U.S. Census (various years);
Mercantile Agency, *The Mercantile Agency's Reference Book of the United States
and British Provinces* (New York: B. Douglass & Co., various years); R.G. Dun &
Co. reports, Baker Library, Harvard Business School; Union of American Hebrew
Congregations, *Statistics of the Jews of the United States, Compiled under the Authority of the Board of Delegates of American Israelites and the Union of American
Hebrew Congregations* ([Philadelphia]: Union of American Hebrew Congrega-
tions, 1880), and several other sources to identify Jewishness, mercantile pres-

ence, and total population. However, in many cases I was still forced to rely on last name only to tentatively determine Jewishness. Population statistics generally use 1878 Jewish statistics and 1880 general census statistics. The towns I use are those that Ransom and Sutch labeled fairly subjectively as important to the cotton industry, plus several others that my research suggests were also central. While the data are not precise, they are directional and paint an accurate picture of the region. For more on the impact of the Shylock stereotype, see David A. Gerber, "Cutting Out Shylock: Elite Anti-Semitism and the Quest for Moral Order in the Mid-Nineteenth-Century American Marketplace," *Journal of American History* 69, no. 3 (1982): 615–637.

34 Settlement followed the pattern uncovered by Louis Kyriakoudes, who concluded that "cotton production, market towns, railroads, and general stores went hand in hand" (Kyriakoudes, "Lower-Order Urbanization and Territorial Monopoly," 195). Again, given extant sources, the results cannot be precise, but they are clearly directional. These sources, as displayed through the map, demonstrate that, in 1878–1880, each and every market town along the Mississippi River between Memphis, Tennessee, and Baton Rouge, Louisiana, one of the strongest cotton-producing regions in the country, saw extremely high concentrations of Jewish general and dry goods store owners. All told, in the major market towns of Vicksburg and the Bends, Jews owned approximately 40–45 percent of all general and dry goods stores. The same pattern holds along the Red River, as well as towns along the Ouachita, Arkansas, Yazoo, and Tennessee Rivers. The pattern also holds for towns along railroads, including the Illinois Central, Texas Pacific, the Tennessee & Virginia Railroad, and the Alabama Great Southern Railroad. Only a handful of towns in the entire region are outliers.

35 While there has been quite a bit of recent work focusing on the Civil War, most American Jewish historiography tends to jump from the end of the war in 1865 to the beginning of the so-called East European period in 1880. Moreover, while American Jewish historians have a general sense that Jews fared well economically in these years, they have been hesitant to explore the story of Jewish economic success, often fearing that it might feed anti-Semitic perceptions of Jewish power and wealth. Of critical importance is the fact that by glossing over this profoundly important era, and by failing to consider its economic history, American Jewish historians have missed a golden opportunity to integrate their work into broader American historiography and to demonstrate the critical ways in which Jews shaped, and were shaped by, their surroundings. The result of this historiographic neglect is a largely unexplored yet fertile territory, with profound possibilities to illuminate both the American Jewish experience and the ways in which economic networks shaped global capitalism.

36 I thank Hasia Diner for helping me to grapple with these three factors.

37 "Down the Mississippi," *American Israelite*, January 21, 1876, 2; and Charles Wessolowsky, *Reflections of Southern Jewry: The Letters of Charles Wessolowsky, 1878–1879*, ed. Louis Schmier (Macon, GA: Mercer University Press, 1982), 64.

38 Herman W. Solomon, *The Early History of the Hebrew Union Congregation of Greenville, Mississippi* (1972; reprint, [Greenville, MS]: Solomon, 2001), 31; "IOBB," *American Israelite*, January 25, 1878, 6. See the papers of the Bayou Sara Lodge, available at the American Jewish Archives, Cincinnati, Ohio. Also see "Woodville, MS," *American Israelite*, August 20, 1891.

39 Temple Sinai minute book, 1893–1909, plus entry from 1940, West Feliciana Historical Society (WFHS), St. Francisville, Louisiana, 59, 66; Wessolowsky, *Reflections of Southern Jewry*, 46–47, 61, 73.

40 Unidentified newspaper clipping, [Baton Rouge, LA]), July 16, 1901, WFHS; "M. & E. Wolf," *True Democrat*, February 24, 1917, 5; "Palimpsests, Reprint of *True Democrat* July 23, 1892," WFHS; and Anne Butler, *Three Generous Generations* (Baton Rouge, LA: Claitor's Publishing Division, 2004), 55, 66. Although the building burned to the ground two years after its construction, it was soon rebuilt.

41 Carolyn Gray LeMaster, *A Corner of the Tapestry: A History of the Jewish Experience in Arkansas, 1820s–1990s* (Fayetteville: University of Arkansas Press, 1994), 508nn233–235. See also James W. Leslie, *Pine Bluff and Jefferson County* (Norfolk, VA: Donning Co., 1981); and Goodspeed Brothers, *Biographical and Historical Memoirs of Mississippi, Embracing an Authentic and Comprehensive Account of the Chief Events in the History of the State, and a Record of the Lives of Many of the Most Worthy and Illustrious Families and Individuals* (Chicago: Goodspeed Publishing Co., 1891), 1036.

42 "Jewish Members of U.S. Congress: House of Representatives (1845–Present)," *Jewish Virtual Library*, n.d., www.jewishvirtuallibrary.org; Isaac Landman, *The Universal Jewish Encyclopedia* (New York: Ktav Publishing House), 7:588; Solomon, *Early History*, 8; John C. Willis, *Forgotten Time: The Yazoo-Mississippi Delta after the Civil War* (Charlottesville: University Press of Virginia, 2000), 209n27; Aaron D. Anderson, *Builders of a New South: Merchants, Capital, and the Remaking of Natchez, 1865–1914* (Jackson: University Press of Mississippi, 2013), 176–177; and Wessolowsky, *Reflections of Southern Jewry*, 71–72, 129–130.

43 "Down the Mississippi," *American Israelite*, June 21, 1876, 2; "General Overview of Natchez History" (Natchez, MS: Historic Natchez Foundation, n.d.), 42; "Woodville, Miss.," *American Israelite*, April 27, 1893, 5; *True Democrat*, March 28, 1903, WFHS; Willis, *Forgotten Time*, 87; Solomon, *Early History of the Hebrew Union Congregation of Greenville, Mississippi*, 37–38.

44 Anton Hieke, *Jewish Identity in the Reconstruction South: Ambivalence and Adaption* (Berlin: De Gruyter, 2013), esp. 108, 164, 307. Hieke contends that the broader Southern society did not view Jews as fully white Southerners, arguing that Jews "were seen as whites of a different shade but not as members of the core of southern society, which was Christian." Instead, he utilizes the term "integrated outsiders" and argues that, "during Reconstruction, southern Jews were subjected to a welcoming public philo-Semitism coupled with a non-public anti-Semitism, i.e., anti-Semitism that is present not only in the private sphere, but

also in the undisclosed sphere of private, political and business correspondence," a concept that he refers to as "covert anti-Semitism." This "non-public, covert, anti-Semitism betrayed the image of southern acceptance and overall integration created by public philo-Semitism," he maintains.

45 Ashkenazi, *The Business of the Jews of Louisiana.*

CHAPTER 1. THE ANTEBELLUM COTTON ECONOMY

1 Friedrich Gerstäcker, *Gerstäcker's Louisiana: Fiction and Travel Sketches from Antebellum Times through Reconstruction,* ed. and trans. Irene S. Di Maio (Baton Rouge: Louisiana State University Press, 2006), 28–31.

2 Gavin Wright, *The Political Economy of the Cotton South: Households, Markets, and Wealth in the Nineteenth Century* (New York: Norton, 1978), 15; Scott D. Marler, "Merchants and the Political Economy of Nineteenth-Century Louisiana: New Orleans and Its Hinterlands" (PhD diss., Rice University, 2007), 18–19, 48–49, 87; and Walter Johnson, *River of Dark Dreams: Slavery and Empire in the Cotton Kingdom* (Cambridge, MA: Harvard University Press, 2013), 5, 256.

3 Johnson, *River of Dark Dreams,* 251; Harold D. Woodman, *King Cotton and His Retainers: Financing and Marketing the Cotton Crop of the South, 1800–1925* (Washington, DC: Beard Books, 2000), 15.

4 Johnson, *River of Dark Dreams,* 266, 274.

5 Woodman, *King Cotton,* 15–19. "Thus," argues Woodman, "through a system of partnerships or other agreements, the factorage system made virtually every cotton market in the world available to the cotton grower," and it was the factor's job to find the market "that netted the planter the highest return."

6 Johnson, *River of Dark Dreams,* 267–271. Johnson argues that "mastery of the cotton trade required factors to imagine the arc of the market in New Orleans, project it into the future, compare the projection to similar ones in New York (adding the two weeks it would take the cotton to move) or in Liverpool (adding four weeks), and then push cotton onto the market just as value crested, and in advance of increasing supply that would dampen the rising price. . . . Those who mastered it had to have the judgment—the confidence—to wait for the moment, and the initiative to seize that moment when it arose" (ibid., 268).

7 Ibid., 274–276.

8 Woodman, *King Cotton,* 30, 33–34, 38.

9 Ibid., 34–35; and Johnson, *River of Dark Dreams,* 259, 261.

10 Woodman, *King Cotton,* 36–37; and Johnson, *River of Dark Dreams,* 259. See Thomas Prentice Kettell, *Southern Wealth and Northern Profits* (New York: George W. & John A. Wood, 1860).

11 Johnson, *River of Dark Dreams,* 262–263.

12 Ibid., 259, 261.

13 Marler, *The Merchants' Capital,* 89, 114.

14 Ibid., 85; and Aaron D. Anderson, *Builders of a New South: Merchants, Capital, and the Remaking of Natchez, 1865–1914* (Jackson: University Press of Mississippi,

2013), 30. Also see Michael Wayne, *The Reshaping of Plantation Society: The Natchez District, 1860–1880* (Urbana: University of Illinois Press, 1990).

15 U.S. Department of the Treasury, *Report on the Internal Commerce of the United States: 1882, 1885, 1887, 1889* (Washington, DC: U.S. Government Printing Office, 1888), year 1888, 5, 7, 9, 270; "From the Interior," *Daily Picayune*, August 4, 1855, 5.

16 Virginia Lobdell Jennings, "Bayou Sara: The Town and Stream," in "Bayou Sara Notes," folder, West Feliciana Historical Society (WFHS), St. Francisville, Louisiana.

17 J. W. Dorr, in Jennings, "Bayou Sara: The Town and Stream," 10.

18 Jennings, "Bayou Sara: The Town and Stream"; and Louise Butler, "West Feliciana, A Glimpse of Its History," *Louisiana Historical Quarterly* 7, no. 1 (1924): 110–111.

19 Anderson, *Builders of a New South*, 31; D. Clayton James, *Antebellum Natchez* (Baton Rouge: Louisiana State University Press, 1968), 208.

20 Lewis E. Atherton, *The Southern Country Store, 1800–1860* (New York: Greenwood Press, 1949), 42, 46–47; Marler, *The Merchants' Capital*, 104. See also Stuart Weems Bruchey, comp. and ed., *Cotton and the Growth of the American Economy: 1790–1860: Sources and Readings* (New York: Harcourt, Brace & World, 1967), 264–270.

21 Marler, *The Merchants' Capital*, 89, 102, 110, 113–114.

22 Louisiana, Vol. 22, p. 243 (hereafter presented as volume:page), R.G. Dun & Co. Credit Report Volumes, Baker Library, Harvard Business School (HBS).

23 Louisiana, 22:240, 254, R.G. Dun & Co. Credit Report Volumes, Baker Library, HBS; also see Marler, *The Merchants' Capital*, 94, 107–108.

24 Louisiana, 22:245, R.G. Dun & Co. Credit Report Volumes, Baker Library, HBS; Jennings, "Bayou Sara: The Town and Stream," 10; and Louisiana, 22:244, 246, R.G. Dun & Co. Credit Report Volumes, Baker Library, HBS.

25 Marler, *The Merchants' Capital*, 96–97, 101, 115–116. Previous scholars have argued that these general stores succeeded because many had a "territorial monopoly" on business in their local communities. This notion has recently been rightly challenged. It is clear that, in towns with multiple stores and outlets for planters' cotton, there was a marketing element to these businesses to bring potential customers through their doors. See Scott P. Marler, "Two Kinds of Freedom: Mercantile Development and Labor Systems in Louisiana Cotton and Sugar Parishes after the Civil War," *Agricultural History* 85, no. 2 (2011): 225–251; and Roger L. Ransom and Richard Sutch, *One Kind of Freedom: The Economic Consequences of Emancipation* (Cambridge: Cambridge University Press, 2001).

26 Hasia Diner, *The Jews of the United States, 1654–2000* (Berkeley: University of California Press, 2006), 99–107, and "Entering the Mainstream of Modern Jewish History: Peddlers and the American Jewish South," in *Jewish Roots in Southern Soil*, ed. Marcie Cohen Ferris and Mark I. Greenberg (Waltham, MA: Brandeis University Press, 2006), 93–95.

27 Alabama, 20:28, R.G. Dun & Co. Credit Report Volumes, Baker Library, HBS; Herbert H. Lehman memoir, Columbia University Archives, Lehman Collection,

box 1297, 2; and Roland Flade, *The Lehmans: From Rimpar to the New World: A Family History* (Würzburg: Konigshausen & Neumann, 1999), 56.

28 Alabama, 20:84, R.G. Dun & Co. Credit Report Volumes, Baker Library, HBS.

29 Louisiana, 22:241, R.G. Dun & Co. Credit Report Volumes, Baker Library, HBS. This link between Isaias Meyer and I. Meyer & Co. is established in New York, 213:447, R.G. Dun & Co. Credit Report Volumes, Baker Library, HBS. This page also connects Isaias Meyer to Meyer, Weis & Co. of Natchez and to Charles Hoffman & Co. of Bayou Sara. Also see Louisiana, 22:240, 247, R.G. Dun & Co. Credit Report Volumes, Baker Library, HBS; and "Bayou Sara, West Feliciana Parish, Louisiana," 1850 U.S. Census, 256B. See Louisiana, 22:243, R.G. Dun & Co. Credit Report Volumes, Baker Library, HBS; and "Bayou Sara: The Town and Stream," 10. There is often a perception that, because of their own history of bondage, Jews did not own slaves. This, however, is not accurate.

30 Anne Butler, *Three Generous Generations* (Baton Rouge, LA: Claitor's Publishing Division, 2004), 6–7. There is uncertainty surrounding this date. See Louisiana, 5:256, R.G. Dun & Co. Credit Report Volumes, Baker Library, HBS. P. Feyan is likely the same person. See Louisiana, 22:258, R.G. Dun & Co. Credit Report Volumes, Baker Library, HBS.

31 Louisiana, 22:250, R.G. Dun & Co. Credit Report Volumes, Baker Library, HBS.

32 Mississippi, 21:80, 6:144, 2:29; Louisiana, 5:51; and Arkansas, 7:189, 13:80, 4:47, 8:5, R.G. Dun & Co. Credit Report Volumes, Baker Library, HBS.

33 "Relief to Bayou Sara," *Daily Picayune*, June 22, 1855, 2.

34 Marler, *The Merchants' Capital*, 16, 18, 40–41, 105. Quotation is from Israel D. Andrews in an 1852 United States Senate Report; *DeBow's Review*, as cited in Johnson, *River of Dark Dreams*, 256.

35 Marler, *The Merchants' Capital*, 15–16, 46, 51–52.

36 Because of New Orleans's reputation for high prices, bad service, and a heightened sense of its own invincibility, shop owners proudly boasted about making purchases in other cities. This trend did not go unnoticed in New Orleans. One local newspaper (cited by Marler) claimed in 1852 that "our country friends send their produce to us, but they do not buy of us." Marler also claims that, "compared to the mutually reinforcing cycles of urban-rural economic development underway in the Midwest, the relationship of New Orleans to its agricultural hinterlands seems to have been pecularly weak." See Marler, "Merchants and the Political Economy of Nineteenth-Century Louisiana," 111–114. Also see Edwin G. Burrows and Mike Wallace, *Gotham: A History of New York City to 1898* (Oxford: Oxford University Press, 1999), 865.

37 Sven Beckert, *The Monied Metropolis: New York City and the Consolidation of the American Bourgeoisie, 1850–1896* (Cambridge: Cambridge University Press, 2001), 17–18.

38 Ibid., 18–19. Beckert argues that "the merchants' activities, in turn strengthened the city's position ever more, making it the center of the nation's trade, information, and transportation networks. Indeed, in contrast to all other urban areas in the

United States, New York dominated not only its hinterland and the northeastern region but also the nation as a whole."

39 Burrows and Wallace, *Gotham*, 736; and Rudolph Glanz, "German Jews in New York City in the 19th Century," in his *Studies in Judaica Americana* (New York: Ktav Publishing House, 1970), 128–131, as cited in Howard B. Rock, *Haven of Liberty: New York Jews in the New World, 1654–1865*, vol. 1 of *City of Promises: A History of the Jews of New York*, general ed. Deborah Dash Moore (New York: New York University Press, 2012).

40 Beckert, *Monied Metropolis*, 18–20, 22; Gene Dattel, *Cotton and Race in the Making of America: The Human Costs of Economic Power* (Chicago: Ivan R. Dee, 2009), 87; and Burrows and Wallace, *Gotham*, xii.

41 Beckert, *Monied Metropolis*, 24; and Dattel, *Cotton and Race*, 71.

42 Beckert, *Monied Metropolis*, 25, 29–30.

43 "Lazard LLC History," *FundingUniverse*, n.d., www.fundinguniverse.com.

44 Johnson, *River of Dark Dreams*, 256, 279; Dattel, *Cotton and Race*, 83; Beckert, *Monied Metropolis*, 84–85; Burrows and Wallace, *Gotham*, 865; and Rock, *Haven of Liberty*, 152–153, 228–229.

45 Beckert, *Monied Metropolis*, 23, 28–29. See also Adam D. Mendelsohn, *The Rag Race: How Jews Sewed Their Way to Success in America and the British Empire* (New York: New York University Press, 2015).

46 David A. Gerber, "Cutting Out Shylock: Elite Anti-Semitism and the Quest for Moral Order in the Mid-Nineteenth-Century American Market Place," *Journal of American History* 69, no. 3 (1982): 627–629, 631, 632; and Elliott Ashkenazi, *The Business of Jews in Louisiana, 1840–1875* (Tuscaloosa: University of Alabama Press, 1988), 74.

47 Susie J. Pak, *Gentlemen Bankers: The World of J. P. Morgan* (Cambridge, MA: Harvard University Press, 2013), esp. 2, 12; and Beckert, *Monied Metropolis*, 31–35. For example, after marrying a son or daughter into a mercantile family, a partner now had ties of kinship with new contacts and business opportunities; see Marler, *The Merchants' Capital*, 90, 107.

48 Marler, *The Merchants' Capital*, 107; and Woodman, *King Cotton*, 18. This firm was in Savannah. See the Julius Weis Autobiography (JWA), n.d., Ida Weis Friend Collection, MSS 287, box 7, Louisiana Research Collection, Tulane University Special Collections (TUSC), 21.

49 Ashkenazi, *The Business of Jews in Louisiana*, 108; and JWA, 13. This particular passage was in reference to 1853–1854.

50 Marler, *The Merchants' Capital*, 90, 107; Ashkenazi, *The Business of Jews in Louisiana*, 109; and Louisiana, 9:75, 9:231, 11:248, R.G. Dun & Co. Credit Report Volumes, Baker Library, HBS.

51 Louisiana, 9:75; and New York, 364:56, 364:69, 369:586, R.G. Dun & Co. Credit Report Volumes, Baker Library, HBS.

52 New York, 364:56; Louisiana, 11:248; and New York, 364:59, 369:586, R.G. Dun & Co. Credit Report Volumes, Baker Library, HBS.

53   Ashkenazi, *Business of Jews in Louisiana*, 109; and Louisiana, 10:324, 10:351, R.G.
     Dun & Co. Credit Report Volumes, Baker Library, HBS.

54   Louisiana, 10:465, 10:325, R.G. Dun & Co. Credit Report Volumes, Baker Library,
     HBS.

55   Louisiana, 10:351, 10:458, 4:2, and 22:93, R.G. Dun & Co. Credit Report Volumes,
     Baker Library, HBS.

56   Florida, 8:9, c R.G. Dun & Co. Credit Report Volumes, Baker Library, HBS.

57   Florida, 8:9; Louisiana, 10:324; and Ohio, 78:212, R.G. Dun & Co. Credit Report
     Volumes, Baker Library, HBS. See also New York, 195:832, 396:125, R.G. Dun &
     Co. Credit Report Volumes, Baker Library, HBS.

58   Ashkenazi, *The Business of Jews of Louisiana*, 110–112; Louisiana, 22:245, R.G.
     Dun & Co. Credit Report Volumes, Baker Library, HBS.

59   Ashkenazi, *The Business of Jews of Louisiana*, 111; Louisiana, 22:245, R.G. Dun &
     Co. Credit Report Volumes, Baker Library, HBS.

60   New York, 369:586; and Louisiana, 9:231, R.G. Dun & Co. Credit Report Volumes,
     Baker Library, HBS.

61   Louisiana, 9:75; New York, 369:586, 364:59; and Louisiana, 9:231, R.G. Dun & Co.
     Credit Report Volumes, Baker Library, HBS.

62   Herbert H. Lehman memoir, 1–4; Kenneth Libo, ed., *Lots of Lehmans: The Family
     of Mayer Lehman of Lehman Brothers: Remembered by His Descendants* (New
     York: Center for Jewish History, 2007), 4–5; Flade, *The Lehmans*, 41, 44–46, 56;
     and Lehman Brothers, *A Centennial: Lehman Brothers, 1850–1950* (New York:
     Lehman Brothers, 1950), 2. Sources differ as to the exact date of Mayer's arrival;
     see Alabama, 20:28, R.G. Dun & Co. Credit Report Volumes, Baker Library,
     HBS.

63   Alabama, 10:110, R.G. Dun & Co. Credit Report Volumes, Baker Library, HBS;
     Flade, *The Lehmans*, 56–57; and Allan Nevins, *Herbert H. Lehman and His Era*
     (New York: Scribner's, 1963), 7.

64   Libo, ed., *Lots of Lehmans*, 6. According to the New York City volumes of the R.G.
     Dun collection, Emanuel may also have been in business with another individual
     while in New York; see Ashkenazi, *Business of Jews in Louisiana*, 127–128; New
     York, 319:500a, R.G. Dun & Co. Credit Report Volumes, Baker Library, HBS.

65   New York, 319:500a, R.G. Dun & Co. Credit Report Volumes, Baker Library, HBS.

66   Alabama, 20:28, R.G. Dun & Co. Credit Report Volumes, Baker Library, HBS.

67   Pak, *Gentlemen Bankers*, 2; *Money Trust Investigation: Investigation of Financial
     and Monetary Conditions in the United States under House Resolutions 429 and
     504 before a Subcommittee of the Committee on Banking and Currency*, Parts 1–29
     (Washington, DC: U.S. Government Printing Office, 1913); New York, 310:500a,
     R.G. Dun & Co. Credit Report Volumes, Baker Library, HBS. Lehman & Ferst
     had credit with John Anderson & Co., presumably a non-Jewish firm.

68   Linton Wells, "The House of Seligman," 1931, typescript, Seligman Family papers,
     New-York Historical Society, New York, 19–21, 25; George Seligman Hellman,
     "Joseph and His Brothers: Or, The Story of the Seligmans," unpublished biography

(New York: New-York Historical Society, 1945), 25–26. Hellman says Cheston, Wells says Clinton.

69 Wells, "The House of Seligman," 24–27; Hellman, "Joseph and his Brothers," 35.

70 Wells, "The House of Seligman," 24–28, 42; Hellman, "Joseph and his Brothers," 35, 37.

71 Isaias Meyer Obituary, *New York Times*, August 25, 1888, reprinted in *Daily Picayune*, August 28, 1888, 4, col. 4. There are varying estimates for Isaias Meyer's birthdate. His *New York Times* obituary of August 25, 1888, says he was born in 1814. New York, 213:447, R.G. Dun & Co. Credit Report Volumes, Baker Library, HBS, says he was born around 1813. And the 1850 U.S. Census from West Feliciana Parish (page 255 stamped/page 2 penned), says he was born around 1817. See *The Commercial Agency Record*, 1861, New-York Historical Society, book A.

72 New York, 213:447; and Louisiana, 22:254, R.G. Dun & Co. Credit Report Volumes, Baker Library, HBS.

73 This firm was known at the time as Meyer, Deutsch & Weis, and Joseph Deutsch was a partner before being joined by Julius Weis. I use "Meyer, Weis & Co." throughout this book for ease in highlighting that this is the same firm. See Louisiana, 9:63, R.G. Dun & Co. Credit Report Volumes, Baker Library, HBS; and "Fifty Years of Southern Progress," *New Orleans Times-Picayune*, November 17, 1895, 7.

74 Louisiana, 9:63; and Mississippi, 2:27, 2:60, R.G. Dun & Co. Credit Report Volumes, Baker Library, HBS.

75 Mississippi, 2:27; and New York, 213:447, 200:375, 197:47, R.G. Dun & Co. Credit Report Volumes, Baker Library, HBS.

76 J. W. Dorr in Jennings, "Bayou Sara: The Town and Stream"; and Louisiana, 22:241, R.G. Dun & Co. Credit Report Volumes, Baker Library, HBS. According to New York, 213:447, R.G. Dun & Co. Credit Report Volumes, Baker Library, HBS, Jacob Meyer was a relative of Isaias Meyer. Also see Louisiana, 22:254; and New York, 213:227, R.G. Dun & Co. Credit Report Volumes, Baker Library, HBS.

77 Records of W. G. Schafer, 3–4, WFHS. In addition to the main partners, the firm also employed Julius Weis's brother and his cousin—both of whom were from the same town as Joseph Deutsch. See Mississippi, 2:27, R.G. Dun & Co. Credit Report Volumes, Baker Library, HBS; Teri D. Tillman, email to author, September 13, 2011; JWA, 14; and see Louisiana, 9:63, and New York, 213:447, R.G. Dun & Co. Credit Report Volumes, Baker Library, HBS.

78 Louisiana, 22:240, R.G. Dun & Co. Credit Report Volumes, Baker Library, HBS. He is also listed as a clerk in the 1850 U.S. Census for West Feliciana Parish (page 5091).

79 Louisiana, 22:240, R.G. Dun & Co. Credit Report Volumes, Baker Library, HBS; "The Great Fire at Bayou Sara," *Daily Picayune*, June 21, 1855; "Great Fire at Bayou Sara," *Daily Picayune*, June 17, 1855; "The Sufferers of the Bayou Sara Fire," *Daily Picayune*, June 22, 1855; and "From the Interior," *Daily Picayune*, August 4, 1855.

80 Louisiana, 22:254, 22:241, R.G. Dun & Co. Credit Report Volumes, Baker Library, HBS; and "From the Interior," *Daily Picayune*, August 4, 1855.

81 Louisiana, 22:241; New York, 213:447, 217:834; and Louisiana, 22:285, 22:260, R.G. Dun & Co. Credit Report Volumes, Baker Library, HBS.

CHAPTER 2. THE WAR YEARS

1 J. David Hacker, "A Census-Based Count of the Civil War Dead," *Civil War History*, 57, no. 4 (December 2011): 307–348. This is a recently revised number, as Hacker demonstrates that the standard figures have undercounted the dead.

2 Scott P. Marler, *The Merchant's Capital: New Orleans and the Political Economy of the Nineteenth-Century South* (Cambridge: Cambridge University Press, 2013), 127, 132.

3 Julius Weis Autobiography (JWA), n.d., Ida Weis Friend Collection, MSS 287, box 7, Louisiana Research Collection, Tulane University Special Collections (TUSC), 10, 15; and New York, Vol. 200, p. 375 (hereafter presented as volume:page), R.G. Dun & Co. Credit Report Volumes, Baker Library, Harvard Business School (HBS).

4 New York, 319:500a, R.G. Dun & Co. Credit Report Volumes, Baker Library, HBS.

5 Sven Beckert, *Empire of Cotton: A Global History* (New York: Knopf, 2014), 243, 247–248.

6 Marler, *The Merchants' Capital*, 120; and Beckert, *Empire of Cotton*, 245.

7 Beckert, *Empire of Cotton*, 250, 256, 261.

8 Marler, *The Merchants' Capital*, 124–126; Howard B. Rock, *Haven of Liberty: New York Jews in the New World, 1654–1865*, vol. 1 of *City of Promises: A History of the Jews of New York*, general ed. Deborah Dash Moore (New York: New York University Press, 2012), 228–229.

9 Jonathan D. Sarna, *When General Grant Expelled the Jews* (New York: Schocken, 2012), 38; and Elliott Ashkenazi, *The Business of Jews in Louisiana, 1840–1875* (Tuscaloosa: University of Alabama Press, 1988), 27.

10 Thelma Peters, "Blockade Running in the Bahamas during the Civil War," *Journal of the Historical Association of Southern Florida* 5 (January 1946): 16–29; Ashkenazi, *The Business of Jews in Louisiana*, 24–27. Jews in Central and Eastern Europe had been subjected to special taxes, which encouraged Jews to trade clandestinely to avoid these harsh levies. Southern Jews might have had friends or relatives who had smuggled in Europe, they were already involved in trade, and they were generally well suited for this occupation. See Sarna, *When General Grant Expelled the Jews*, 39; and JWA, 15–16. Weis told of this smuggling incident in an early draft of his memoir, although he crossed out the story, and it did not appear in the final draft.

11 "Aunt Mellie's Story: John Mayer and His Wife, Jeanette Reis (as recorded by Clara Lowenburg Moses—for nephews & nieces Ike, Ret, Frank and Margaret)," email from Carol Mills-Nichol, September 29, 2012.

12 Sarna, *When General Grant Expelled the Jews*, 40–42.

13 Ibid., 40.

14 "In the Court of Claims," December Term, 1893–1894, Levi M. Lowenburg, 2, 8, 10, 18, and "Defendant's Brief on Merits," December Term, 1893, Levi M. Lowenburg, 2, National Archives and Record Administration (NARA), E22, Congressional Jurisdiction, Case Files 3756, Record Group (RG) 123, Stack area 163E. Lowenburg's story also reveals nuances of religious life during the war. When Lowenburg was drafted, he purportedly asked an official, "Why didn't the Catholic priest and Dr. Marshall go?" The official asked "what that had to do with it," and Lowenburg "told him I was a clergyman," as well. After that, Lowenburg claimed, the official "came back and told me that I was exempt." See "In the Court of Claims," Levi M. Lowenburg, folder C.d. 3756, 2–3, NARA, E22, Congressional Jurisdiction, Case Files 3756, RG 123, Stack area 163E. Moreover, according to one witness, Lowenburg received sugar and molasses "for service as a rabbi in performing circumcision," apparently during the conflict.

15 Marler, *The Merchants' Capital*, 132; and "In the Court of Claims," December Term, 1893–1894, Levi M. Lowenburg, folder C.d. 3756, 9–10, and "In the Court of Claims," Levi Lowenburg, October 1892, folder C.d. 3756, 3, NARA, E22, Congressional Jurisdiction, Case Files 3756, RG 123, Stack area 163E.

16 Records of W. G. Schafer, West Feliciana Historical Society (WFHS), 20–21.

17 "In the Court of Claims," October 1892, Levi M. Lowenburg, folder C.d. 3756, M. Bodenheim, 5, and "In the Court of Claims," December Term, 1891–1892, Levi M. Lowenburg, folder C.d. 3756, Charles Lehman, 16, NARA, E22, Congressional Jurisdiction, Case Files 3756, RG 123, Stack area 163E.

18 JWA, 15–16.

19 Jay Silverberg, "Louisiana Letters, 1855–1871: The Story of an Immigrant Family," *Southern Jewish Historical Society Journal* 18 (2005): 104–110, 159; Louisiana, 22:240 and New York, 320:570, R.G. Dun & Co. Credit Report Volumes, Baker Library, HBS. See also Jay Silverberg, email to author, December 15, 2014.

20 Ashkenazi, *The Business of Jews in Louisiana*, 72, 74.

21 Sarna, *When General Grant Expelled the Jews*, 18–19; David M. Delo, *Peddlers and Post Traders: The Army Sutler on the Frontier* (Helena, MT: Kingfisher Books, 1998), 1–2, 127.

22 Delo, *Peddlers and Post Traders*, 109; Sarna, *When General Grant Expelled the Jews*, 19; and "Aunt Mellie's Story."

23 John D. Winters, *The Civil War in Louisiana* (Baton Rouge: Louisiana State University Press, 1963), 85–102; and Marler, *The Merchants' Capital*, 176–177.

24 Winters, *The Civil War in Louisiana*, 96; Marler, *The Merchants' Capital*, 146; "A Statement of Facts, relatively to the destruction of Cotton in this City on the 24th, 25th of April 1862 and following days," New-York Historical Society, Misc MSS, New Orleans, folder 1.

25 Marler, *The Merchants' Capital*, 176–177, 179, 181–182. Marler has corrected what he calls "minor discrepancies, probably attributable to typographical errors." See the charts that he provides; and *Debow's Review*, February 1866, 202–203, and

November 1866, 415. While much of the decline in New Orleans' cotton receipts was due to the sharp reduction in interior production, it was also due to increased cotton smuggling and marketing in the interior and transportation via overland rail lines to other cities. This shift would be far more pronounced in the postbellum years.

26 Marler, *The Merchants' Capital*, 179; and Sarna, *When General Grant Expelled the Jews*, 43–44.

27 Marler, *The Merchants' Capital*, 150–152, 156–157, 177; Sarna, *When General Grant Expelled the Jews*; and Jonathan D. Sarna and Benjamin Shapell, *Lincoln and the Jews* (New York: St. Martin's Press, 2015), 138.

28 Sarna, *When Grant Expelled the Jews*, 39, 44–45.

29 Ibid., 44–45, 47–49. This work also contains a more complete portrait of General Order no. 11 and its implications.

30 Ashkenazi, *Business of Jews in Louisiana*, 73; "In the Court of Claims," October 1892, Levi M. Lowenburg, James Conklin, 2, NARA, E22, Congressional Jurisdiction, Case Files 3756, RG 123, Stack area 163E; records of W. G. Schafer, WFHS, 10; and JWA, 15. Also see "In the Court of Claims," October 1892, Levi M. Lowenburg, M. Bodenheim, 5, NARA, E22, Congressional Jurisdiction, Case Files 3756, RG 123, Stack area 163E.

31 While Clinton was cut off from New Orleans, Emanuel Meyer purchased cotton, although he did so with the financial assistance of Abraham Levy. See Ashkenazi, *The Business of Jews in Louisiana*, 73–74. See also Stanley Lebergott, "Through the Blockade: The Profitability and Extent of Cotton Smuggling, 1861–1865," *Journal of Economic History* 41, no. 4 (1981): 867–884; and records of W. G. Schafer, WFHS, 15–17.

32 Marler, *The Merchants' Capital*, 165, 177–178, 181–182. See *Debow's Review*, February 1866, 202–203, and November 1866, 415, as cited in ibid. The Crescent City was instrumental in the resumption of trade. The number of "legal" cotton bales during the war was 444,095—310,931 bales of which went through the Port of New Orleans. This suggests on the surface that New Orleans was playing a key role in the wartime cotton economy, but the drop in New Orleans receipts was significant, although the total value was not. For example, in the 1860–1861 season, New Orleans receipts were just over 1.849 million bales, with a total value of over $92,000,000. While the 1864–1865 crop totaled over $73,000,000, the actual number of bales was just over 271,000. Thus the artificially high prices created the illusion that New Orleans was returning to a central role in the industry. See "Report of Acting Rear-Admiral Lee, US Navy, transmitting report of Lieutenant Commander Cornwell, U. S. Navy, commanding Second District, covering February 8-M, 1865," in *Official Records of the Union and Confederate Navies in the War of the Rebellion* (Washington, DC: U.S. Naval War Records Office, 1865); and Beckert, *Empire of Cotton*, 261–262.

33 Woodman, *King Cotton*, 207–214.

34 JWA, 17.

35 Roland Flade, *The Lehmans: From Rimpar to the New World: A Family History* (Würzburg: Königshausen & Neumann, 1999), 63, 65; Lehman Brothers, *A Centennial: Lehman Brothers, 1850–1950* (New York: Lehman Brothers, 1950), 9–10; and New York, 319:500/G, R.G. Dun & Co. Credit Report Volumes, Baker Library, HBS.

36 "Report of Acting Rear-Admiral Lee"; and records of W. G. Schafer, WFHS, 19–20.

37 Hacker, "A Census-Based Count," 311, 313.

38 Virginia Lobdell Jennings, "Bayou Sara: The Town and Stream," in "Bayou Sara Notes," folder, 10; Historical Data Systems, comp., *U.S., Civil War Soldier Records and Profiles, 1861–1865*, online database (Provo, UT: Ancestry.com Operations, Inc., 2009); *The War of the Rebellion: A Compilation of the Official Records of the Union and Confederate Armies, Part I* (Washington, DC: U.S. Government Printing Office, 1884), 490; and Louisiana, 22:254, R.G. Dun & Co. Credit Report Volumes, Baker Library, HBS.

39 Milton P. Barschdorf, *A History of an Inland River Port* ([Greenville, MS?]: E. & M. Barschdorf, 1997), 12; Herman W. Solomon, *The Early History of the Hebrew Union Congregation of Greenville, Mississippi* (1972; reprint, [Greenville, MS]: Solomon, 2001), 4.

40 "Yankee Grave Dixie Decorates Reveals Strange Tale: Man Who Shelled Louisiana Village Lies Buries There: Bombardment Halted to Give Self-Slain Leader Last Rites," transcription in WFHS, source given as *Times-Picayune*, October 14, 1937; "General Overview of Natchez History" (Natchez, MS: Historic Natchez Foundation, n.d.), 36–37; and records of W. G. Schafer, WFHS, 13–14. I am appreciative of Mimi Miller's insight on this subject.

41 "General Overview of Natchez History," 40; and Joe Gray Taylor, *Louisiana Reconstructed, 1863–1877* (Baton Rouge: Louisiana State University Press, 1974), 320.

42 Taylor, *Louisiana Reconstructed*, 317–319; and James T. Currie, *Enclave: Vicksburg and Her Plantations, 1863–1870* (Jackson: University Press of Mississippi, 1980), 220.

43 JWA, 16.

44 Marler, *The Merchants' Capital*, 17; Alabama, 20:24, R.G. Dun & Co. Credit Report Volumes, Baker Library, HBS; Flade, *The Lehmans*, 63; and Louisiana, 12:180, R.G. Dun & Co. Credit Report Volumes, Baker Library, HBS.

45 T. H. Watts to Jefferson Davis, December 14, 1864, document 0536_0005; M. Lehman and I. T. Tichenor, agents of the State of Alabama, to Lieutenant General Grant, January 11, 1865, Herbert H. Lehman Papers, document 0506_0006, Rare Book and Manuscript Library, Columbia University Library.

46 Aaron D. Anderson, *Builders of a New South: Merchants, Capital, and the Remaking of Natchez, 1865–1914* (Jackson: University Press of Mississippi, 2013), 32.

47 "In the Court of Claims," October 1892, Levi M. Lowenburg, 1, 2, 4, 5, 6, and "In the Court of Claims," December Term, 1893–1894, Levi M. Lowenburg, NARA, E22, Congressional Jurisdiction, Case Files 3756, RG 123, Stack area 163E, 2; and Mississippi, 2:122, R.G. Dun & Co. Credit Report Volumes, Baker Library, HBS.

48 On the difficulty of quantification, how, for example, do we count merchants who returned after Grant opened the region, but who subsequently left during the waning years of the war? How do we count merchants who came during the early years of the conflict and who remained into the postbellum years? And how do we count merchants who left the region during the conflict but returned before Dun recorders came to town? Because of the disruption of war, determining specific movement of individuals and businesses is particularly difficult. See Louisiana, 3:1, 3:9, R.G. Dun & Co. Credit Report Volumes, Baker Library, HBS.

49 New York, 217:834, R.G. Dun & Co. Credit Report Volumes, Baker Library, HBS. This reference was also made on April 21, 1861, suggesting that the firm might have been out of business before the war. A reference in New York, 372:1084, R.G. Dun & Co. Credit Report Volumes, Baker Library, HBS, says that they dissolved during the war. I also have found no further records in the postbellum years linking Meyer to the Natchez firm; see Louisiana, 22:254, R.G. Dun & Co. Credit Report Volumes, Baker Library, HBS.

50 "Freyhan, Julius," West Feliciana Historical Society, transcription of Michael F. Howell, "Feliciana Confederates," 221; and Anne Butler, *Three Generous Generations* (Baton Rouge, LA: Claitor's Publishing Division, 2004), 23–24. See Louisiana, 22:258, R.G. Dun & Co. Credit Report Volumes, Baker Library, HBS; and "M. & E. Wolf," *True Democrat*, February 24, 1917, 5.

51 Louisiana, 22:250, R.G. Dun & Co. Credit Report Volumes, Baker Library, HBS. Scott Marler argues that the Wolf Brothers ran several country stores in the northern part of the parish. Dun recorders noted that Gustave Wolf's firm involved two brothers, and Gustave and Abram are listed together in the Dun ledgers with the notation "two bros. both the same store." See Marler, *The Merchants' Capital*, 239; and Louisiana, 22:247, 22:278, 22:244, and 22:243, R.G. Dun & Co. Credit Report Volumes, Baker Library, HBS.

52 Louisiana, 22:260, R.G. Dun & Co. Credit Report Volumes, Baker Library, HBS; and Jennings, "Bayou Sara: The Town and Stream," 10.

53 Ashkenazi, *The Business of Jews in Louisiana*, 73; Jay Silverberg, "Louisiana Letters, 1855–1871: The Story of an Immigrant Family," *Southern Jewish Historical Society Journal* 18 (2005): 106; New York, 320:570, R.G. Dun & Co. Credit Report Volumes, Baker Library, HBS.

54 Ferdinand Goldsmith, "Life and Doings of Ferdinand Goldsmith," American Jewish Archives, Cincinnati, Ohio, SC-4063, 1–2.

55 JWA, 16–18.

56 Ibid., 17. This last quotation does not appear in the typewritten manuscript at Tulane University Special Collections or in Jacob Rader Marcus's *Memoirs of American Jews*. However, it does appear in "Fifty Years of Southern Progress," *Times-Picayune*, November 17, 1895, 7, as cited at "Julius Weis," memorial no. 124527131, *Find a Grave*, February 2, 2014, www.findagrave.com.

57 Ibid., 16–18.

58 New York, 200:375, R.G. Dun & Co. Credit Report Volumes, Baker Library, HBS.

59 "Report of Acting Rear-Admiral Lee."

60 Ashkenazi, *The Business of Jews in Louisiana*, 27.

CHAPTER 3. TIMING IS EVERYTHING

1 Harold D. Woodman, *King Cotton and His Retainers: Financing and Marketing the Cotton Crop of the South 1800–1925* (Washington, DC: Beard Books, 2000), 273, 275. See *Bradstreet's*, April 10, 186, 226–227, as cited in Woodman, *King Cotton*, 275; and Sven Beckert, *Empire of Cotton: A Global History* (New York: Knopf, 2014), 318.

2 Woodman, *King Cotton*, 273, 275; and Joseph Nimmo, Jr., *First Annual Report on the Internal Commerce of the United States*, 44th Congress, 2nd session, House Executive Document 46, pt. 2 (Washington, DC: U.S. Government Printing Office, 1877), 143.

3 Perry Anderson Snyder, "Shreveport, Louisiana, during the Civil War and Reconstruction" (PhD thesis, Florida State University, 1979), 158; and Gary D. Joiner and Ernie Roberson, *Lost Shreveport: Vanishing Scenes from the Red River Valley* (Charleston, SC: History Press, 2010), 15.

4 "The Louisiana Parishes," *New York Times*, October 6, 1874, 4.

5 James T. Currie, *Enclave: Vicksburg and Her Plantations, 1863–1870* (Jackson: University Press of Mississippi, 1980), 221; and Edward King, *The Great South*, ed. W. Magruder Drake and Robert R. Jones (Baton Rouge: Louisiana State University Press, 1972), 290.

6 Milton P. Barschdorf, *A History of an Inland River Port* ([Greenville, MS?]: E. & M. Barschdorf, 1997), 12. See various editions of Mercantile Agency, *The Mercantile Agency's Reference Book of the United States and British Provinces* (New York: B. Douglass & Co., various years); "Port Gibson: Its Past and Present," *Jackson Clarion*, June 20, 1883; and "A Mississippi Mayor," *St. Louis Daily Globe-Democrat*, September 12, 1883, 8, col. 7.

7 "Almost any town of consequence" had cotton compresses and the telegraph by the turn of the twentieth century, and one periodical noted that "the sending of cotton buyers into the interior, shipping cotton they buy on through bills of lading, avoiding heavy charges at the ports, has cut considerably into business formerly exclusively enjoyed by those ports." See Woodman, *King Cotton*, 273, 275–276; and *Bradsteet's* 13 (April 10, 1886): 226. Also see Nimmo, *First Annual Report on the Internal Commerce of the United States*, 146.

8 "General Overview of Natchez History" (Natchez, MS: Historic Natchez Foundation, n.d.), 49; Barschdorf, *A History of an Inland River Port*, 3; "The Louisiana Parishes," *New York Times*, October 6, 1874, 4; Ann M. McLaurin, ed., *Glimpses of Shreveport* (Natchitoches, LA: Northwestern State University Press, 1985), 49–50; Joiner and Roberson, *Lost Shreveport*, 15; Snyder, "Shreveport, Louisiana, during the Civil War and Reconstruction," 161; and Currie, *Enclave*, 220.

9 Robert Somers, *The Southern States since the War* (London: MacMillian & Co., 1871), 166; Currie, *Enclave*, 223.

10 Ibid., 150, 166.

11 A key component in the move to the interior was the coming of the railroad. "Every town," notes Harold Woodman, "indeed, virtually every stop on the railroad, had become a market town where the grower could sell his crop." See Woodman, *King Cotton*, 274. Also see Somers, *The Southern States since the War*, 166–167.

12 Somers, *The Southern States since the War*, 167–168.

13 George S. Bush, *An American Harvest: The Story of Weil Brothers Cotton* (Englewood Cliffs, NJ: Prentice-Hall, 1982), 44–59, 71.

14 King, *The Great South*, 312; Somers, *The Southern States since the War*, 150–151; and Richelle Putnam, *Lauderdale County, Mississippi: A Brief History* (Charleston, SC: History Press, 2011), 60, 64, 79.

15 Union of American Hebrew Congregations, *Statistics of the Jews of the United States, Compiled under the Authority of the Board of Delegates of American Israelites and the Union of American Hebrew Congregations* ([Philadelphia]: Union of American Hebrew Congregations, 1880), 26; Mississippi, Vol. 12, pages 383/0 and 12:383/p (hereafter presented as volume:page), R.G. Dun & Co. Credit Report Volumes, Baker Library, Harvard Business School (HBS); "Meridian: Historical Overview," Institute of Southern Jewish Life, n.d., www.isjl.org; Mississippi, 12:450, R.G. Dun & Co. Credit Report Volumes, Baker Library, HBS; and Putnam, *Lauderdale County*, 73.

16 Thomas Owen, *History of Alabama and Dictionary of Alabama Biography* (Chicago: S. J. Clarke Publishing Co., 1921), 1:24–28; U.S. Census of Population and Housing, "1990: Population and Housing Unit Counts: United States" (Washington, DC: U.S. Department of Commerce, Bureau of the Census, 1993), 594, table 46: "Population Rank of Incorporated Places of 100,000 Population or More, 1990; Population, 1790 to 1990; Housing Units: 1940 to 1990," www.census.gov.; population growth as cited in "Birmingham's Population, 1880–2000," Birmingham Public Library, n.d., www.bplonline.org; and "Birmingham, Alabama," *The Mercantile Agency's Reference Book* (1880, 1890).

17 Mercantile Agency, *The Mercantile Agency's Reference Book*.

18 Woodman, *King Cotton*, 275.

19 Roger L. Ransom and Richard Sutch, "Debt Peonage in the Cotton South after the Civil War," *Journal of Economic History* 32, no. 3 (September 1972): 643–650.

20 Louisiana, 22:253, R.G. Dun & Co. Credit Report Volumes, Baker Library, HBS; and Virginia Lobdell Jennings, "Bayou Sara: The Town and Stream," in "Bayou Sara Notes," folder, West Feliciana Historical Society (WFHS), St. Francisville, Louisiana, 12. See Mann, Fischer & Co. Account Books, 1:16, November 1873, MSS 896, Louisiana State University Special Collections.

21 Somers, *The Southern States since the War*, 171; Ransom and Sutch argue that, "since the banking system was either unable or unwilling to extend loans to small farmers, it fell to the local merchant to extend the seasonal credit necessary for farming." See Ransom and Sutch, "Debt Peonage," 651.

22 Somers, *The Southern States since the War*, 171; Sven Beckert, *The Monied Metropolis: New York City and the Consolidation of the American Bourgeoisie, 1850–1896* (Cambridge: Cambridge University Press, 2001), 162. Stanley Coben notes that "only one important northeastern business group was strongly attracted by investment opportunities in the South immediately after the war: New York financiers, the true 'masters of capital,' who had long-standing commercial ties with the South, and had sufficient funds to risk large amounts in a turbulent era." See Stanley Coben, "Northeastern Business and Reconstruction," in *Reconstruction: An Anthology of Revisionist Writings*, ed. Kenneth Milton Stampp and Leon Litwack (Baton Rouge: Louisiana State University Press, 1969), 86; and Woodman, *King Cotton*, 263.

23 Kate Stone, *Brokenburn: The Journal of Kate Stone, 1861–1868* (Baton Rouge: Louisiana University Press, 1955), as cited in Joe Gray Taylor, *Louisiana Reconstructed, 1863–1877* (Baton Rouge: Louisiana State University Press, 1974), 344.

24 Woodman, *King Cotton*, 249–250. This quote refers to Georgia, but the dearth of cotton for legal shipment appears to have been present in the Gulf South as well.

25 Taylor, *Louisiana Reconstructed*, 344; records of W. G. Schafer, West Feliciana Historical Society (WFHS), 22; Coben, "Northeastern Business and Reconstruction," 85.

26 W. G. Schafer diary, WFHS packet 2, 24.

27 Taylor, *Louisiana Reconstructed*, 345. See Richard W. Griffin, "Problems of Southern Cotton Planters after the Civil War," *Georgia Historical Quarterly* 39 (June 1955): 111. See *Harper's Weekly*, October 9, 1869, 643; and "How the Country Looks," *New Orleans Times-Picayune*, April 19, 1868, 1.

28 Louisiana, 22:260, R.G. Dun & Co. Credit Report Volumes, Baker Library, HBS.

29 Louisiana, 3:56, R.G. Dun & Co. Credit Report Volumes, Baker Library, HBS.

30 Alabama, 20:84, R.G. Dun & Co. Credit Report Volumes, Baker Library, HBS.

31 Meyer had been successful before the war in Natchez, Bayou Sara, and New York, and by the end of the war he had dissolved both his Bayou Sara and Natchez partnerships. He did forge a new, short-lived partnership in Bayou Sara with Abraham Hirsch, and the pair was conducting a large business ("No. 1") by mid-1866, but by summer, however, Meyer appears to have left the business. See Louisiana, 22:254–255; New York, 320:600/o; and Mississippi, 21:79, R.G. Dun & Co. Credit Report Volumes, Baker Library, HBS.

32 New York, 320:600/o; Arkansas, 7:223, R.G. Dun & Co. Credit Report Volumes, Baker Library, HBS.

33 Julius Weis Autobiography (JWA), n.d., Ida Weis Friend Collection, MSS 287, box 7, Louisiana Research Collection, Tulane University Special Collections (TUSC), 18–19; Louisiana, 12:19, R.G. Dun & Co. Credit Report Volumes, Baker Library, HBS.

34 Louisiana, 12:19, R.G. Dun & Co. Credit Report Volumes, Baker Library, HBS; JWA, 19; and Louisiana, 12:80, R.G. Dun & Co. Credit Report Volumes, Baker Library, HBS.

35 Louisiana, 22:250, 22:268, R.G. Dun & Co. Credit Report Volumes, Baker Library, HBS.

36 Louisiana, 22:261, 22:264, R.G. Dun & Co. Credit Report Volumes, Baker Library, HBS.

37 Records of W. G. Schafer, WFHS, 21–22, 24–26; Louisiana, 22:263, R.G. Dun & Co. Credit Report Volumes, Baker Library, HBS.

38 This counters the notion, often repeated, that Jews were "carpetbaggers" who came down from the North to take jobs away from the native population. Though contemporaries were right in noticing Jewish overrepresentation in this sector of the economy, the statistics question their contention that a mass influx of Jews arrived from the North and drove out existing businesses. Here, the example of Bayou Sara is particularly illustrative. We see tremendous continuity in the town between the Jewish businesses operating immediately before and immediately after the war. Nearly all the Jewish businesses in the cotton economy that were operational in 1860 were still in business in 1866—thus many of the Jewish merchants whom contemporaries noticed had been in the South prior to the war. Further casting doubt on the assumption that all carpetbaggers were Jews is that twelve new Jewish businesses opened between 1865 and 1870, and twenty new non-Jewish businesses opened over the same period.

39 Louisiana, 22:245, 22:262, R.G. Dun & Co. Credit Report Volumes, Baker Library, HBS.

40 Louisiana, 22:263, 22:261, R.G. Dun & Co. Credit Report Volumes, Baker Library, HBS.

41 Louisiana, 22:262–263, R.G. Dun & Co. Credit Report Volumes, Baker Library, HBS.

42 It is not clear whether each brother's tenure at the helm should be considered the same or different establishments. My best deduction from extant sources suggests that these firms should be considered one and the same. Bernard later operated a small store in Bayou Sara from 1869 through 1890, but it is unclear if he took over this store or operated his own; see Louisiana, 22:258, 22:269, R.G. Dun & Co. Credit Report Volumes, Baker Library, HBS; and Mercantile Agency, *The Mercantile Agency's Reference Book* (various years).

43 Louisiana, 22:263, R.G. Dun & Co. Credit Report Volumes, Baker Library, HBS.

44 Louisiana, 22:268, 22:255, 22:264, R.G. Dun & Co. Credit Report Volumes, Baker Library, HBS.

45 Mississippi, 21:17, R.G. Dun & Co. Credit Report Volumes, Baker Library, HBS; Mercantile Agency, *The Mercantile Agency's Reference Book*.

46 Mississippi, 2:120, R.G. Dun & Co. Credit Report Volumes, Baker Library, HBS; "General Overview of Natchez History," Historic Natchez Foundation, 48.

47 Shreveport was a particularly attractive place to settle because there was less damage from battles on Caddo Parish cotton plantations during the war. Although cotton production was down along the Red River, Shreveport's production was close to normal. This may have made Shreveport a more attractive place to settle,

but it by no means guaranteed success. Many growers did not benefit from this, as treasury agents often seized bales of cotton before they reached the market. See Taylor, *Louisiana Reconstructed*, 316–317, 372; and Mercantile Agency, *The Mercantile Agency's Reference Book* (1900).

48 Taylor, *Louisiana Reconstructed*, 351.

49 Ibid., 87–88, 378, 401; and Harold Woodman, "Southern Agriculture and the Law," *Agricultural History* 53, no. 1 (January 1979): 319–337. Lien laws were passed in Alabama, January 15, 1866, Acts, 1865–1866, 44; Mississippi, February 18, 1867, Acts, 1867, 569; Georgia, December 15, 1866, Acts, 1866, 141; South Carolina, 1869, 13 Stat. 380; and North Carolina, Public Laws, 1866–1867, 3. Laws changed in the early 1870s. See Woodman, "Southern Agriculture and the Law," 328–329, esp. n18. See also Floyd M. Clay, "Economic Survival of the Plantation System within the Feliciana Parishes, 1865–1880" (MA thesis, Louisiana State University, 1962); and James T. Currie, *Enclave: Vicksburg and Her Plantations*, 161–162. For more data on Natchez, see Aaron D. Anderson, *Builders of a New South: Merchants, Capital, and the Remaking of Natchez, 1865–1914* (Jackson: University Press of Mississippi, 2013), 87, 130; and Woodman, *King Cotton*, 298. The lien laws were also to have an added bonus for landowners—binding the workforce to the land. Planters assumed that they would be the ones acquiring credit from the merchants and that they could then extend that credit to sharecroppers and tenant farmers at interest rates of their choosing. Without any other means to purchase goods, and because farmers needed to see the cotton through to harvest before they would be paid, landowners believed they had served a dual purpose: They would have access to credit while they also had control over their labor force. This, however, was not to be, as the law of unintended consequences took over. Freedmen in particular generally preferred to work directly with merchants as a means of asserting their independence. In this way, lien laws ironically allowed workers to break free of total control by their landlords, though they hardly gave them the freedoms for which they had hoped would follow the abolition of slavery. See Harold D. Woodman, *New South—New Law: The Legal Foundations of Credit and Labor Relations in the Postbellum Agricultural South* (Baton Rouge: Louisiana State University Press, 1995), 10, 23–24.

50 Taylor, *Louisiana Reconstructed*, 403–405; Berkert, *Empire of Cotton*, 286. Historiography has been largely focused on the question of interest rates and whether or not they were justified, given the inherent financial risks of the era. There is already a significant literature on this topic, and it is not my aim to engage this question.

51 Abraham Levy to Emanuel Meyer, December 21, 1868, as translated in Jay Silverberg, "Louisiana Letters, 1855–1871: The Story of an Immigrant Family," *Southern Jewish Historical Society Journal* 18 (2005): 156–157.

52 These statistics are culled primarily from the R.G. Dun collection (Baker Library, Harvard Business School) and Mercantile Agency, *The Mercantile Agency's Reference Books* (various years).

53 Ibid.

54 Eric Foner, *Reconstruction: America's Unfinished Revolution, 1863–1877* (New York: Harper & Row, 1988), 1; and Beckert, *Empire of Cotton*, 280.

55 Beckert, *Empire of Cotton*, 283, 285; and Gene Dattel, *Cotton and Race in the Making of America: The Human Costs of Economic Power* (Chicago: Ivan R. Dee, 2009), 321.

56 Beckert, *Empire of Cotton*, 285–286.

57 Ibid., 269–271, 283–284; Dattel, *Cotton and Race*, 251; Eric Foner, *A Short History of Reconstruction, 1863–1877*, updated ed. (New York: Harper Perennial Modern Classics, 2015), 182, 186, and *Politics and Ideology in the Age of the Civil War* (Oxford: Oxford University Press, 1981),122; and Kate Kelly, *Election Day: An American Holiday, an American History* (New York: ASJA Press, 1991), 126.

58 Foner, *A Short History of Reconstruction*, 49, 146; and Daniel R. Weinfeld, "Samuel Fleischman: Tragedy in Reconstruction-Era Florida," *Southern Jewish History* 8 (2005): 48–49.

59 Foner, *A Short History of Reconstruction*, 52–53; and records of W. G. Schafer, 25.

60 Foner, *A Short History of Reconstruction*, 195, 215.

61 "The Louisiana Parishes," *New York Times*, October 6, 1874, 4.

62 Louisiana, 22:258, 22:250–251, 22:288, R.G. Dun & Co. Credit Report Volumes, Baker Library, HBS.

63 Louisiana, 22:273, 22:291, R.G. Dun & Co. Credit Report Volumes, Baker Library, HBS; "Adolph Teutsch," memorial no. 66779414, *Find a Grave*, March 11, 2011, www.findagrave.com.

64 Louisiana, 22:261, 22:277, R.G. Dun & Co. Credit Report Volumes, Baker Library, HBS; Mercantile Agency, *The Mercantile Agency's Reference Book* (1880).

65 Mitchell's name was often used interchangeably with the French version "Michel." There were several individuals by the name of Jacob Mitchell or Jacob Michael in the region. See Louisiana, 22:267, 22:269, R.G. Dun & Co. Credit Report Volumes, Baker Library, HBS.

66 Louisiana, 22:244, 22:255, 22:247, R.G. Dun & Co. Credit Report Volumes, Baker Library, HBS.

67 Louisiana, 22:272–273, R.G. Dun & Co. Credit Report Volumes, Baker Library, HBS. Meyer Bros. may have been in business for a brief while from 1866 to 1867. See Louisiana, 22:59, 22:275, 22:277, 22:279, R.G. Dun & Co. Credit Report Volumes, Baker Library, HBS; and Mercantile Agency, *The Mercantile Agency's Reference Book* (1880).

68 Louisiana, 22:278, R.G. Dun & Co. Credit Report Volumes, Baker Library, HBS.

69 Mississippi, 21:26, 21:11, R.G. Dun & Co. Credit Report Volumes, Baker Library, HBS; and William Alexander Percy, *Lanterns on the Levee: Recollections of a Planter's Son* (New York: Knopf, 1966), 17. Statistics are compiled from R.G. Dun & Co. Credit Report Volumes, Baker Library, HBS; and Mercantile Agency, *The Mercantile Agency's Reference Book*.

70 Mississippi, 6:144/o, 6;144/e, 6:144/m, R.G. Dun & Co. Credit Report Volumes, Baker Library, HBS.

71 Louisiana, 3:91; Alabama, 14:239, 15:287, 15:299, R.G. Dun & Co. Credit Report Volumes, Baker Library, HBS.

72 Louisiana, 22:270, 22:249, 22:276, 22:272, R.G. Dun & Co. Credit Report Volumes, Baker Library, HBS.

73 Louisiana, 22:284, 22:288, 22:272, 22:263, 22:267; Mississippi, 6:144/o, R.G. Dun & Co. Credit Report Volumes, Baker Library, HBS.

74 "Democratic Work in Louisiana," *New York Times*, March 8, 1877, WFHS; "A Cowardly Crime," *Donaldsonville Chief*, March 10, 1877, 2, col. 1, as quoted at "Don A. Weber," memorial no. 152348219, *Find a Grave*, September 15, 2015, www.findagrave.com.

75 Beckert, *Monied Metropolis*, 195; Beckert, *Empire of Cotton*, 287; Foner, *A Short History of Reconstruction*, 235, 250–251; and "Arrest of Intimidators in Louisiana," *New York Times*, October 31, 1876, 1, WFHS.

76 Michael Perman, *The Road to Redemption: Southern Politics, 1869–1879* (Chapel Hill: University of North Carolina Press, 1984), 248–250.

77 Ibid., 248–249. Also in an attempt to increase their hegemony, legislatures in nearly every Southern state passed laws in the 1870s that defined the sharecropper as a wage laborer. See Woodman, *New South*, 45, 64–65, 68–69.

78 Edwin G. Burrows and Mike Wallace, *Gotham: A History of New York City to 1898* (Oxford: Oxford University Press, 1999), 1020; and Beckert, *Monied Metropolis*, 207.

79 Beckert, *Monied Metropolis*, 207–208. They were "were in the hands of receivers"; see Burrows and Wallace, *Gotham*, 1022.

80 Beckert, *Monied Metropolis*, 208–209.

81 Frederic Cople Jaher, *The Urban Establishment: Upper Strata in Boston, New York Charleston, Chicago, and Los Angeles* (Urbana: University of Illinois Press, 1982), 602–603; and Frances Dinkelspiel, *Towers of Gold: How One Jewish Immigrant Named Isaias Hellman Created California* (New York: St. Martin's Press, 2008), 87–90.

82 Taylor, *Louisiana Reconstructed*, 359–360.

83 Ibid., 359–362; and Beckert, *Empire of Cotton*, 286–287.

84 Taylor, *Louisiana Reconstructed*, 360. Taylor also notes significant flooding in 1876. See the excerpt "The Mississippi flood has overflowed . . . ," *Highland Weekly* (Hillsboro, North Carolina), February 21, 1874; the excerpt "At a mass meeting of the citizens . . . ," *Ouachita Telegraph* (Monroe, Louisiana), May 1, 1874; and the excerpt "To sum up the flood from Memphis to the Passes . . . ," *Caucasian* (Shreveport, Louisiana), May 16, 1874, all at D.E.B., "Flooding of the Mighty Mississippi, Part One—The Great Overflow of 1874," *Roots from the Bayou*, March 23, 2015, rootsfromthebayou.blogspot.com.

85 Herman W. Solomon, *The Early History of the Hebrew Union Congregation of Greenville, Mississippi* (1972; reprint, [Greenville, MS]: Solomon, 2001), 10–12.

86 Eric J. Brock, *Shreveport Chronicles: Profiles from Louisiana's Port City* (Charleston, SC: History Press, 2009), 30–31; "Pioneer Woman Tells of Yellow Fever Epidemic, Caddo Parish [Louisiana]—1873," *Shreveport Journal*, June 27, 1935, Centennial edition, from the collection of Mildred Legg Carver (copy of newspaper clipping, found in the papers of Mildred Legg Carver), submitted January 1998 by Gaytha Carver Thompson, *USGenWeb Archives*, n.d., http://usgwarchives.net; and Taylor, *Louisiana Reconstructed*, 433–434.

87 Another from the Hebrew Benevolent Association also called for assistance. "Aid for the South," *Jewish Messenger*, August 23, 1878, 2.

88 Solomon, *The Early History*, 14–15.

89 JWA, 19.

90 Louisiana, 22:250, 22:274, R.G. Dun & Co. Credit Report Volumes, Baker Library, HBS; and Mercantile Agency, *The Mercantile Agency's Reference Book* (1880).

91 Louisiana, 22:274, 22:255, 13:384, 13:97, R.G. Dun & Co. Credit Report Volumes, Baker Library, HBS.

92 Louisiana, 3:56, 3:126/h, 3:140/26, R.G. Dun & Co. Credit Report Volumes, Baker Library, HBS; and Mercantile Agency, *The Mercantile Agency's Reference Book* (1880).

93 Alabama, 10:192Z/23, R.G. Dun & Co. Credit Report Volumes, Baker Library, HBS.

94 Mississippi, 2:120, 2:170, R.G. Dun & Co. Credit Report Volumes, Baker Library, HBS.

95 Mississippi, 24:287, 24:317, 24:312/c, R.G. Dun & Co. Credit Report Volumes, Baker Library, HBS; and Goodspeed Brothers, *Biographical and Historical Memoirs of Mississippi, Embracing an Authentic and Comprehensive Account of the Chief Events in the History of the State, and a Record of the Lives of Many of the Most Worthy and Illustrious Families and Individuals* (Chicago: Goodspeed Publishing Co., 1891), 725.

96 New York, 405a:1200/a4, 405a:1200/a17, R.G. Dun & Co. Credit Report Volumes, Baker Library, HBS; and vol. 539: 64, 65, 68, 138, 144, Lehman Brothers Records, Baker Library, Harvard Business School.

97 Louisiana, 22:264, R.G. Dun & Co. Credit Report Volumes, Baker Library, HBS; Scott P. Marler, *The Merchants' Capital: New Orleans and the Political Economy of the Nineteenth-Century South* (Cambridge: Cambridge University Press, 2013), 239; Alabama, 5:24, 5:56–57; Louisiana, 22:269, 22:278, R.G. Dun & Co. Credit Report Volumes, Baker Library, HBS; and Jennings, "Bayou Sara: The Town and Stream," 10.

98 New York, 323:900a/2, 323:900a/38, R.G. Dun & Co. Credit Report Volumes, Baker Library, HBS.

99 "Henry Bodenheim," *Brooklyn (New York) Daily Eagle*, May 7, 1875, 2; "New York City News," *Pomeroy's Democrat* (New York, NY), May 15, 1875, [5], col. 4; digital images, *GenealogyBank*, n.d., www.genealogybank.com; "Suicide of a Merchant," *Evening Star* (Washington, DC), May, 7, 1875, 1; "Over the State," *Canton*

(Mississippi) Mail, May 15, 1875, 2; "Henry Bodenheim," *Daily Phoenix* (Columbia, SC), May 13, 1875, 3; and New York, 323:900a/38, R.G. Dun & Co. Credit Report Volumes, Baker Library, HBS.

100 Louisiana, 22:269, 22:278, R.G. Dun & Co. Credit Report Volumes, Baker Library, HBS.

101 David Glasner and Thomas F. Cooley, eds., *Business Cycles and Depressions* (New York: Garland, 1997), 149.

102 Ibid., 149–150.

103 Ibid., 150–151, 517–518.

104 Woodman, *King Cotton*, 334–335; and U.S. Senate, *Report of the Committee on Agriculture and Forestry on Condition of Cotton Growers in the United States, the Present Prices of Cotton, and the Remedy*, 53d Congress, 3d session, Senate Report 986 (Washington, DC: U.S. Government Printing Office, February 23, 1895), 1:3.

CHAPTER 4. NETWORKS FROM ABOVE

1 Louisiana, Vol. 12, p. 180; New York, Vol. 319, p. 500/a53 (hereafter presented as volume:page), R.G. Dun & Co. Credit Report Volumes, Baker Library, Harvard Business School (HBS).

2 Roland Flade, *The Lehmans: From Rimpar to the New World: A Family History* (Würzburg: Königshausen and Neumann, 1999), 68; New York, 319:500/g, 319:500/a13, 319:500 a/53, 319:500 a/72, R.G. Dun & Co. Credit Report Volumes, Baker Library, HBS.

3 New York, 319:500/g, 319:500/a72, 319:500/a26, R.G. Dun & Co. Credit Report Volumes, Baker Library, HBS; and Elliot Ashkenazi, "Jewish Commercial Interests between North and South: The Case of the Lehmans and the Seligmans," *American Jewish Archives* 43 (Spring/Summer 1991): 35.

4 Lehman Brothers, *A Centennial: Lehman Brothers, 1850–1950* (New York: Lehman Brothers, 1950), 9–10, 13–15; Ashkenazi, "Jewish Commercial Interests between North and South," 33, 35; and Louisiana, 12:180, R.G. Dun & Co. Credit Report Volumes, Baker Library, HBS.

5 Louisiana, 12:180, 12:1a, R.G. Dun & Co. Credit Report Volumes, Baker Library, HBS.

6 Henry Abraham was a brother-in-law of Lewis Goldsmith's son Ferdinand. See Flade, *The Lehmans*, 68; Louisiana, 12:1a, 12:3b, 12:ae, R.G. Dun & Co. Credit Report Volumes, Baker Library, HBS.

7 Louisiana, 12:3b, 12:3ae, R.G. Dun & Co. Credit Report Volumes, Baker Library, HBS; and vol. 539:292, Lehman Brothers Records, Baker Library, Harvard Business School. There were two transactions of $25,000 with State and one transaction of $25,000 with Citizens.

8 Ashkenazi, "Jewish Commercial Interests between North and South," 35; Susie J. Pak, *Gentlemen Bankers: The World of J. P. Morgan* (Cambridge, MA: Harvard University Press, 2013), 14–15.

9 Pak, *Gentlemen Bankers*, 13–14, 83, 91, 99.

10 Ibid., 80, 82–83; and 539:50–51, 326–329, 350, 408–415, 427, 762, 774–775, 540:885, 899, 927, 542:1177, Lehman Brothers Records, Baker Library, Harvard Business School. See Mira Wilkins, *The History of Foreign Investment in the United States to 1914* (Cambridge, MA: Harvard University Press, 2004), 120; "Lazard LLC History," *FundingUniverse*, n.d., www.fundinguniverse.com.

11 Adam D. Mendelsohn, *The Rag Race: How Jews Sewed Their Way to Success in America and the British Empire* (New York: New York University Press, 2015); Ashkenazi, "Jewish Commercial Interests between North and South," 27–29, 31–33; Ross L. Muir and Carl J. White, *Over the Long Term . . . : The Story of J. & W. Seligman & Co.* (New York: J. & W. Seligman & Co., 1964), 75; Charles William Smith (of Liverpool), *International Commercial and Financial Gambling in "Options and Futures" (*Marchés à Terme*): The Economic Ruin of the World* (London: P. S. King & Son), 279.

12 Linton Wells, "The House of Seligman," 1931, typescript, Seligman Family papers, New-York Historical Society, New York, 26, 78; Ashkenazi, "Jewish Commercial Interests between North and South," 29–31.

13 George S. Hellman, "Joseph and his Brothers," New-York Historical Society, n.p., 102A, 202A; "Theodore Hellman," *San Francisco Bulletin*, July 6, 1872, 1; "Theodore Hellman," *Ancestry*, n.d., www.ancestry.com; and "Auction Sales," *New Orleans Times Picayune*, December 4, 1881, 16.

14 Joseph Seligman to Max Hellman, February 27, 1867, and Joseph Seligman to Max Hellman, March 1867, as quoted in Wells, "The House of Seligman," 78; Louisiana, 13:237, 9:286/r, 16:203, R.G. Dun & Co. Credit Report Volumes, Baker Library, HBS; Muir and White, *Over the Long Term*, 71; and "I Told You So," *New Orleans Times Picayune*, July 18, 1877, 1.

15 Louisiana, 16:203, R.G. Dun & Co. Credit Report Volumes, Baker Library, HBS; and 539:334–337, 349, 357–358, 360, 362, 606, 724, 781, Lehman, Abraham & Co., Lehman Brothers Records, Baker Library, Harvard Business School.

16 Isaias Hellman, together with Benjamin Newgass and Meyer Lehman, "created their own informal financial syndicate that moved capital from Britain to New York to California and to other parts of the country." See Frances Dinkelspiel, *Towers of Gold: How One Jewish Immigrant Named Isaias Hellman Created California* (New York: St. Martin's Press, 2008), 3, 54, 56. Also see 539:1–2, Lehman Brothers Records, Baker Library, Harvard Business School.

17 Dinkelspiel, *Towers of Gold*, 92–93, 141; and Isaias Hellman to Benjamin Newgass, March 28, 1890, California Historical Society, San Francisco (CHS), box 29, 9:21–22. I thank Frances Dinkelspiel for alerting me to these documents.

18 Dinkelspiel, *Towers of Gold*, 56, 152–154. They were "buying and selling stocks and bonds for various enterprises, extending credit, and investing in one another's ventures in railroads, banks, and commodities," argues Dinkelspiel. See Isaias W. Hellman to Benjamin Newgass, MS 981, June 13, 1891, CHS, box

30, 11:460; and Benjamin Newgass to Isaias Hellman, CHS, unidentified box of letters, 1871–1915, July 3, 1891. I thank Frances Dinkelspiel for alerting me to these documents.

19 Louisiana, 12:3/b, R.G. Dun & Co. Credit Report Volumes, Baker Library, HBS; Ashkenazi, "Jewish Commercial Interests between North and South," 35; Louisiana, 12:3/a/e; New York, 319:500 a/13, R.G. Dun & Co. Credit Report Volumes, Baker Library, HBS; and Elliott Ashkenazi, *The Business of Jews in Louisiana, 1840–1875* (Tuscaloosa: University of Alabama Press, 1988), 130–131.

20 Louisiana, 12:3/1/a, R.G. Dun & Co. Credit Report Volumes, Baker Library, HBS.

21 Louisiana, 22:33, R.G. Dun & Co. Credit Report Volumes, Baker Library, HBS. They may have been born in Rodney, Mississippi. See Louisiana, 22:49, 22:16, 22:33, 6:240/6, R.G. Dun & Co. Credit Report Volumes, Baker Library, HBS.

22 Louisiana, 22:16, 22:33, R.G. Dun & Co. Credit Report Volumes, Baker Library, HBS.

23 Louisiana, 22:33, 22:49, R.G. Dun & Co. Credit Report Volumes, Baker Library, HBS.

24 Ibid.

25 Vol. 542, Lehman Brothers Records, Baker Library, Harvard Business School; Mississippi, 21:81a, 21:129, 21:186, 21:353, R.G. Dun & Co. Credit Report Volumes, Baker Library, HBS.

26 Emily Ford and Barry Stiefel, *The Jews of New Orleans and the Mississippi Delta: A History of Life and Community along the Bayou* (Charleston, SC: History Press, 2012), list Simon Metzger as Jewish. Also see 539:25, 353, 363, 552–53, 662, Lehman Brothers Records, Baker Library, Harvard Business School; Mississippi, 21:206, R.G. Dun & Co. Credit Report Volumes, Baker Library, HBS; and Mercantile Agency, *The Mercantile Agency's Reference Book of the United States and British Provinces* (New York: B. Douglass & Co., 1890).

27 Mississippi, 6:176, 6:144, 6:168, R.G. Dun & Co. Credit Report Volumes, Baker Library, HBS.

28 Ibid.

29 Mississippi, 6:168, R.G. Dun & Co. Credit Report Volumes, Baker Library, HBS.

30 Mississippi, 6:144/d, 6:144/o, R.G. Dun & Co. Credit Report Volumes, Baker Library, HBS.

31 Mississippi, 6:144/d, 6:144/x, 6:144/o, R.G. Dun & Co. Credit Report Volumes, Baker Library, HBS.

32 Mississippi, 6:144/d, 6:144/x, 6:144/o, R.G. Dun & Co. Credit Report Volumes, Baker Library, HBS; 542:979, Lehman Brothers Records, Baker Library, Harvard Business School.

33 Arkansas, 9:257, 9:270, R.G. Dun & Co. Credit Report Volumes, Baker Library, HBS; Carolyn Gray LeMaster, *A Corner of the Tapestry: A History of the Jewish Experience in Arkansas, 1820s–1990s* (Fayetteville: University of Arkansas Press,

1994), 168; and 540:752–754, Lehman Brothers Records, Baker Library, Harvard Business School.

34 Alabama, 10:155, 10:193, 10:3.16, R.G. Dun & Co. Credit Report Volumes, Baker Library, HBS.

35 Alabama, 14:26, 5:24, 15:56–57, R.G. Dun & Co. Credit Report Volumes, Baker Library, HBS.

36 Louisiana, 13:132, 16:136, R.G. Dun & Co. Credit Report Volumes, Baker Library, HBS; and vol. 540:334–369, 600–619, Lehman Brothers Records, Baker Library, Harvard Business School.

37 Louisiana, 16:136; Mississippi, 21:40; Louisiana, 9:286/11, 16:288, R.G. Dun & Co. Credit Report Volumes, Baker Library, HBS.

38 Louisiana, 3:81, 3:98, R.G. Dun & Co. Credit Report Volumes, Baker Library, HBS; 539:663, Lehman Brothers Records, Baker Library, Harvard Business School.

39 Louisiana, 19:50, 19:68, 19:81, R.G. Dun & Co. Credit Report Volumes, Baker Library, HBS.

40 Ibid.

41 Ibid.

42 Louisiana, 19:82, R.G. Dun & Co. Credit Report Volumes, Baker Library, HBS.

43 Louisiana, 19:82, 19:76, R.G. Dun & Co. Credit Report Volumes, Baker Library, HBS; 539:68, 346, 605–608, 706, Lehman Brothers Records, Baker Library, Harvard Business School.

44 Arkansas, 13:80, 8:5, R.G. Dun & Co. Credit Report Volumes, Baker Library, HBS.

45 Arkansas, 13:80, 13:109, vol. 4, R.G. Dun & Co. Credit Report Volumes, Baker Library, HBS.

46 Arkansas, 13:139, 13:109, 13:168, R.G. Dun & Co. Credit Report Volumes, Baker Library, HBS.

47 Louisiana, 9:286/0, 16:344, R.G. Dun & Co. Credit Report Volumes, Baker Library, HBS.

48 Vols. 539:334, 678; 540:921, 994, Lehman Brothers Records, Baker Library, Harvard Business School.

49 Arkansas, 13:108, R.G. Dun & Co. Credit Report Volumes, Baker Library, HBS.

50 Arkansas, 13:108, 13:122, R.G. Dun & Co. Credit Report Volumes, Baker Library, HBS.

51 Arkansas, 13:108, 13:138, 13:170, 13:174, R.G. Dun & Co. Credit Report Volumes, Baker Library, HBS; 539:346, 440–441, Lehman Brothers Records, Baker Library, Harvard Business School.

52 LeMaster, *A Corner of the Tapestry*, 137; Arkansas, 11:211, R.G. Dun & Co. Credit Report Volumes, Baker Library, HBS; 539:516–517, Lehman Brothers Records, Baker Library, Harvard Business School.

53 LeMaster, *A Corner of the Tapestry*, 137; Arkansas, 11:211, 11:321, R.G. Dun & Co. Credit Report Volumes, Baker Library, HBS; 540:915, Lehman Brothers Records, Baker Library, Harvard Business School.

54 LeMaster, *A Corner of the Tapestry*, 146, 499n318. For another example of women operating stores, see the memoir of Julie Kaufman, who operated businesses in Louisiana, American Jewish Archives, Cincinnati, Ohio, SC-13790, Goodwin, Julie.

55 LeMaster, *A Corner of the Tapestry*, 146–147. Also see the entry for Bluma Gans, "Jewish Oakland (Hebrew) Cemetery, Pulaski County, Arkansas," *Arkansas Gravestones*, August 28, 2009, http://arkansasgravestones.org.

56 LeMaster, *A Corner of the Tapestry*, 29, 182. Also see *Pine Bluff Daily Graphic*, December 4, 1917. Members of this firm included Adolph Meyer. Arkansas, 7:243/6, R.G. Dun & Co. Credit Report Volumes, Baker Library, HBS.

57 Arkansas, 7:189, 7:223, 7:243/s, R.G. Dun & Co. Credit Report Volumes, Baker Library, HBS.

58 Arkansas, 7:189, 7:223, 7:243/s, 7:243/6, R.G. Dun & Co. Credit Report Volumes, Baker Library, HBS; and LeMaster, *A Corner of the Tapestry*, 182.

59 Arkansas, 7:223, 7:189, 7:243/s, R.G. Dun & Co. Credit Report Volumes, Baker Library, HBS; 540:994, 539:773, 775, Lehman Brothers Records, Baker Library Historical Collections, Harvard Business School.

60 Richelle Putnam, *Lauderdale County, Mississippi: A Brief History* (Charleston, SC: History Press, 2011), 72; Mississippi, 12:399, 12:439, 12:416, R.G. Dun & Co. Credit Report Volumes, Baker Library, HBS; and 540:1006, Lehman Brothers Records, Baker Library, Harvard Business School.

61 Mississippi, 12:416, 12:439, R.G. Dun & Co. Credit Report Volumes, Baker Library, HBS.

62 New York, 204:800/l, 800/w, 800/z, R.G. Dun & Co. Credit Report Volumes, Baker Library, HBS.

63 New York, 204:800/l; Louisiana, 16:70, 16:291, R.G. Dun & Co. Credit Report Volumes, Baker Library, HBS; and 539:1, Lehman Ledgers, 488–489, Lehman Brothers Records, Baker Library, Harvard Business School.

CHAPTER 5. NETWORKS FROM BELOW

1 "M. & E. Wolf," *True Democrat*, February 24, 1917, 5; "Palimpsests," *True Democrat*, July 23, 1892, West Feliciana Historical Society (WFHS).

2 "Julius Freyhan Passport," April 1873, WFHS; Louisiana, Vol. 5, p. 256 (hereafter presented as volume:page), R.G. Dun & Co. Credit Report Volumes, Baker Library, Harvard Business School (HBS); Anne Butler, *Three Generous Generations* (Baton Rouge, LA: Claitor's Publishing Division, 2004), 6–9, 23; Michael F. Howell, "Feliciana Confederates," WFHS, 221; Louisiana, 22:258, R.G. Dun & Co. Credit Report Volumes, Baker Library, HBS. The example of Freyhan demonstrates how deserters could be welcomed back into society after the war, and Freyhan's wartime actions did not impede his postbellum success. In fact, he became one of the parish's most influential citizens, as well as the largest merchant in West Feliciana Parish.

3 "M. & E. Wolf," *True Democrat*, February 24, 1917, 5; Louisiana, 22:258–259, R.G. Dun & Co. Credit Report Volumes, Baker Library, HBS; Butler, *Three Generous Generations*, 34.

4 Butler, *Three Generous Generations*, 34–35; "Palimpsests," *True Democrat*, July 23, 1892; Louisiana, 22:258–259, R.G. Dun & Co. Credit Report Volumes, Baker Library, HBS.

5 "M. & E. Wolf," *True Democrat*, February 24, 1917, 5.

6 Ibid.; Louisiana, 22:259, 22:282, R.G. Dun & Co. Credit Report Volumes, Baker Library, HBS. A 4,000 bale estimate was revised downward to 3,000 the following year.

7 "Bayou Sara/St. Francisville, La." (Sanborn Map & Publishing Co., 1885, 1891), Sanborn Map Collection, Library of Congress, www.loc.gov. There are additional maps at the Library of Congress. Also see Butler, *Three Generous Generations*, 38–39.

8 Butler, *Three Generous Generations*, 38–40.

9 January 29, 1879, Vendee Conveyance Records, Excerpted by Ann S. Weller, Notarial Record S, 1878–1882, WFHS; Louisiana, 22:258, R.G. Dun & Co. Credit Report Volumes, Baker Library, HBS; 539:657, 540:762–766, Lehman Brothers Records, Baker Library, Harvard Business School. Also see Butler, *Three Generous Generations*, 61.

10 "M. & E. Wolf," *True Democrat*, February 24, 1917, 5; Jeanet S. Dreskin to Ann [Butler], October 21, 2004, WHFS.

11 Records in the Elizabeth Dart Collection, Louisiana State University Special Collections, Freyhan Folder, February 29, 1896; April 1, 1896; May 1, 1896; and June 1, 1896. See Suzanne Turner, ed., *The Garden Diary of Martha Turnbull, Mistress of Rosedown Plantation* (Baton Rouge: Louisiana State University Press, 2012).

12 Records in the Elizabeth Dart Collection, Louisiana State University Special Collections, Freyhan Folder, purchases for June 1896; August 1, 1896; September 1, 1896; October 1, 1896; November 2, 1896; and October 14, 1895.

13 Beulah Watts Smith, *Bayou Sara, 1900–1975, Then and Now* (Baton Rouge, LA: Claitor's Publishing Division, 1976), WFHS, 9.

14 "M. & E. Wolf," *True Democrat*, February 24, 1917, 5.

15 "Palimpsests," *True Democrat*, July 23, 1892.

16 Henry Clay Applewhite to Julius Freyhan, June 11, 1874, Vendee Conveyance Records, Excerpted by Ann S. Weller, Book R, 26–27, WFHS; sheriff's sale, January 3, 1874, Vendee Conveyance Records, Excerpted by Ann S. Weller, Notarial Record Book Q, 593, WFHS; Louisiana, 22:259, R.G. Dun & Co. Credit Report Volumes, Baker Library, HBS; Butler, *Three Generous Generations*, 27, 38, 60–61; November 10, 1871, Vendee Conveyance Records, Excerpted by Ann S. Weller, Notarial Record Book Q, 206, WFHS; September 15, 1887, Vendee Conveyance Records, Excerpted by Ann S. Weller, Notarial Record U, 1886–1891, WFHS; March 9, 1895, Vendee Conveyance Records, Excerpted by Ann S. Weller, Book V, 388, WFHS; Vendor, June 22, 1903, Vendee Conveyance Records, Excerpted by Ann S. Weller, Conveyance Records Y, 1904–1907, 197–198, WFHS.

17 Vol. 540:726–729, Lehman Brothers Records, Baker Library, Harvard Business School.

18 Louisiana, 22:264–265, R.G. Dun & Co. Credit Report Volumes, Baker Library, HBS; Carol Mills-Nichol, *Louisiana's Jewish Immigrants from the Bas-Rhin, Alsace, France* (Santa Maria, CA: Janaway Publishing, 2014), 361–362; Louisiana, 22:279, R.G. Dun & Co. Credit Report Volumes, Baker Library, HBS; Butler, *Three Generous Generations*, 40; and Sanborn Map, "Bayou Sara/St. Francisville, La.," map, May 1885.

19 Louisiana, 22:261, 22:277, R.G. Dun & Co. Credit Report Volumes, Baker Library, HBS; Mercantile Agency, *Mercantile Agency's Reference Book* (1880); Louisiana, 22:279, R.G. Dun & Co. Credit Report Volumes, Baker Library, HBS.

20 Louisiana, 22:274, 22:241, R.G. Dun & Co. Credit Report Volumes, Baker Library, HBS; Mercantile Agency, *Mercantile Agency's Reference Book* (1880).

21 The earliest discovered transaction between Lehman brothers and S. & A. Jacobs was for $141.50 in July 1879. See 539:367, Lehman Brothers Records, Baker Library, Harvard Business School; and Aaron D. Anderson, *Builders of a New South: Merchants, Capital, and the Remaking of Natchez, 1865–1914* (Jackson: University Press of Mississippi, 2013), 61.

22 Mississippi, 2:124, 2:87, 2:154, R.G. Dun & Co. Credit Report Volumes, Baker Library, HBS; and Anderson, *Builders of a New South*, 87–88, 207–208. Anderson argues that this figure was approximately double that of several of the other most successful merchant families in Natchez.

23 Vol. 539:334, Lehman Brothers Records, Baker Library, Harvard Business School; Mississippi, 21:66, R.G. Dun & Co. Credit Report Volumes, Baker Library, HBS. In 1875, the firm purchased $40,000 worth of stock in New York, although it is unclear from whom; see John C. Willis, *Forgotten Time: The Yazoo-Mississippi Delta after the Civil War* (Charlottesville: University Press of Virginia, 2000), 126. There were conflicting reports of where Wilczinski came from prior to his arrival in Greenville. One report suggested that he arrived in Greenville in 1868 after living in Tennessee and Louisiana; see Goodspeed Brothers, *Biographical and Historical Memoirs of Mississippi, Embracing an Authentic and Comprehensive Account of the Chief Events in the History of the State, and a Record of the Lives of Many of the Most Worthy and Illustrious Families and Individuals* (Chicago: Goodspeed Publishing Co., 1891), 1036. One report claimed that Wilczinski had filed for bankruptcy in New York in 1869; see Mississippi, 21:25, R.G. Dun & Co. Credit Report Volumes, Baker Library, HBS.

24 Mississippi, 21:25, 21:65–66, R.G. Dun & Co. Credit Report Volumes, Baker Library, HBS.

25 The information about the transactions between the Wilczinskis and their customers is derived from the excellent, extensive research of John C. Willis. For more detailed information, as well as a list of the specific sources consulted, see Willis, *Forgotten Time*, 126–127.

26 Ibid., 63.

27 Ibid., 65.

28 Ibid., 65–66.

29 Ibid., 127; see Goodspeed Brothers, *Biographical and Historical Memoirs of Mississippi*, 1036.

30 Leo E. Turitz and Evelyn Turitz. *Jews in Early Mississippi* (Jackson: University Press of Mississippi, 1983), 66, 69; Mississippi, 21:64, R.G. Dun & Co. Credit Report Volumes, Baker Library, HBS.

31 Again, the information about the transactions between Greenville merchants and their customers is derived from the excellent, extensive research of John C. Willis. For more detailed information, as well as a list of the specific sources consulted, see Willis, *Forgotten Time*, esp. 66–68.

32 Vol. 539:16, 25, 344, 349, 359, Lehman Brothers Records, Baker Library, Harvard Business School; and Julius Weis Autobiography (JWA), n.d., Ida Weis Friend Collection, MSS 287, box 7, Louisiana Research Collection, Tulane University Special Collections (TUSC), 20–21.

33 "Fifty Years of Southern Progress," *New Orleans Times-Picayune*, November 17, 1895, 7, as cited at "Julius Weis," memorial no. 124527131, *Find a Grave*, February 2, 2014, www.findagrave.com; New York, 200:375; Mississippi, 2:60, R.G. Dun & Co. Credit Report Volumes, Baker Library, HBS.

34 Mississippi, 2:103, R.G. Dun & Co. Credit Report Volumes, Baker Library, HBS; and JWA, 19.

35 Mississippi, 2:103, R.G. Dun & Co. Credit Report Volumes, Baker Library, HBS.

36 JWA, 18; and Louisiana, 12:19, R.G. Dun & Co. Credit Report Volumes, Baker Library, HBS.

37 JWA, 18–19, 21.

38 Louisiana, 12:80, R.G. Dun & Co. Credit Report Volumes, Baker Library, HBS; JWA, 19; and Louisiana, 16:229, R.G. Dun & Co. Credit Report Volumes, Baker Library, HBS.

39 Louisiana, 16:229, R.G. Dun & Co. Credit Report Volumes, Baker Library, HBS. This refers to V & A Meyer, after the firm changed hands. Also see JWA, 9.

40 Anderson, *Builders of a New South*, 59, 98, 156. By Anderson's estimate they handled as much as a million dollars' worth of cotton annually from the area around Natchez. See also the memoir of Clara Lowenburg Moses, TUSC, 808.8 M911a.

41 Mississippi, 2:129, 2:148, R.G. Dun & Co. Credit Report Volumes, Baker Library, HBS; and Anderson, *Builders of a New South*, 134, 166.

42 Mississippi, 2:148, R.G. Dun & Co. Credit Report Volumes, Baker Library, HBS; and Anderson, *Builders of a New South*, 157, 160–161.

43 The information about the transactions between Lowenburg and his customers is derived from the excellent, extensive research of Aaron D. Anderson. For more detailed information, as well as a list of the specific sources consulted, see Anderson, *Builders of a New South*, 76–77, 87.

44 Ibid., 76–77.

45 Ibid., 102, 134.

46 Ibid., 87, 121, 124, 128–129.

47 Ibid., 112–113, 116.

48 Ibid., 127, 136; and Charles Wessolowsky, *Reflections of Southern Jewry: The Letters of Charles Wessolowsky, 1878–1879*, ed. Louis Schmier (Macon, GA: Mercer University Press, 1982), 47.

49 Again, this detail is from the research of Anderson, *Builders of a New South*, 120, 122–123, 137, 139.

50 Ibid., 61, 87, 125.

51 Ibid., 60–61, 99–100. There is uncertainty as to when Friedler arrived and set up shop. He claimed in May 1871 to have begun three years' prior, suggesting around 1868 or 1869. The first reference is in February 1870. Anderson, *Builders of a New South*, 60, says that he came to the Natchez area in 1866 or 1867. See Louisiana, 4:228–229, R.G. Dun & Co. Credit Report Volumes, Baker Library, HBS.

52 The information about Friedler's business interests and his transactions with Julius Weis is derived from the excellent, extensive research of Aaron D. Anderson. For more detailed information, as well as a list of the specific sources consulted, see Anderson, *Builders of a New South*, 61, 96, 125–126.

53 Mississippi, 2:122, R.G. Dun & Co. Credit Report Volumes, Baker Library, HBS.

54 Ibid.

55 Mississippi, 2:164, 2:173, R.G. Dun & Co. Credit Report Volumes, Baker Library, HBS.

56 Mississippi, 2:173, 2:141, 2:238, 2:235, 2:244, R.G. Dun & Co. Credit Report Volumes, Baker Library, HBS.

57 Anderson, *Builders of a New South*, 98; Mississippi, 21:15, R.G. Dun & Co. Credit Report Volumes, Baker Library, HBS.

58 Mississippi, 21:15–16, 21:59, R.G. Dun & Co. Credit Report Volumes, Baker Library, HBS.

59 Mississippi, 21:17, 21:26, R.G. Dun & Co. Credit Report Volumes, Baker Library, HBS. This firm is spelled differently depending on the source.

60 Mississippi, 21:30, R.G. Dun & Co. Credit Report Volumes, Baker Library, HBS.

61 Mississippi, 21:88, a, R.G. Dun & Co. Credit Report Volumes, Baker Library, HBS.

62 Mississippi, 6:144/e, R.G. Dun & Co. Credit Report Volumes, Baker Library, HBS. Kaufman is later referred to as a nephew of M. Kaufman, Sr. One recorder claimed in 1874 that Kaufman "encourages negroes to steal jewelry and [spoons?] and he buys [them?] in quantity" and argued that Kaufman was "a thief."

63 Edward King, *The Great South*, ed. W. Magruder Drake and Robert R. Jones (Baton Rouge: Louisiana State University Press, 1972), 290; and Louisiana, 22:4, 14, 41–42, 44, R.G. Dun & Co. Credit Report Volumes, Baker Library, HBS.

64 Louisiana, 22:4, 14, 41–42, 44, R.G. Dun & Co. Credit Report Volumes, Baker Library, HBS.

65 Ibid.

66 Louisiana, 22:267, R.G. Dun & Co. Credit Report Volumes, Baker Library, HBS; and U.S. States Census, 1860, entry for Jacob Mitchell, West Feliciana Parish, Louisiana, 123, *Ancestry*, www.ancestry.com.

67 Louisiana, 22:267, 22:269, 22:278, R.G. Dun & Co. Credit Report Volumes, Baker Library, HBS.

68 Louisiana, 3:121, 3:57, R.G. Dun & Co. Credit Report Volumes, Baker Library, HBS.

69 Ibid.; Louisiana, 3:140/14, 140/17, R.G. Dun & Co. Credit Report Volumes, Baker Library, HBS; and Mercantile Agency, *The Mercantile Agency's Reference Book* (1900).

70 Louisiana, 19:23, 19:34, 19:55, R.G. Dun & Co. Credit Report Volumes, Baker Library, HBS.

71 Louisiana, 19:34, 19:55, R.G. Dun & Co. Credit Report Volumes, Baker Library, HBS.

CHAPTER 6. THE END OF THE NICHE ECONOMY

1 Sven Beckert, *The Monied Metropolis*, 242–244.

2 Ibid.

3 Sven Beckert argues that "trades on these exchanges no longer rested on trust networks forged by religious, kin, or place-of-origin solidarities. Instead, these institutions were impersonal marketplaces in which anyone at any time could trade in any quantity and quality of cotton for immediate or future delivery, or could speculate on the future price movements of cotton that had not been shipped, or perhaps not even grown." See Beckert, *Empire of Cotton: A Global History* (New York: Knopf, 2014), 320, 345.

4 Beckert, *Empire of Cotton*, 320–322; [Lee Richardson and Thomas Godman], *In and About Vicksburg: An Illustrated Guide Book to the City of Vicksburg, Mississippi* (Vicksburg, MS: Gibraltar Publishing Co., 1890); and Peter Chapman, *The Last of the Imperious Rich: Lehman Brothers, 1844–2008* (New York: Portfolio, 2010), 34–35.

5 Chapman, *The Last of the Imperious Rich*, 34; and New York, Vol. 319, p. 500 a/13; Louisiana, Vol. 12, p. 1a (hereafter presented as volume:page), R.G. Dun & Co. Credit Report Volumes, Baker Library, Harvard Business School (HBS).

6 Beckert, *Empire of Cotton*, 323, 345; and Amy A. Quark, *Global Rivalries: Standards Wars and the Transnational Cotton Trade* (Chicago: University of Chicago Press, 2013), chapter 2, esp. 38–39.

7 Beckert, *Empire of Cotton*, 319–320, 344–345, 348, 357. Beckert argues that "colonial cotton symbolized the new symbiosis of a powerful nation-state with powerful national industries. This symbiosis in fact characterized a new form of global capitalism centered on the strengthening of national capital in rival capitalist nations."

8 Ibid., 377–378, 381–382, 399, 401, 409–410, 431.

9 Ibid., 336. For more on the term "invisible hand," see Adam Smith, *The Wealth of Nations* (London: Strahan, 1776).

10 Beckert, *Empire of Cotton*, 319–320.

11 "Advertisement," *True Democrat*, April 11, 1908; "Bank of Commerce," *True Democrat*, February 24, 1917, sec. 2, 3; and Roger L. Ransom and Richard Sutch,

One Kind of Freedom: The Economic Consequences of Emancipation (Cambridge: Cambridge University Press, 2001), 197. These new businesses demonstrate how Jews began to transition into other fields—beyond investment banking—as their opportunities as cotton merchants declined.

12 Julius Weis Autobiography (JWA), n.d., Ida Weis Friend Collection, MSS 287, box 7, Louisiana Research Collection, Tulane University Special Collections (TUSC), 19–21. The claim about fifty million dollars was typewritten in the memoir, but then crossed out by hand, and no figure was included. See Louisiana, 16:229, R.G. Dun & Co. Credit Report Volumes, Baker Library, HBS; and Mercantile Agency, *The Mercantile Agency's Reference Book of the United States and British Provinces* (New York: B. Douglass & Co., 1890). V. & A. Meyer is listed in the 1890 *Mercantile Reference Book* for New Orleans, but not for 1895. Weis claims that he took over the Lazard Frères account in 1891 after V&A Meyer had gone out of business; see JWA, 20–21.

13 Anne Butler, *Three Generous Generations* (Baton Rouge, LA: Claitor's Publishing Division, 2004), 60–62, 71–72, 76. See the *New Orleans Jewish Ledger*, October 12, 1904, as quoted in Butler, 76. The home was at 5225 St. Charles Avenue.

14 Butler, 60; "M. & E. Wolf," *True Democrat*, February 24, 1917, 5; and Beulah Watts Smith, *Bayou Sara, 1900–1975, Then and Now* (Baton Rouge, LA: Claitor's Publishing Division, 1976), West Feliciana Historical Society (WFHS), 10–11.

15 Mercantile Agency, *Mercantile Agency's Reference Book* (1905, 1910, 1915); Butler, *Three Generous Generations*, 40; "Bayou Sara: Pawn of the Mississippi," *Morning Advocate*, November 23, 1952, WFHS; and "Quarrantine Violated," *Feliciana Sentinel*, August 24, 1878, 3, WFHS.

16 "Bayou Sara: Pawn of the Mississippi," *Morning Advocate*, November 23, 1952.

17 "Palimpsests," reprint of *True Democrat*, July 23, 1892, WFHS; and *New York Times* articles "Bayou Sara under Water," April 22, 1890; "Louisiana's Great Peril," April 23, 1890; and "Bayou Sara Inundated," June 20, 1892, 1.

18 "Bayou Sara Greets the Nation's Chief," *True Democrat*, October 30, 1909.

19 "Bayou Sara Levee Breaks, Washing Away Many Buildings; No Serious Accidents," *True Democrat*, May 4, 1912, 2.

20 "Bayou Sara: The Town and Stream," 14, WFHS; and "Bayou Sara: Pawn of the Mississippi," *Morning Advocate*, November 23, 1952, WFHS.

21 Fabian Lange, Alan L. Olmstead, and Paul W. Rhode, "The Impact of the Boll Weevil, 1892–1932," working paper (Davis: University of California, February 2008), 3–5; and "General Overview of Natchez History," Historic Natchez Foundation, 51–52.

22 "Agricultural Development of the Felicianas," *True Democrat*, February 24, 1917, sec. 1, 3; "Bank of Commerce," *True Democrat*, February 24, 1917, sec. 2, 3; and "M. & E. Wolf," *True Democrat*, February 24, 1917, 5.

23 Aaron D. Anderson, *Builders of a New South: Merchants, Capital, and the Remaking of Natchez, 1865–1914* (Jackson: University Press of Mississippi, 2013), 210–211, 218; and "General Overview of Natchez History," Historic Natchez Foundation, 52. This did not resume until the 1980s.

24 Anderson, *Builders of a New South*, 210–211, 218. See "General Overview of Natchez History," Historic Natchez Foundation, 51.

25 By the late nineteenth century, one contemporary observed that "there is a good deal of excitement here about what is called whitecaps. They are running all the darkeys off from people's mills and farms at a dreadful rate. It is rumored that all the Jews in Summit are going to Jerusalem." Whitecaps operated in secrecy, had their own rituals, may have emerged as an outgrowth of the Ku Klux Klan, and they operated with local support in the Florida Parishes of Louisiana—including West Feliciana. See Samuel C. Hyde, Jr., *Pistols and Politics: The Dilemma of Democracy in Louisiana's Florida Parishes, 1810–1899* (Baton Rouge: Louisiana State University Press, 1996), 208–210.

26 "Anti-Semitic Outrages," *American Israelite*, March 25, 1887, 7; and Patrick Mason, *The Mormon Menace: Violence and Anti-Mormonism in the Postbellum South* (New York: Oxford University Press, 2011), 175. See "Anti-Semites in Louisiana, *American Hebrew*, April 1, 1887.

27 "Anti-Semitic Outrages," *American Israelite*, March 25, 1887, 7; and Carol Mills-Nichol, *The Forgotten Jews of Avoyelles Parish, Louisiana* (Santa Maria, CA: Janaway Publishing, 2012), 473.

28 "Mobbing Merchants," *American Israelite*, October 31, 1889, 6; "Delhi's Dark Deed," *Daily Picayune*, October 31, 1889, 3; "The Outrages at Delhi," *Daily Picayune*, November 8, 1889, 8; and *Jewish Messenger*, November 15, 1889, 4.

29 "War on the Jew," *American Israelite* (reprinted from *Morning Star*), January 30, 1890, 7; "The Crusade against the Jews," *Baton Rouge Advocate*, October 30, 1889, 2; "Delhi's Dark Deed," *Daily Picayune*, October 31, 1889, 3; and "Mobbing Merchants," *American Israelite*, October 31, 1889, 6.

30 "The Outrages at Delhi," *Daily Picayune*, November 8, 1889, 8.

31 "Delhi's Dark Deed," *Daily Picayune*, October 31, 1889, 3; "War on the Jew," *American Israelite* (reprinted from *Morning Star*), January 30, 1890, 7; and "The Outrages at Delhi," *Daily Picayune*, November 8, 1889, 8.

32 "More Anti-Jewish Outbreaks," *Daily Advocate*, November 17, 1889, 2; "The Southern States," *Daily Picayune*, November 21, 1889, 3; and "The Louisiana Outrages," *American Israelite*, November 21, 1889, 6.

33 "Jottings," *Jewish Messenger*, March 29, 1895, 4 (this newspaper may have been from Memphis); "The City," *New Orleans Daily Picayune*, October 29, 1871, 2; Herman W. Solomon, *The Early History of the Hebrew Union Congregation of Greenville, Mississippi*, (1972; reprint, [Greenville, MS]: Solomon, 2001), 38–39; "Double Shooting in Mississippi," *Cincinnati Commercial Tribune*, June 9, 1884, 1; "Vicksburg: the Indictment of the Murderers of Taylor Rucks at Greenville," *New Orleans Daily Picayune*, July 4, 1884; Charles Wessolowsky, *Reflections of Southern Jewry: The Letters of Charles Wessolowsky, 1878–1879*, ed. Louis Schmier (Macon, GA: Mercer University Press, 1982), 50; and Mason, *The Mormon Menace*, 175.

34 *American Hebrew*, December 6, 1889, 117; "Lawlessness in Louisiana," *American Hebrew*, January 17, 1890, 242; and *American Hebrew*, January 31, 1890, 281.

35 "Natchez, Mississippi," Institute of Southern Jewish Life, n.d., www.isjl.org; "Bayou Sara, LA," *American Israelite*, February 15, 1894, 7. The *True Democrat* noted that, at the founding of Temple Sinai, "the Hebrew population was larger than [in 1917], being decreased by deaths and the removal of a number of wealthy families." The congregation later dissolved, and in 1922, Temple Sinai was sold to a Presbyterian Church. See "Forty-Seven Prosperity Street," WFHS, 7.

36 Sven Beckert, *The Monied Metropolis: New York City and the Consolidation of the American Bourgeoisie, 1850–1896* (Cambridge: Cambridge University Press, 2001), 243; Allan Nevins, *Herbert H. Lehman and His Era* (New York: Scribner's, 1963), 13; New York, 319:500 a/26, 319:500 a/72, R.G. Dun & Co. Credit Report Volumes, Baker Library, HBS; and Elliot Ashkenazi, "Jewish Commercial Interests between North and South: The Case of the Lehmans and the Seligmans," *American Jewish Archives* 43 (Spring/Summer 1991): 35.

37 Vol. 539:64–65, 68, 138, 144, Lehman Brothers Records, Baker Library, Harvard Business School; and JWA, 21.

INDEX

A. Beer & Co., 44
Abraham, Henry, 128
Adams, Henry, 107. *See also* Lehman,
    Abraham & Co.
Alexander the Great, 65
Anaconda Plan, 59
antebellum years, 4; banking structure in,
    92–93; capital in, 24; cotton prices in,
    26, 27–28; freedmen in, 108, 111; global
    capitalism and, 19–20, 24; interior
    river towns in, 30–31; Jewish merchant
    success in, 16, 19–20, 24–25, 57; Jewish
    population in South in, 34–35; for
    Lehman Brothers, 49–50, 52, 126; New
    Orleans in, 38–39; New York in, 40–42;
    North-South networks in, 52; Shreve-
    port in, 30; steamboat traffic in, 26;
    structural factors in, 199–200. *See also*
    Bayou Sara, antebellum; factors; gen-
    eral and dry goods stores; networks,
    family and ethnic
Ashkenazi, Elliott, 11

Baer & Bro., 137; credit for, 138
Baer & Mann, 142–44
banking: in antebellum years, 92–93; in
    Depression of 1882–1885, 122; Euro-
    pean, 41–42; Hellman, I., and, 115;
    Lazard Frères, 41–42; National Banking
    Act (1863), 93, 129; Panic of 1873 and,
    114–15; postbellum Southern, 92–93;
    Robinson Mumford and, 93. *See also*
    investment banking
Banks, Nathaniel, 68, 70

Baring Brothers, 41
Baum, Joseph, 90–91
Baum, Leon, 90–91
Baum & Co., *90*, 90–91
Bayou Sara, antebellum, 30; cotton
    economy in, 37–38; Dorr at, 31–32,
    93, 120; general stores in, 33–34; great
    fire (1855) in, 55–56; importance of, 31;
    Meyer, Isaias, in, 53–54, 55; reputa-
    tion of, 32; Toorain in, 33. *See also* St.
    Francisville
Bayou Sara, postbellum, *85*, 229n38;
    Civil War damage and, 74; disease in,
    187–88; downturn of 1866–1867 in,
    100–101; fires in, 187; flooding in, 95,
    188–89, *189*, *190*; freedmen and Jewish
    firms in, 108–10; M. & E. Wolf in, 187;
    Meyer, Weis & Co. providing credit in,
    178–79; postbellum period for, 104–5;
    Robinson Mumford banking house in,
    93; Taft visiting, 188–89. *See also* Julius
    Freyhan & Co.; St. Francisville
Beckert, Sven, 3
Belmont, August, 41, 114
Berg, Meyer, 146–47
Bernheimer, Samuel, 138; capital for, 140;
    credit for, 139, 140; S. Bernheimer &
    Sons and, 140
black farmers, 106; Jacobs and, 162;
    Lincoln, Henry, as, 170–71; Lincoln,
    Lucinda, as, 170–71; Spearman, 163–64;
    Toler, 164–65
black political participation and represen-
    tation, 106–7

247

Block, Solomon, 144–45. *See also* Block & Feibelman
blockade, 6, 20, 200; demand and, 60, 61; as economic warfare, 59; Lehman Brothers and, 59–60; smuggling and blockade-running, 61–62, 221n10; Weis on, 59
Block & Feibelman, 144; Camden branch of, 145; New Orleans branch of, 145–46
Bodenheim, Henry, 97, 121
Bodenheim, M., 63
Bodenheim, Meyer & Co., 98, 120, 121; Meyer, G., and, 149–50
boll weevil, 190; in Natchez, 191, 192, 197
Bowman, Sarah T., 158
Burgas, Morris, 157–58
Butler, Benjamin, 68
B. Weil & Bro., 179–80

Cahn, William, 139
capital: in antebellum years, 24; Bernheimer and, 140; Civil War and, 6, 61, 81; and ethnic networks in Gulf South, 43, 135; Europe and, 41; general and dry goods stores and, 33; for investment banking, 181; Lehman Brothers flow of credit and, 36, 124, *125*, 134–35, 165; in postbellum period, 99, 117
Charles Hoffman & Co., 37; growth of, 56; Meyer, Isaias, and, 53–54; networks of, 54, 56
Civil War, 4; Anaconda Plan in, 59; Banks in, 68, 70; battle of Vicksburg in, 20, 70, 74, 79–80; Bayou Sara damage from, 74; capital and, 6, 61, 81; Confederate currency in, 63–64, 82; cotton as payment during, 64, 75–76; cotton prices during, 68, 81; deaths in, 73; Dun reports and, 77–78; economic warfare in, 59; end of, 81; European cotton trade and, 60–61; exports during, 59, 60; first phase of, 58, 67; Grant in, 68–69; Hoffman and, 78; interior merchants and, 58–59;

Jewish firms reopening and, 76–79; legal trade during, 62–64, 67–72, 200; Lehman Brothers and, 73, 75–78, 126; looting in, 75; Meridian in, 89; Meyer, Isaias, and, 78; Natchez and, 74, 76; New Orleans during, 67–68, 69, 70, 223n32; railroads in, 75; second phase of, 58–59, 67; Shreveport and, 77–78; start of, 58; structural factors in, 200; sutlers in, 64–67, *65*, *66*; town and plantation damages in, 74–75; Weis trading in, 63–64, 70, 79–81. *See also* blockade; Confederates; smuggling and blockade-running; Union
Clark, Thomas, 11
colonial expansion, 181; cotton production and, 184
communication technology, 83, 92, 207n12
Concerning the Jews (Twain), 10
Confederate currency, 63–64, 82
Confederates: Civil War trade and, 71–72; cotton burned by, 72–73
Confederate States of America, 58
Conklin, James, 69
cotton, 25, 27, *91*, *92*; competition for, 42; as export, 3, 9–10, 40, 59, 60, 181–82; global production of, 184; market process for, 26–27; modern world and, 3; slavery and, 3, 25, *26*, 42; state roles in, 183–84; weight of bales of, 25. *See also specific topics*
cotton economy. *See* credit system; general and dry goods stores
cotton exchanges, 182–83, 243n3
cotton prices: in antebellum years, 26, 27–28; Civil War and, 68, 81; communication technology and, 83; Europe and, 184; Julius Freyhan & Co. and, 156; postbellum, 94–95
credit system, 4, 199, 210n23; for Baer & Bro., 138; for Bernheimer, 139, 140; cycle of debt and, 29–30; downturn of 1866–1867 and, 96; end of niche economy

and, 182, 185; ethnicity and, 201; Freyhan access to, 157, 158; general and dry goods stores and, 6, 8, 19, 42, 92–94, 158; in Greenville, 163–64; interior merchants and towns and, 6, 124, 150–51; Jewish merchants role in, 8, 41, 42, 182, 185; Julius Freyhan & Co. customers and, 158, 159–60; Lehman Brothers flow of capital and, 36, 124, *125*, 134–35, 165; leniency in, 153; Leopold Wilczinski & Co. and, 162–63; Lowenburg and, 169; Meyer, G., and, 149–50; Meyer, Isaias, and, 119–20; Meyer, Weis & Co. and, 165, 168, 172–74, 176–77, 178–79; New York and, 41, 42–43; Panic of 1873 and, 114; for Picard & Weil, 160, 161; in postbellum years, 8, 82, 92–94, 118, 119–21, 123, 178–79; risk and, 1, 164; small businesses and, 22; for Weis, 1, 44–45; Wise, Moss & Co. and, 177. *See also* general and dry goods store; Lehman Brothers; Meyer, Weis & Co.; networks, family and ethnic; networks, from below
crop failures, 21, 200; downturn of 1866–1867 and, 82, 96, 102; Meyer, Weis & Co. and, 166, 167; risk and, 29–30
crop liens, 103; Georgia and, 113; Jacobs and, 162; Lowenburg and, 170–71

Delhi, Louisiana, *193*, 194–96
Democrats, 113
demographic profile, of Jews, 12; niche economy and, 13–15, *14, 15*, 16
Depression of 1882–1885, 122
Deutsch, Joseph, 53
Dorr, J. W., 31–32, 93, 120
downturn of 1866–1867: Bayou Sara and, 100–101; capital in, 96–97, 99, 102; creditors in, 96; crop failures in, 82, 96, 102; environmental factors in, 95–96; firms opening during, 100–101; Mann and, 98–99; Meyer, Isaias, and, 97–98; Natchez in, 101; non-Jewish merchants

and firms and, 99–102; Shreveport and, 101–2; structural factors in, 102; Weis in, 98
Dreyfus, Benjamin, 135; Panic of 1873 and, 137
Dun reports: Civil War and, 77–78; quantifying Jewish merchants in, 11–15, *14, 15*, 211n32, 212n33
Durr, John Wesley, 73, 128

E & B Jacobs, 77, 95–96; postbellum period for, 118
Eiseman, Meyer, 166
entrepreneurship, self-employed, 204n4
environmental factors: boll weevil as, 190–92, 197; downturn of 1866–1867 and, 95–96; end of niche economy and, 186–92, *189, 190*; fire as, 55–56, 116, 157, 160–61, 187; flooding as, 95–96, 115–16, 188–90, *189, 190. See also* Bayou Sara, postbellum
ethnicity, 1; credit system and, 201; global capitalism and, 2, 23, 124, 199, 202; Hellman, Isaias, and, 133; success and, 2–3. *See also* Jews; networks, family and ethnic; trust
ethnic trust. *See* networks, family and ethnic
Europe: banking and, 41–42; capital and, 41; Civil War and cotton trade for, 60–61; colonial expansion of, 181, 184; cotton prices and, 184; Lehman Brothers and investment from, 94, 124, 129, 130, 153, 202; market in, 130–31; sutlers in, 65
exports, 9–10; Civil War and, 59, 60; New York and, 3, 40, 181–82

factors, 4, 6, 23, 200, 206n11; bad crop year for, 30; general stores challenging, 32–33, 36, 92; J. W. Seligman & Co. and, 130; markets and, 28; postbellum decline of, 82–83, 209n17; supplies provisioned by, 28–29

Farrelly, Charles, 100

Feibelman, Edward, 144–45, 146. *See also* Block & Feibelman

Ferst, Moses, 49–50

Forcheimer & Bro., 47

Forcheimer family, 46–47

Frank, Henry, 62, 66–67; postbellum years for, 119

Frankfurt, 51; J. W. Seligman & Co. and, 131

freedmen, 102–3, 123, 200, 207n13, 207n17; Adams, 107; in antebellum years, 108, 111; in Bayou Sara, 108–10; economic coercion of, 106–7; Emancipation Proclamation and, 105; Freyhan and, 108, 111, 155; Jewish merchants and firms and, 4, 21, 109–12, 208n16; land ownership for, 105–6; Long and, 141; Mann and, 108, 111; Mitchell and, 178; Natchez left by, 191–92; non-Jewish businesses and, 111; peddlers and, 110, 208n15; Picard & Weil and, 108–9; racial segregation and, 113; racism and, 192; Redeemer politicians and, 113; Republicans and, 106–7, 112; as sharecroppers, 106; S. Weil & Bro. and, 161; Teutsch and, 108; violence against, 107–8; Weber and, 112. *See also* black farmers

Freyhan, Julius, 17–18, 153, *154*, 197; background of, 37–38, 155; business complex of, 156; credit system access for, 157, 158; as deserter, 78, 155, 238n2; diversification for, 186–87; family and ethnic network for, 157–58; fires and, 157; freedmen and, 108, 111, 155; interest rates for, 154–55; Lehman Brothers credit for, 154, 157, 158, 159–60; postbellum business success of, 38; property of, 160. *See also* Julius Freyhan & Co.

Friedler, Isaac: background of, 173; Meyer, Weis & Co. credit for, 172–74

Gans, Bluma DeYoung: husband of, 147, 148; Mrs. B. Gans Company of, 147–48, *148*

Gans, Simon, 147

general and dry goods stores, 13, 24, 30, 200, 216n25; in antebellum Bayou Sara, 33–34; Bernheimer and, 138–39; Block & Feibelman as, 144–46; capital and, 33; cotton economy and, 36–37; credit system and, 6, 8, 19, 42, 92–94, 158; factors challenged by, 32–33, 36, 92; functions of, 34; Goldsmith, Forcheimer & Bro. as, 46; growth of, 33; Isaacs operating, 174; of Michael, 55; Mitchell owning, 178–79; Morrison, Haber & Co. as, 45–46; in Natchez, 32; Seelig, Moses, and, 175–76; Teutsch and, 108; Weil & Kohn as, 36; Winter owning, 77. *See also* Freyhan, Julius; Goldsmith, Haber & Co.; interior merchants and towns; Meyer, Isaias; Meyer, Weis & Co.; networks, family and ethnic; Picard & Weil; postbellum period

Gensburger, M., 176–77

geographic information systems (GIS), 12–13

Gerstäcker, Friedrich, 24, 26

GIS. *See* geographic information systems

global capitalism, 1, 3; antebellum years and, 19–20, 24; ethnicity and, 2, 23, 124, 199, 202; investment banking and, 181; Lazard Frères and, 41–42, 165, 166; Lehman Brothers and, 94, 124, 129, 130, 134, 153, 202; niche economy and, 22, 184–85, 201; structural forces and, 181, 199

G. Meyer & Bro., 149. *See also* Meyer, Gabe

Goldman, Marcus, 8

Goldman Sachs, 8

Goldsmith, Ferdinand, 79

Goldsmith, Forcheimer & Bro., 46

Goldsmith, Haber & Co.: branches of, 45–46; debts of, 47–48; family and ethnic networks for, 45–47; Morrison, Haber & Co. and, 45–46; New York market and, 45, 47–48; trust for, 47, 48–49

Goldsmith, Lewis, 49; peddling of, 45

Goldsmith, Manuel, 46–47

Goldstein, Nathan, 17, 164–65

Grant, Ulysses S.: Jews and, 69; trade and, 68–69

Greek networks, 9–10

Greenville, Mississippi, 4, *14*, *125*; anti-Jewish violence in, 196; Civil War and, 74, 86; credit in, 163–64; downturn of 1866–1867 and, 101; 1868 to 1873 postbellum period in, 105, 110; fires in, 116; Gresenberger in, 176–77; Jewish integration in, 19; Meyer, Weis & Co. credit in, 175, 176–77, 179; politics in, 18; population of, 5, *15*, *136*; railroad in, 86–87; Seelig in, 175–76; Wilczinski & Co. in, 162–64; yellow fever in, 117

Gulf South, 3, 5; cotton economy in, 37–38; cutting costs in, 185; ethnic networks and capital in, 43, 135; global forces and, 22–23; Lehman Brothers impact in, 161; market share of, 25; Panic of 1873 and, 115; quantifying Jewish merchants in, 11–15, *14*, *15*, 211n32, 212n33. *See also* antebellum years; Bayou Sara, antebellum; Bayou Sara, postbellum; freedmen; North-South cotton trade; postbellum period; Vicksburg and the Bends

Haber, Isaac, 151

Hatch, W. D., 37

Hellman, Isaias, 115; ethnicity for, 133; Lehman, M., and, 133–34

Hellman, Max, 131

Hellman, Theodore, 131–32

Herold, Simon, 179

Herzberg, Heyman, 62

Heyman, Abraham, 142; bankruptcy of, 143–44; Panic of 1873 and, 143

Hirsch, Aaron, 62

Hoffman, Charles: Civil War and, 78; as peddler, 53–54. *See also* Charles Hoffman & Co.

Industrial Revolution, 103

integration, Jewish, 2, 17, 199; integrated outsiders and, 19, 214n44; politics and, 18; social, 15, 18–19

interior merchants and towns: in antebellum years, 30–31; Civil War and, 58–59; communication technology and, 83, 92, 207n12; credit system and, 6, 124, 150–51; Lehman Brothers credit for, 124, 150–51; New Orleans and, 39–40; peddling and, 6; postbellum period and, 4, 5, 6, 83, 84, 86, 92, 93–94, 123; railroad and, 87, 88, 92

investment banking, 8, 22; capital for, 181; economic diversification and, 181–82; ethnic networks and, 180; global capitalism and, 181; global investment and, 124, 126, 165, 180; Industrial Revolution and, 103

Irvine, J. F., 120

Isaac Haber & Co., 151

Isaacs, Abraham, 174

Jacobs, Simon, 161; black farmers and, 162; Lehman Brothers credit for, 162

Jewish merchants, 35, 211n31, 229n38; American Jewish map and, 36, 199; antebellum years and success of, 16, 19–20, 24–25, 57; anti-Jewish violence and, 23, 181, 192–96, *193*; Berg as, 146–47; Civil War and returning, 76–77; cotton and, 1–2; cotton exchanges and, 182–83, 243n3; credit system role of, 8, 41, 42, 182, 185; diversification for, 186–87, 197; freedmen and, 4, 21, 109–12, 208n16; Friedler as, 172–74;

Jewish merchants (*cont.*)
  GIS and, 12–13; industrial goods and,
  182; Jacobs as, 161–62; Jewish community investment by, 16–17; land
  control and, 172; in Meridian, 90–91;
  as minority, 10–11; Natchez middle-
  class, 32; in postbellum period, 104–5,
  109–11, 123; quantifying, 11–15, *14, 15,*
  211n32, 212n33; smuggling for, 61–62;
  states and, 183; structural factors and,
  94; success of, 2–3, 15–17; suicides of,
  121, 192–93. *See also* Civil War; credit
  system; general and dry goods stores;
  Goldsmith, Haber & Co.; interior
  merchants and towns; networks, family and ethnic; networks, from below;
  postbellum period; violence
Jews: Alsatian and Bavarian, 34–35; in
  antebellum New York, 40–41; anti-
  Jewish violence, 23, 181, 192–96, *193;*
  demographic profile of, 12, 13–15, *14,*
  15, 16; discrimination of, 7; Grant and,
  69; immigration by, 16; integration for,
  2, 15, 17–19, 199, 214n44; internal community dynamics for, 199; Sephardic,
  16; social and economic prominence
  of, 197; as sutlers, *65,* 65–67, *66;* yellow
  fever and, 117. *See also* demographic
  profile, of Jews; peddling, of Jews
Jim Crow laws, 113
J. P. Morgan & Co., 8, 124, 129–30
Julius Freyhan & Co., 78–79; cotton prices
  and, 156; credit for customers of, 158,
  159–60; loan default and, 159; M. &
  E. Wolf and, 187; wholesale and, 160;
  yearly customer cycle for, 158. *See also*
  Freyhan, Julius
J. W. Seligman & Co.: diversification for,
  197; European market and, 130–31;
  factorage system and, 130; networks
  for, 50–51, 52; New Orleans branch
  of, 131; New York and, 51; Seligman,
  Hellman & Co. and, 51, 131

Kaufman, Moses, Jr., 111, 177
Kaufman, Moses, Sr., 111
King, Edward, 10, 89
Kuhn, Loeb & Co., 130
Ku Klux Klan, 106, 107
Ku Klux Klan Act of 1871, 107

land control, 172
Lazard Frères: banking of, 41–42; diversi-
  fication for, 197; global capitalism and,
  41–42, 165, 166; Meyer, Weis & Co.
  and, 165, 166
Leake, Felix, 34
Lebret & Hearsey, 33–34
Lehman, Abraham & Co., 128, 137; Jacobs
  and, 161–62
Lehman, Durr & Co., 73, 128
Lehman, Emanuel, 126, 128; Ferst partnering with, 49–50
Lehman, Henry, 36
Lehman, Mayer, 73, 126, *127,* 128; Hellman, I., and, 133–34; New York Cotton
  Exchange and, 183
Lehman Brothers, 8, 120; antebellum
  years for, 49–50, 52, 126; Baer & Mann
  and, 142–43; Bernheimer and, 138–40;
  in Black Belt region, 141; blockade
  and, 59–60; Block & Feibelman and,
  144–46; branches of, 128; Civil War
  and, 73, 75–78, 126; collapse of, 127;
  as cotton commission business, 128;
  cotton exchange and, 183; credit and
  capital flow from, 36, 124, *125,* 134–35,
  165; credit reports for, 50, 126–27; diversification for, 197; Dreyfus and, 135,
  137; ethnic network of, 9, 21–22, 49–50,
  52, 130, 134, 151–52, 153; Freyhan credit
  from, 154, 157, 158, 159–60; Gans and,
  147; global capitalism and, 94, 124, 129,
  130, 134, 153, 202; Gulf South impacted
  by, 161; Hellman, I., and, 133; Heyman
  and, 142–44; interior merchants and,
  124, 150–51; international networks of,

129; investments of, 94, 127–28; Jacobs credit from, 162; J. W. Seligman & Co. and, 130; Kuhn, Loeb & Co. and, 130; Leopold Wilczinski & Co. credit from, 162–63; Levy & Bodenheimer and, 142; Marks & Lichtenstein and, *150*, 150–51; Meyer, G., and, 148–49; Meyer, Weis & Co. credit from, 165; Mrs. B. Gans Company and, 147–48, *148*; New Orleans branch of, 128–29; New York and, 49–50, 59–60, 126; non-Jewish firms and, 141–42, 150; Panic of 1873 and, 135; Picard & Weil credit from, 160, 161; Renfro & Andrews and, 141; Seelig and, 140–41; Seligman, Hellman & Co. and, 132–33; Sussman & Metzger and, 138; trust and, 1; in Vicksburg and the Bends, 135, 137–41

Lehman & Ferst, 49–50

Lehman & Smiley, 174–75

Leopold Wilczinski & Co.: credit issued by, 163; Lehman Brothers credit for, 162–63; Spearman and, 163–64

Levy, Abraham, 64, 79; 1868 mercantile activities for, 104

Levy, S., 142

Levy & Bodenheimer, 142

Levy brothers, 47–48

lien laws, 103, 230n49; Lowenburg, Isaac, and, 170–71; in postbellum period, 103, 112–13; Toler and, 165

Lincoln, Abraham, 58; Emancipation Proclamation of, 105

Lincoln, Henry, 170–71

Lincoln, Lucinda, 170–71

Liverpool: credit network and, 21; factors and, 28; J. H. Schroder & Co. in, 131; Lehman Brothers and, *125*, 128, 129, 130; New York merchants and, 41; Ralli family and, 9

London, 9, 129; Baring Brothers and, 41; J. W. Seligman & Co. and, 131; Lazard Frères in, 41–42; Lehman Brothers and, *125*

Long, H., 141

Lowenberg, Levi, 63, 76–77, 222n14

Lowenburg, Isaac, 66–67, 76, *169*; credit for, 169; liens for, 170–71; Meyer, Weis & Co. and, 168–72; plantation operation for, 172; success of, 170; trust deeds for, 171–72

Mann, Moses, 38, 78; downturn of 1866–1867 for, 98–99; freedmen and, 108, 111; in postbellum period and, 98–99, 117–18

markets: European, 130–31; factors and, 28; process of bringing cotton to, 26–27

Marks & Lichtenstein, *150*, 150–51

May, Augustus H., 141, 142

Meridian: Baum & Co. in, *90*, 90–91; Civil War and, 89; Jewish merchants in, 90–91; Marks & Lichtenstein in, *150*, 150–51; postbellum, 89–90

M. & E. Wolf, 187

Meyer, Adolph, 166

Meyer, Emanuel, 64, 79; peddling of, 70

Meyer, Gabe, 148; Bodenheim, Meyer & Co. and, 149–50; credit for, 149–50

Meyer, Isaac: diversification for, 186; Meyer, Weis & Co. and, 53, 186

Meyer, Isaias, 197; in antebellum Natchez, 52–53, 55; in Bayou Sara, 53–54, 55; Charles Hoffman & Co. and, 53–54; Civil War and, 78; credit networks of, 119–20; downturn 1866–1867 and, 97–98; economic relationships of, 54; ethnic and family networks of, 52–55; Meyer, Weis & Co. and, 53, 55; Meyer & Co. of, 120–21; in postbellum period, 97, 119–20. *See also* Bodenheim, Meyer & Co.; Pelgram & Meyer

Meyer, Louis, 47

Meyer, Weis & Co., 22, 52; V. & A. Meyer and, 186; Bayou Sara and, 178–79; B. Weil & Bro. and, 179–80; Civil War and, 165–66; commission business for, 167; credit system and, 165, 168, 172–74, 176–77, 178–79; crop failure impacting, 166, 167; dry goods and, 167; family and ethnic network for, 166, 168, 180; Friedler and, 172–73; global capital for, 165; Herold and, 179; Isaacs and, 174; Lazard Frères and, 165, 166; Lehman Brothers providing credit to, 165; Lehman & Smiley and, 174–75; Lowenburg, Isaac, and, 168–72; Meyer, Isaias, and, 53, 55; Mitchell and, 178–79; Natchez-area cotton businesses and, 53, 168–75; Radjesky and, 176; Seelig, Simon, and, 175–76; in Shreveport, 179; in Vicksburg and the Bends, 175–79; wholesale trade and, 165

Michael, Jacob: Bayou Sara fire and, 55–56; dry goods store of, 55; legal trouble for, 56

Mitchell, Jacob, 109; freedmen and, 178; Meyer, Weis & Co. and, 178–79

Morgan, J. P., 1; on trust, 6–7, 50. See also J. P. Morgan & Co.

Morrison, Haber & Co., 45–46. See also Goldsmith, Haber & Co.

Mrs. B. Gans Company, 147–48, 148. See also Gans, Bluma DeYoung

M. Schwartz & Co., 118–19

Mumford, Robinson, 93

Natchez, 30; boll weevil in, 191, 192, 197; Civil War and, 74, 76; downturn 1866–1867 and, 101; freedmen leaving, 191–92; merchant suicides in, 192–93; Meyer, Isaias, in antebellum, 52–53, 55; Meyer, Weis & Co. working in, 53, 168–75; middle-class merchants in, 32. See also Friedler, Isaac; Lowenburg, Isaac

National Banking Act (1863), 129

networks, family and ethnic, 1, 7, 57, 210n20; battle of Vicksburg and, 79–80; capital in Gulf South and, 43, 135; of Charles Hoffman & Co., 54, 56; cotton exchanges minimizing, 182–83, 243n3; Freyhan and, 157–58; global investment and, 124, 126, 180; Goldsmith, Haber & Co. and, 45–47; Greek firms and, 9–10; investment banking and, 180; J. P. Morgan & Co. and, 8, 124, 129–30; J. W. Seligman & Co. and, 50–51, 52; Lehman Brothers and, 9, 21–22, 49–50, 52, 130, 134, 151–52, 153; of Meyer, Isaias, 52–55; Meyer, Weis & Co. and, 166, 168, 180; new economic sectors and, 197–98; non-Jews and, 9, 43–44; Panic of 1873 and, 114–15; Picard & Weil and, 161; postbellum period and, 123; Seligman, Hellman & Co. and, 131–32; trust and, 21–22, 42, 135, 180, 201–2; Weis and, 79–80; yellow fever and, 117. See also credit system

networks, from above. See Lehman Brothers

networks, from below: creditor leniency in, 153; crop liens in, 170–71; Jacobs and, 161–62; Lehman Brothers credit flow and, 165; Leopold Wilczinski & Co. and, 162–63; plantation operation and, 172; trust deeds and, 171–72; wholesale trade in, 153, 160, 165, 180. See also crop liens; Freyhan, Julius; Julius Freyhan & Co.; Meyer, Weis & Co.; Picard & Weil

Newgass, Benjamin, 128, 134

New Orleans, 1, 38, 217n36; antebellum years for, 38–39; Block & Feibelman branch in, 145–46; during Civil War, 67–68, 69, 70, 223n32; interior merchants and, 39–40; J. W. Seligman & Co. branch in, 131; Lehman Brothers branch in, 128–29; long-term development problems for, 39; Panic of 1873 and, 115

New York: antebellum years, 40–42; cotton economy and, 41; credit and, 41, 42–43; exports and, 3, 40, 181–82; Goldsmith, Haber & Co. in, 45, 47–48; Jewish presence in, 40–41; J. W. Seligman & Co. and, 51; Lehman Brothers in, 49–50, 59–60, 126; Lehman & Ferst in, 49–50; Meyer, Isaias, in, 52; Morrison, Haber & Co. in, 45; slavery and, 42

New York Cotton Exchange, 182–83; Lehman, M., and, 183

niche economy, 203n3; anti-Jewish violence and, 23; background of, 2, 201n5, 205n6; demographic profile of Jews and, 13–15, 14, 15, 16; economic environment and, 202; global capitalism and, 22; impact of, 15–16; integration and, 2, 15, 17–19, 199, 214n44; investment banking impacting, 181–82; place and time and, 2, 205n6, 205n7, 213n35; postbellum years and, 82, 94, 102–3; real or perceived, 10–11; self-employed entrepreneurship and, 204n4; structural factors changing, 2, 181. See also networks, family and ethnic; networks, from below

niche economy, end of, 202; anti-Jewish violence and, 181, 192–96, 193, 201; banking and purchasing changes and, 185–86; cheap production and, 185; colonial expansion and, 181, 184; cotton exchange and, 182–83, 243n3; credit system and, 182, 185; diversification and, 186–87, 197; environmental factors and, 186–92, 189, 190; European economy and, 181, 184; global capitalism and, 184–85, 201; state roles in, 183–84. See also investment banking

non-Jewish merchants and firms, 21; downturn of 1866–1867 and, 99–102;

freedmen and, 111; J. P. Morgan & Co. and, 8, 124, 129–30; Lehman Brothers and, 141–42, 150; in postbellum period, 99–102, 120; Renfro & Andrews as, 141; Richardson & May as, 141, 142, 162

North-South cotton trade: antebellum networks in, 52; Civil War and legal, 62–64, 67–72, 200; smuggling and blockade-running for, 61–62, 221n10. See also blockade; New York

Nutt, Julia, 74

Olmsted, Frederick Law, 10

Opelika, Alabama, 89

Panic of 1873, 40, 83, 200–201; banking and, 114–15; credit and, 114; Dreyfus and, 137; ethnic networks and, 114–15; Gulf South and, 115; Heyman and, 143; Lehman Brothers and, 135; New Orleans and, 115; recovery from, 121; Seelig, Moses, and, 176; Seligman, Hellman & Co. and, 132; violence and, 21

Panic of 1893, 122

peddling, of Jews, 2, 16, 179–80, 199; Alsatian and Bavarian Jews and, 34–35; early settlers and, 35–36; freedmen and, 110, 208n15; of Goldsmith, L., 45; Hoffman and, 53–54; interior merchants and, 6; Meyer, E., and, 70

Pelgram & Meyer, 119–20, 197

Picard & Weil: ethnic and family network for, 161; fire and, 160–61; freedmen and, 108–9; Lehman Brothers credit for, 160, 161; wholesale of, 160

Pierpont, John. See Morgan, J. P.

politics: black participation and representation in, 106–7; Democrats in, 113; Jewish integration and, 18; Redeemer politicians, 113; Republicans in, 106–7, 112

Port Gibson, Mississippi: antebellum years in, *15*, 18, 38; anti-Jewish violence in, *193*, 196; Bernheimer in, 138–40; Kaufman, M., Jr., store in, 177; merchant-freedmen relationships in, 111–12; Meyer, Weis & Co. in, 177, 179; politics in, 18; postbellum years in, 110–11, *136*

postbellum period, 4, 200; banking structure in, 92–93; capital in, 99, 117; as challenge, 112–13; communication technology in, 83, 92, 207n12; compression systems in, 83–84, 96; cotton industry challenges in, 122–23; cotton prices in, 94–95; credit system in, 8, 82, 92–94, 118, 119–21, 123, 178–79; Democrats in, 113; Depression of 1882–1885, 122; E & B Jacobs in, 118; ethnic networks in, 123; factorage system decline in, 82–83, 209n17; failed businesses in, 120–21; fires in, 116; flooding in, 95–96, 115–16; Frank in, 119; Freyhan success in, 38; Greenville in 1868 to 1873, 105; interest rates in, 103–4; interior merchants and stores in, 4, *5*, 6, 83, 84, 86, 92, 93–94, 123; Jewish firms and merchants in, 104–5, 109–11, 123; Jim Crow laws in, 113; Levy, A., in, 104; lien laws in, 103, 112–13; for Mann, 98–99, 117–18; Meridian in, 89–90; Meyer, Isaias, in, 97, 119–20; niche economy and, 82, 94, 102–3; non-Jewish merchants in, 99–102, 120; Panic of 1893 in, 122; quantifying Jewish merchants in, 11–15, *14*, *15*, 211n32, 212n33; railroad in, 82, 86–87, *87*, 88, 89–90, 122; Schaefer in, 119; Seligman, Hellman & Co. in, 132; sharecroppers in, 106; in Shreveport, 101–2, 105; structural factors in, 20–21, 82, 102, 112, 200–201; suicides in, 121, 192–93; Vicksburg and the Bends importance in, 3–4, 84, 86; violence in, 113; Weis and, 98, 117; Wright, Frazier & Co. in, 120; yellow fever in, 96, 116–17. *See also* Bayou Sara, postbellum; downturn of 1866–1867; freedmen; Lehman Brothers; networks, from below; Panic of 1873

Radjesky, Joseph, 176

railroads: Civil War and, 75; expansion of 1880 of, 122; interior merchants and, 87, 88, 92; Meridian and, 89–90; Opelika and, 89; postbellum expansion of, 82, 86–87, *87*; Weil brothers and, 89

Ralli family, 9

Ransom, Roger, 10–11

Renfro & Andrews, 141

Republicans: election of 1872 for, 107; freedmen and, 106–7, 112

R. G. Dun & Co. records. *See* Dun reports

Richardson, Edmund, 140–41

Richardson & May, 141, 162; credit reporters and, 142

risk, 110; credit system and, 1, 164; crop failure and, 29–30; interest rates and, 103–4; trust and, 22

San Francisco: Hellman, I., and, 133; J. W. Seligman & Co. in, 131; Lazard Frères and, 41; Lehman Brothers and, *125*; Seligman brothers in, 51

S. Bernheimer & Sons, 140

Schaefer, Emile, 119

Schafer, W. G., 70, 95–96, 99

Schiff, Jacob, 7, 117, 130

Schneider, Leonard, 34

Seelig, Moses: Meyer, Weis & Co. and, 175–76; Panic of 1873 and, 176

Seelig, Simon, 140–41

Seligman, Hellman & Co., 51; family network for, 131–32; Lehman Brothers and, 132–33; Panic of 1873 and, 132

Seligman, Joseph, 7

Seligman brothers, 50–51

Selma, Alabama, 88–89

Sephardic Jews, 16

Seward, William H., 60–61, 67, 71
sharecroppers, 106
Shreveport, Louisiana, 105, 229n47; antebellum, 30; Civil War and, 77–78; downturn of 1866–1867 in, 101–2; Meyer, Weis & Co. in, 179; yellow fever in, 116–17
slavery: cotton and, 3, 25, 26, 42; end of, 81; prices of, 42
smuggling and blockade-running, 221n10; Herzberg and, 62; Hirsch and, 62; Weis and, 61–62
Solitude Plantation, 158
Somers, Robert, 10, 87, 93; on Meridian, 89–90
Spearman, Lewis, 163–64
St. Francisville, Louisiana. See Bayou Sara
structural factors: antebellum years and, 199–200; Civil War and, 200; downturn of 1866–1867 and, 102; global capitalism and, 181, 199; Jewish merchants and, 94; niche economy and, 2, 181; in postbellum years, 20–21, 82, 102, 112, 200–201; Weis and, 3. See also niche economy, end of
suicides, mercantile: Bodenheim, H., and, 121; in Natchez, 192–93
Sussman & Metzger, 138
Sutch, Richard, 10–11
sutlers, 64; history of, 65; Jews as, 65, 65–67, 66
S. Weil & Bro., 161
synagogue, 16–17

Taft, William Howard, 188–89
telegraph, 83
Teutsch, Adolph, 108
Toler, William, 164–65
Toorain, Charles, 33; death of, 73–74
trade, Civil War and, 62–64, 67, 200; Confederates and, 71–72; Grant against, 68–69; New Orleans capture and, 70; permits for, 68

trust, 1, 56–57; ethnic and family networks and, 21–22, 42, 135, 180, 201–2; Goldsmith, Haber & Co. and, 47, 48–49; Lehman Brothers and, 1; Morgan on, 6–7, 50; risk and, 22
trust deeds, 171–72
Twain, Mark, 10

Union: Mississippi River controlled by, 70–71; New Orleans controlled by, 67–68; Seward and, 60–61; trade and, 68–69. See also blockade

V. & A. Meyer, 186
Vicksburg, battle of, 20, 70, 74; networks after, 79–80
Vicksburg, Mississippi, 4, 5, 6, 97; antebellum years in, 38; battle of, 20, 70, 74, 79–80; Bodenheim, H., in, 97, 121; Civil War and, 58, 63, 67, 70, 74, 75, 76–77, 79; Jewish-owned general and dry goods in, 14, 15; levee at, 71; Lowenberg, L., in, 63, 76; population in, 136; port of, 84, 86; railroad in, 86, 88; synagogue built in, 17
Vicksburg and the Bends, 4, 5, 6, 136; Baer & Bro. in, 137–38; battle of Vicksburg, 20, 70, 74, 79–80; cotton economy in, 38; Gresenberger in, 176–77; Jewish demographics in, 13; Kaufman, M., Jr., in, 177; Lehman Brothers in, 135, 137–41; Meyer, Weis & Co. in, 175–79; position of, 84, 86; postbellum importance of, 3–4, 84, 86; Radjesky and, 176; roads in, 88; Seelig in, 175–76; Sussman & Metzger in, 138; Wise, Moss & Co. in, 177–78. See also Greenville; Natchez; Port Gibson; Vicksburg
violence: anti-Jewish, 23, 181, 192–96, 193, 201; in Delhi attack, 194–95; freedmen and, 107–8; Panic of 1873 and, 21; in postbellum period, 113; Whitecaps and, 192, 245n25

Ward, George Cabot, 41

Waterproof, Louisiana: Dreyfus in, 135; Wise, Moss & Co. in, 177, 178

Weber, Emile, 100–101; freedmen and, 112

Weil, Simon, 160. *See also* Picard & Weil

Weil Brothers, 89

Weil & Kohn, 36

Weis, Julius, *44*, 53, 168, 197–98; on blockade, 59; Civil War trading for, 63–64, 70, 79–81; commission business for, 167; Confederates burning cotton of, 72–73; credit for, 1, 44–45; diversification for, 186; downturn of 1866–1867 and, 98; networks and, 79–80; in postbellum period, 98, 117; smuggling of, 61–62; structural factors and, 3. *See also* Meyer, Weis & Co.

Weiss, Morris, 17, 164–65

Weiss & Goldstein, 17, 164–65

Wessolowsky, Charles, 17

western Anatolia, 9

Whitecaps, 192, 245n25

Whiteman, John, 37

white supremacy, 106–7

wholesale trade, 40, 153, 180; Julius Freyhan & Co. and, 160; Meyer, Weis & Co. and, 165; Picard & Weil and, 160

Wilcox, Carlos, 100

Wilczinski, Leopold, 162–64

Winter, A., 77

Wise, Moss & Co., 177–78

Wolf, Abram, 78–79

Wolflin, Charles, 79

women: in ethnic economy, 147–48; Gans, B., business, 147–48, *148*

Wright, Frazier & Co., 120

yellow fever, 96; ethnic networks and, 117; outbreak of 1878 of, 116–17

ABOUT THE AUTHOR

Michael R. Cohen is Associate Professor and Chair of Jewish Studies at Tulane University, where he holds a Sizeler Professorship. He is the author of *The Birth of Conservative Judaism: Solomon Schechter's Disciples and the Creation of an American Religious Movement*, as well as several articles and reviews. He earned his Ph.D. from Brandeis University and his A.B. from Brown University.